Building Modern Networks

Create and manage cutting-edge networks and services

Steven Noble

BIRMINGHAM - MUMBAI

Building Modern Networks

First published: July 2017

Production reference: 1280717

Published by Packt Publishing Ltd.
Livery Place
35 Livery Street
Birmingham
B3 2PB, UK.
ISBN 978-1-78646-697-6

www.packtpub.com

Credits

Author
Steven Noble

Reviewer
George Wong

Commissioning Editor
Kartikey Pandey

Acquisition Editor
Namrata Patil

Content Development Editor
Radhika Atitkar

Technical Editor
Bhagyashree Rai

Copy Editor
Tom Jacob

Project Coordinator
Kinjal Bari

Proofreader
Safis Editing

Indexer
Rekha Nair

Graphics
Kirk D'Penha

Production Coordinator
Melwyn Dsa

About the Author

Steven Noble has been working on computer networks for over 25 years. He has designed, built, and installed networks for companies such as Foundation Health and Exodus Communications. Steven has spent significant time in the open source community and is the President of the Board of the Network Device Education Foundation (NetDEF) focusing on Quagga, an open source routing stack and network testing. Steven has held roles from network engineer to CTO and is currently working at Big Switch Networks as an Open Networking Evangelist.

About the Reviewer

George Wong, Director of Business Development at Qualcomm, has over 20 years of both wired and wireless networking experience. He is currently leveraging Qualcomm technologies and developing ecosystems to accelerate IoT deployment in enabling the vision of Smart Cities.

Prior to Qualcomm, George was at Broadcom for 9 years, growing the Ethernet portfolio he managed five folds. Broadcom Ethernet switches were the first series of products used for OpenFlow development. He has also held product management positions at Juniper, Bay Networks, and other networking companies.

George holds both a master's in Engineering from California State University, Los Angeles, and an MBA from Pepperdine University.

www.PacktPub.com

For support files and downloads related to your book, please visit www.PacktPub.com. Did you know that Packt offers eBook versions of every book published, with PDF and ePub files available? You can upgrade to the eBook version at www.PacktPub.com and as a print book customer, you are entitled to a discount on the eBook copy. Get in touch with us at service@packtpub.com for more details. At www.PacktPub.com, you can also read a collection of free technical articles, sign up for a range of free newsletters and receive exclusive discounts and offers on Packt books and eBooks.

https://www.packtpub.com/mapt

Get the most in-demand software skills with Mapt. Mapt gives you full access to all Packt books and video courses, as well as industry-leading tools to help you plan your personal development and advance your career.

Why subscribe?

- Fully searchable across every book published by Packt
- Copy and paste, print, and bookmark content
- On demand and accessible via a web browser

Customer Feedback

Thanks for purchasing this Packt book. At Packt, quality is at the heart of our editorial process. To help us improve, please leave us an honest review on this book's Amazon page at https://www.amazon.com/dp/178646697X. If you'd like to join our team of regular reviewers, you can email us at customerreviews@packtpub.com. We award our regular reviewers with free eBooks and videos in exchange for their valuable feedback. Help us be relentless in improving our products!

Table of Contents

Preface

Building Modern Networks will brush up your knowledge of modern networking concepts and help you apply them to your software-defined infrastructure. Modern networking revolves around the construction, design, and usage of network. What describes a modern network? The latest development is that networking is the concept of Next Generation Networks (NGNs), which is the USP of this book. The book further allows you to study different types of NGNs with a deeper understanding.

As you master the NGN concepts, you will slowly move toward one of the major concepts of networking—understanding OpenFlow. As rightly stated by the Open Networking Foundation, OpenFlow is the first standard communications interface defined between the control and forwarding layers of an SDN architecture. OpenFlow allows direct access to and manipulation of the forwarding plane of network devices such as switches and routers, both physical and virtual. You will not only learn OpenFlow but also explore the Thrift and REST API in order to comprehend and control switches.

After OpenFlow, we will move on to grasp VMware NSX and ACI ideas. These concepts are like the building blocks of modern network. Eventually, we will move to the best part of learning all these concepts—implementing them! As we complete our take on initial concepts, we will move to actually building a modern network! In the last section of the book, we will apply all the notions of a modern network and design a NGN. As you learn how to build a modern network, we will also secure the network while working on its quality.

What this book covers

Chapter 1, *Open and Proprietary Next Generation Networks*, starts our journey from with concepts of NGNs, including hardware, software, and controllers. Here, we will also explore concepts such as open hardware, Open Source Network Operating Systems (ONOS), proprietary hardware, proprietary Network Operating Systems (NOS), and open source and proprietary software controllers.

Chapter 2, *Networking Hardware and Software*, discusses the multitude of open and closed hardware and software systems available to network architects. We will discuss the Open Compute Project (OCP), its goals, and members including Juniper Networks and Cisco, who are both mostly in the proprietary networking space.

Chapter 3, *Exploring OpenFlow*, talks about programmable networks. Specifically, it discusses how OpenFlow works, the different OpenFlow controllers available, and the hardware that can use OpenFlow.

Chapter 4, *Using REST and Thrift APIs to Manage Switches*, discusses the API-driven routing/switching applications. This concept allows you to have easier automation and management. Instead of programming systems box by box, you will now be able to use a central server or application to manage multiple systems.

Chapter 5, *Using Postman for REST API Calls*, teaches how to install Postman, use it to configure, and get the configuration from a switch running SnapRoute's FlexSwitch software. You will also consider how to program FlexSwitch using some of the extra features of Postman.

Chapter 6, *OpenFlow Deep Dive*, teaches the history of OpenFlow, why it was invented, and what issues it solves. We will also consider how OpenFlow works internally and how an OpenFlow agent and controller work together. Finally, we will set up ODL and ONOS.

Chapter 7, *VMware NSX*, gives you an idea about VMware NSX, its history, features, and use cases. You will now have a general understanding of what VMware NSX is and how you can integrate it into an existing or new SDDC.

Chapter 8, *Cisco ACI*, talks about Cisco ACI and how to navigate the CLI, GUI, and RESTful interfaces. We will also discuss how to set up a new APIC-driven network; configure the management network, users, tenants, and interfaces; and add a BGP ASN to the configuration.

Chapter 9, *Where to Start When Building a Next Generation Network*, talks about choosing between open and proprietary hardware and software. We will cover the support levels that can be expected and how your support needs may guide your decisions. We will cover the RFI and PoC concepts and how to handle them.

Chapter 10, *Designing a Next Generation Network*, teaches about determining the size and type of installation the equipment will be going in to. You will also learn about designing the network hardware layout based on the RFI/RFQ information and finally, you will understood how to assemble a final list of equipment to construct the NGN.

Chapter 11, *Example NGN Designs,* discusses designs using OpenFlow, SnapRoute, Cisco ACI, and NSX to design and build networks. We refer back to the chapters examining each to see how to do the deep configuration.

Chapter 12, *Understanding and Configuring Quality of Service,* explains QoS, how it works and how to use it with NGN technologies. Examples of simple QoS on both Linux and Windows will be shown along with the basic concepts of QoS in both OpenFlow and VMware NSX. We will cover both flat and hierarchical QoS and their uses in both enterprise and service provider networks.

Chapter 13, *Securing the Network,* teaches about general security concepts and how to apply them to different next generation systems. Using the OPNFV project, we will look at configuring switches using OpenFlow and virtual firewalls.

What you need for this book

To practice the examples and best practices explained in the book, you should have the following:

- Postman
- Access VirtualBox or another pc based hypervisor running Linux(r) to work with
    - OpenDaylight
    - ONOS
    - OVS
- Cisco Nexus switch running NX-OS
- Indigo (included with Broadcom OF-DPA)
- Floodlight
- Access to a non-production VMware system running NSX
- Access to a non-production Cisco network using APIC

Who this book is for

This book is for network engineers and network administrators who are taking their first steps when deploying software-defined networks. Network architects will also find this book useful when designing and building modern networks.

Conventions

In this book, you will find a number of text styles that distinguish between different kinds of information. Here are some examples of these styles and an explanation of their meaning. Code words in text, database table names, folder names, filenames, file extensions, pathnames, dummy URLs, user input, and Twitter handles are shown as follows: "In Rescue mode, you can run the `onie-nos-install` command to install an image from a web server or the `onie-self-update` command to upgrade ONIE".

A block of code is set as follows:

```
"NextHopList": [
  {
    "NextHopIntRef": "fpPort3",
    "NextHopIp": "192.168.30.2",
    "Weight": 0
  }
]
```

When we wish to draw your attention to a particular part of a code block, the relevant lines or items are set in bold:

```
"NextHopList": [
  {
    "NextHopIntRef": "fpPort3",
    "NextHopIp": "192.168.30.2",
    "Weight": 0
  }
]
```

Any command-line input or output is written as follows:

```
curl -X GET http://10.1.1.1:8080/public/v1/state/BGPGlobal | python -m
json.tool
```

New terms and **important words** are shown in bold. Words that you see on the screen, for example, in menus or dialog boxes, appear in the text like this: "Once you click on **Send**, you should be logged in to the APIC server."

Warnings or important notes appear in a box like this.

Tips and tricks appear like this.

Reader feedback

Feedback from our readers is always welcome. Let us know what you think about this book—what you liked or disliked. Reader feedback is important for us as it helps us develop titles that you will really get the most out of. To send us general feedback, simply email feedback@packtpub.com, and mention the book's title in the subject of your message. If there is a topic that you have expertise in and you are interested in either writing or contributing to a book, see our author guide at www.packtpub.com/authors.

Customer support

Now that you are the proud owner of a Packt book, we have a number of things to help you to get the most from your purchase.

Downloading the color images of this book

We also provide you with a PDF file that has color images of the screenshots/diagrams used in this book. The color images will help you better understand the changes in the output. You can download this file from http://www.packtpub.com/sites/default/files/downloads/BuildingModernNetworks_ColorImages.pdf.

Errata

Although we have taken every care to ensure the accuracy of our content, mistakes do happen. If you find a mistake in one of our books-maybe a mistake in the text or the code-we would be grateful if you could report this to us. By doing so, you can save other readers from frustration and help us improve subsequent versions of this book. If you find any errata, please report them by visiting http://www.packtpub.com/submit-errata, selecting your book, clicking on the **Errata Submission Form** link, and entering the details of your errata. Once your errata are verified, your submission will be accepted and the errata will be uploaded to our website or added to any list of existing errata under the Errata section of that title. To view the previously submitted errata, go to https://www.packtpub.com/books/content/support and enter the name of the book in the search field. The required information will appear under the **Errata** section.

Piracy

Piracy of copyrighted material on the Internet is an ongoing problem across all media. At Packt, we take the protection of our copyright and licenses very seriously. If you come across any illegal copies of our works in any form on the Internet, please provide us with the location address or website name immediately so that we can pursue a remedy. Please contact us at copyright@packtpub.com with a link to the suspected pirated material. We appreciate your help in protecting our authors and our ability to bring you valuable content.

Questions

If you have a problem with any aspect of this book, you can contact us at questions@packtpub.com, and we will do our best to address the problem.

1
Open and Proprietary Next Generation Networks

The term **Next Generation Network** (**NGN**) has been around for over 20 years, and refers to the current state-of-the-art network equipment, protocols, and features. In this chapter, we will discuss networking concepts such as hyperscale networking, software-defined networking, network hardware, and software design along with a litany of network design ideas utilized in NGN.

A big driver in NGN is the constant newer, better, and faster forwarding ASICs coming out of companies such as Barefoot, Broadcom, Cavium, and Nephos (MediaTek). The advent of commodity networking chips has shortened the development time for generic switches, allowing hyperscale networking end users to build equipment upgrades into their network designs.

At the time of writing, multiple companies have announced 6.4 Tbps switching chips. In layman terms, a 6.4 Tbps switching chip can handle 64x100 GbE of evenly distributed network traffic without losing any packets. To put the number in perspective, the entire internet in 2004 was about 4 Tbps, so all of the internet traffic in 2004 could have crossed this one switching chip without any issues (internet traffic 1.3 EB/month; `http://blogs.ci sco.com/sp/the-history-and-future-of-internet-traffic`).

 A hyperscale network is one that is operated by companies, such as Facebook, Google, and Twitter, that add hundreds if not thousands of new systems a month to keep up with demand.

Examples of next generation networking

At the start of the commercial internet age (1994), software routers running on minicomputers such as BBNs PDP-11-based IP routers designed in the 1970s were still in use and hubs were simply dumb hardware devices that broadcast traffic everywhere.

At that time, the state of the art in networking was the Cisco 7000 series router, introduced in 1993. The next generation router was the Cisco 7500 (1995), while the Cisco 12000 series (gigabit) routers and the Juniper M40 were only concepts.

In this book, we will cover the current and near future of networking. When we say next generation, we are speaking of the current state of the art and the near future of networking equipment and software. For example, 100 GB Ethernet is the current state of the art, while 400 GB Ethernet is in the pipeline.

The definition of a modern network is that it is a network that contains one or more of the following concepts:

- **Software-defined Networking (SDN)**
- Network design concepts
- Next generation hardware
- Hyperscale networking
- Open networking hardware and software
- **Network Function Virtualization (NFV)**
- Highly configurable traffic management

Both open and closed network hardware vendors have been innovating at a high rate of speed with the help of and due to hyperscale companies such as Google, Facebook, and others who have the need for next generation high speed network devices. This provides the network architect with a reasonable pipeline of equipment to be used in designs.

Google and Facebook are both companies with hyperscale networks. A hyperscale network is one where the data stored, transferred, and updated on the network grows exponentially. Hyperscale companies deploy new equipment, software, and configurations weekly or even daily to support the needs of their customers. These companies have needs that are outside of the normal networking equipment available, so they must innovate by building their own next generation network devices, designing multi-tiered networks (like a three-stage Clos network), and automating the installation and configuration of the next generation networking devices.

The need for hyperscalers is well summed up by Google's Amin Vahdat in a 2014 *Wired* article: *"We couldn't buy the hardware we needed to build a network of the size and speed we needed to build."*

In this chapter, we will cover the basics of modern or next generation networking. When you are done with this chapter, you will have a good grasp of the following:

- Network protocols
- Next generation networking concepts
- Network design planning
- Open networking hardware and software
- Proprietary networking hardware and software
- Open source software controllers
- Closed source software controllers
- Network function virtualization
- Traffic engineering concepts
- Tools we will use in this book

Terms and concepts used in this book

Here you will find the definition of terms that we will use in this book. They have been broken into groups of similar concepts.

Routing and switching concepts

In network devices and network designs, there are many important concepts to understand. Here we'll begin with the way data is handled. The easiest way to discuss networking is to look at the OSI layer and point out where each device sits.

The OSI layer with respect to routers and switches is as follows:

- **Layer 1 (Physical)**: This layer includes cables, hub, and switch ports. This is how all of the devices connect to each other, including copper cables (CatX), fiber optics, and **Direct Attach Cable (DAC)**, which connect SFP ports without fiber.
- **Layer 2 (Data link layer)**: This layer includes the raw data sent over the links and manages the **Media Access Control (MAC)** addresses for Ethernet.
- **Layer 3 (Network layer)**: This layer includes packets that have more than just layer 2 data, such as IP, IPX (Novell Networks protocol), and AFP (Apple's protocol).

Routers and switches

In a network, you will have equipment that switches and/or routes traffic. A **switch** is a networking device that connects multiple devices, such as servers, provides local connectivity, and provides an uplink to the core network. A **router** is a network device that computes paths to remote and local devices, providing connectivity to devices across a network. Both switches and routers can use copper and fiber connections to interconnect. There are a few parts to a networking device: the forwarding chip, the TCAM, and the network processor. Some newer switches have **Baseboard Management Controllers** (**BMCs**) which manage the power, fans, and other hardware, lessening the burden on the **Network Operating System** (**NOS**) to manage these devices.

Currently, routers and switches are very similar as there are many layer 3 forwarding capable switches and some layer 2 forwarding capable routers. Making a switch layer 3 capable is less of an issue than making a router layer 2 forwarding as the switch already is doing layer 2 and adding layer 3 is not an issue. However, a router does not do layer 2 forwarding in general, so it has to be modified to allow for ports to switch rather than route.

Control plane

The **control plane** is where all of the information about how packets should be handled is kept. Routing protocols live in the control plane and are constantly scanning information received to determine the best path for traffic to flow. This data is then packed into a simple table and pushed down to the data plane.

Data plane

The **data plane** is where forwarding happens. In a software router, this would be done in the device's CPU, and in a hardware router, this would be done using the forwarding chip and associated memories:

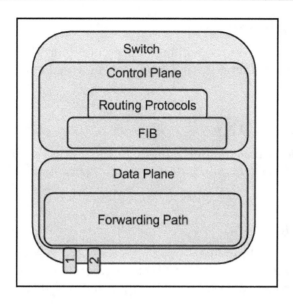

VLAN/VXLAN

A **Virtual Local Area Network** (**VLAN**) is a way of creating separate logical networks within a physical network. VLANs are generally used to separate/combine different users or network elements such as phones, servers, and workstations. You can have up to 4,096 VLANs on a network segment.

Virtual Extensible LAN (**VXLAN**) was created for large, dynamic isolated logical networks, virtualized networks, and multiple tenant networks. You can have up to 16 million VXLANs on a network segment versus 4,096 VLANs.

A **VXLAN Tunnel Endpoint** (**VTEP**) is a set of two logical interfaces—inbound, which encapsulates incoming traffic into VXLANs, and outbound, which removes the encapsulation of outgoing traffic from VXLANs back to its original state.

Network design concepts

Network design requires the knowledge of the physical structure of the network so that the proper design choices are made. For example, in a data center, you would have a local area network; if you have multiple data centers near each other, they would be considered a metro area network.

Local Area Network (LAN)

A LAN is generally considered to be within the same building. These networks can be bridged (switched) or routed. In general, LANs are segmented into areas to avoid large broadcast domains.

Metro Area Network (MAN)

A MAN is generally defined as multiple sites in the same geographic area or city, that is, a metropolitan area. A MAN generally runs at the same speed as a LAN, but is able to cover larger distances.

Wide Area Network (WAN)

A WAN is essentially everything that is not a LAN or MAN. WANs generally use fiber optic cables to transmit data from one location to another. WAN circuits can be provided via multiple connections and data encapsulations, including MPLS, ATM, and Ethernet.

Most large network providers utilize **Dense Wavelength Division Multiplexing** (DWDM) to put more bits on their fiber networks. DWDM puts multiple colors of light onto the fiber, allowing up to 128 different wavelengths to be sent down a single fiber.

DWDM has just entered open networking with the introduction of Facebook's Voyager system.

The leaf-spine design

In a leaf-spine network design, there are leaf switches (that connect to the servers), sometimes called **Top of Rack** (ToR) switches, connected to a set of spine switches (that connect leaves), sometimes called **End of Rack** (EoR) switches:

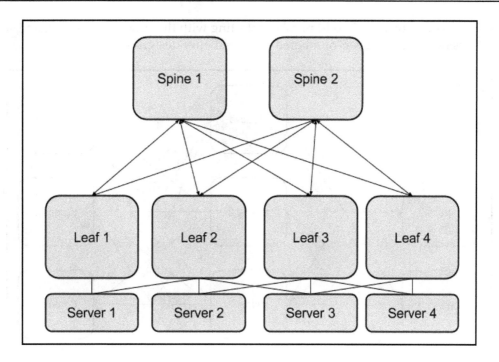

The Clos network

A Clos network is one of the ways to design a multi-stage network. Based on the switching network design by Charles Clos in 1952, a three-stage Clos is the smallest version of a Clos network. It has an ingress, a middle, and an egress stage. Some hyperscale networks use a five-stage Clos, where the middle is replaced with another three-stage Clos. In a three-stage Clos, there is an ingress, a middle ingress, a middle, a middle egress, and an egress stage. All stages are connected to their neighbor, so in the example shown here, **Ingress 1** is connected to all four of the middle stages just as **Egress 1** is connected to all four of the middle stages.

A Clos network can be built in odd numbers starting with three, so a five, seven, and so on stage Clos is possible. For even-numbered designs, Benes designs are usable:

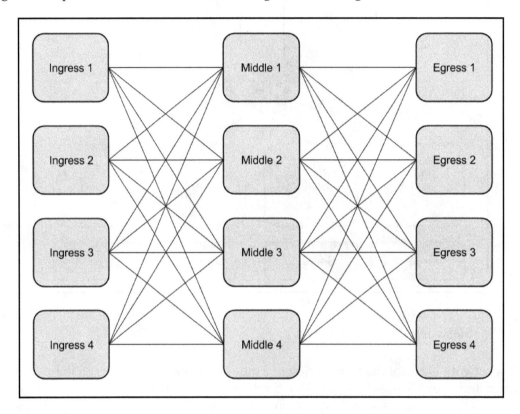

The Benes network

A Benes design is a non-blocking Clos design where the middle stage is 2 x 2 instead of N x N. A Benes network can have even numbers of stages. Here is a four-stage Benes network:

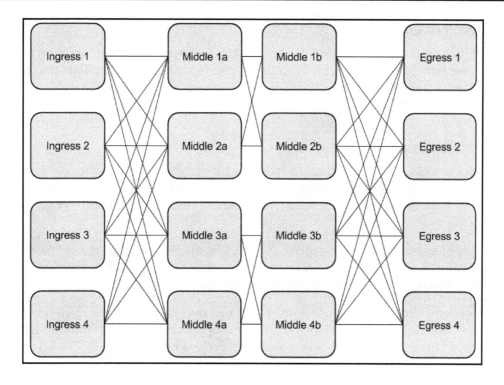

Network controller concepts

Here we will discuss the concepts of network controllers. Every networking device has a controller, whether built in or external to manage the forwarding of the system.

Controllers

A **controller** is a computer that sits on the network and manages one or more network devices. A controller can be built into a device, like the Cisco Supervisor module, or be standalone, like an OpenFlow controller.

The controller is responsible for managing all of the control plane data and deciding what should be sent down to the data plane.

Generally, a controller will have a **Command-line Interface** (**CLI**) and more recently a web configuration interface. Some controllers will even have an **Application Programming Interface** (**API**).

The OpenFlow controller

An OpenFlow controller, as it sounds, is a controller that uses the OpenFlow protocol to communicate with network devices. The most common OpenFlow controllers that people hear about are OpenDaylight and ONOS. People who are working with OpenFlow would also know of Floodlight and RYU.

The Supervisor module

A route processor is a computer that sits inside of the chassis of the network device you are managing. Sometimes, the route processor is built in to the system, while at other times, it is a module that can be replaced/upgraded. Many vendor multislot systems have multiple route processors for redundancy.

An example of a removable route processor is the Cisco 9500 series Supervisor module. There are multiple versions available, including revision A, with a 4-core processor and 16 GB of RAM, and revision B, with a 6-core processor and 24 GB of RAM.

Previous systems such as the Cisco Catalyst 7600 had options such as the SUP720 (Supervisor Module 720) of which they offered multiple versions—the standard SUP720 had a limited number of routes that it could support (256k) versus the SUP720 XL which could support up to 1 M routes:

Juniper Routing Engine

In Juniper terminology, the controller is called a **Route Engine** (**RE**). These are similar to the Cisco Route Processor/Supervisor modules. Unlike Cisco Supervisor modules, which utilize special CPUs, Juniper's REs generally use common x86 CPUs. Like Cisco, Juniper multislot systems can have redundant processors.

Juniper has recently released the information about the **Next Generation Route Engines** (**NG-REs**). One example is the new RE-S-X6-64G, a 6-core x86 CPU-based routing engine with 64 GB DRAM and 2x64 GB SSD storage available for MX240/MX480/MX960. These NG-REs allow for containers and other virtual machines to be run directly.

Built-in processor

When looking at single **Rack Unit** (**RU**) or pizza box design switches, there are some important design considerations. Most 1 RU switches do not have redundant processors or field replaceable route processors. In general, the **Field Replaceable Units** (**FRUs**) that the customer can replace are power supplies and fans. If the failure is outside of the available FRUs, the entire switch must be replaced in the event of a failure. With white-box switches, this can be a simple process as white-box switches can be used in multiple locations of your network, including the customer edge, provider edge, and core. Sparing (keeping a spare switch) is easy when you have the same hardware in multiple parts of the network.

Recently, commodity switch fabric chips have come with built-in low power ARM CPUs that can be used to manage the entire system, leading to cheaper and less power-hungry designs.

Facebook Wedge microserver

The Facebook Wedge is different from most white-box switches as it has its controller as an add-in module, the same board that is used in some of the OCP servers. By separating the controller board from the switch, different boards can be put in place, such as higher memory, faster CPUs, and different CPU types.

Routing protocols

A **routing protocol** is a daemon that runs on a controller and communicates with other network devices to exchange route information. For this section, we will use common words to demonstrate the way the routing protocol is working; these should not be construed as the actual way that the protocols talk.

Border Gateway Protocol (BGP)

BGP is a path-vector-based **External Gateway Protocol** (**EGP**) that makes routing decisions based on paths, network policies, or rules (route-maps on Cisco). Though designed as an EGP, BGP can be used as both an interior (iBGP) and exterior (eBGP) routing protocol. BGP uses keepalive packets (are you there?) to confirm that neighbors are still accessible.

BGP is the protocol that is utilized to route traffic across the internet, exchanging routing information between different **Autonomous System Numbers** (**ASNs**). An ASN comprises all of the connected networks under the control of a single entity, such as Level 3, which has **Autonomous System 1** (**AS1**) or Sprint (AS1239).

When two different ASNs interconnect, BGP peering sessions are set up between two or more network devices that have direct connections with each other.

In an eBGP scenario, AS1 and AS1239 would set up BGP peering sessions that would allow traffic to route between their AS.

In an iBGP scenario, the same AS would peer with other routers with the same AS and transfer the routes that are defined on the system. While iBGP is used internally in most networks, iBGP is used in large corporate networks because other **Interior Gateway Protocols** (**IGPs**) may not scale.

Consider these examples:

- **iBGP next-hop self**: In this scenario, **AS1** and **AS2** are peered with each other and exchange one prefix each. **AS1** advertises **192.168.1.0/24** and **AS2** advertises **192.168.2.0/24**. Each network has two routers, one border router, which connects to other ASNs, and one internal router, which gets its routes from the border router. The routes are advertised internally with the next-hop set as the border router. This is a standard scenario when you are not running an IGP inside, to distribute the routes for the border router external interfaces:

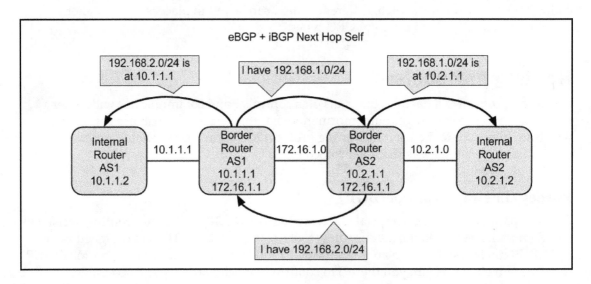

The conversation goes like this:

AS1 -> **AS2**: Hi **AS2**, I am **AS1**

AS2 -> **AS1**: Hi **AS1**, I am **AS2**

AS1 -> **AS2**: I have the following route, **192.168.1.0/24**

AS2 -> **AS1**: I have received the route, I have **192.168.2.0/24**

AS1 -> **AS2**: I have received the route

AS1 -> **Internal Router AS1**: I have this route, **192.168.2.0/24**, you can reach it through me at **10.1.1.1**

AS2 -> **Internal Router AS2**: I have this route, **192.168.1.0/24**, you can reach it through me at **10.1.1.1**

- **iBGP next-hop unmodified:** In the next scenario, the border routers are the same, but the internal routers are given a next-hop of the external (other AS) border router:

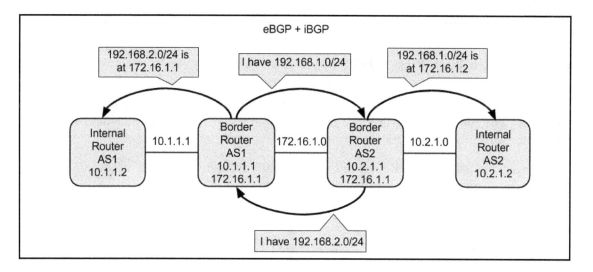

- The last scenario is where you peer with a router server, a system that handles peering, filtering the routes based on what you have specified you send. The routes are then forwarded onto your peers with your IP as the next-hop:

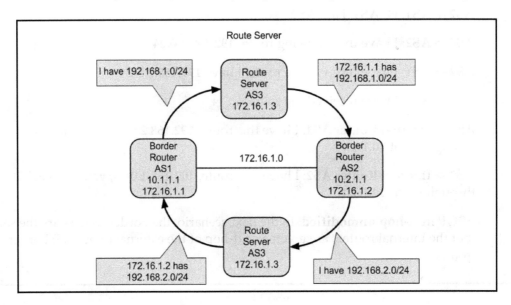

Open Shortest Path First (OSPF)

OSPF is a relatively simple protocol. Different links on the same router are put into the same or different areas. For example, you would use Area 1 for the interconnects between campuses, but you would use another area, such as Area 10, for the campus itself. By separating areas, you can reduce the amount of cross-talk that happens between devices.

There are two versions of OSPF, v2 and v3. The main difference between v2 and v3 is that v2 is for IPv4 networks and v3 is for IPv6 networks:

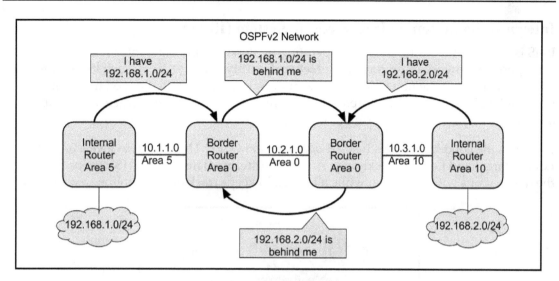

When there are multiple paths that can be taken, the cost of the links must be taken into account. In the following diagram, you can see where there are two paths, one has a total cost of 20 (*5+5+10*) and the other, 16 (*8+8*), so the traffic will take the lowest-cost link:

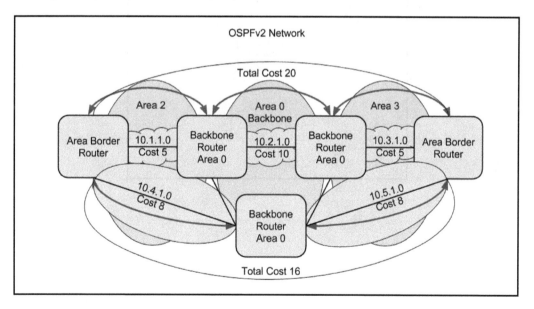

Intermediate System to Intermediate System (IS-IS)

IS-IS is a link-state routing protocol, operating by flooding link-state information throughout a network of routers using **Network Entity Titles** (**NETs**). Each IS-IS router has its own database of the network topology, built by aggregating the flooded network information. IS-IS is used by companies who are looking for fast convergence, scalability, and rapid flooding of new information.

IS-IS uses the concept of levels instead of areas as in OSPF. There are two levels in IS-IS, Level 1 (area) and Level 2 (backbone). A Level 1 **Intermediate System** (**IS**), keeps track of the destinations within its area, while a Level 2 IS keeps track of paths to the Level 1 areas:

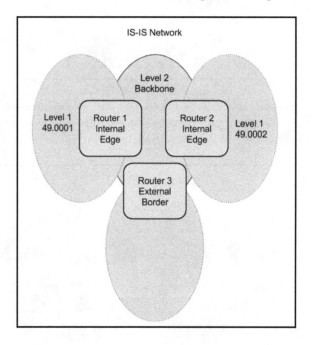

Enhanced Interior Gateway Routing Protocol (EIGRP)

EIGRP is Cisco's proprietary routing protocol. It is hardly ever seen in current networks, but if you see it in yours, then you need to plan accordingly. Replacing EIGRP with OSPF is suggested so that you can interoperate with non-Cisco devices.

Routing Information Protocol (RIP)

If RIP is being used in your network, it must be replaced during the design. Most newer routing stacks do not support RIP. It is one of the original routing protocols, using the number of hops (routed ports) between the device and remote location to determine the optimal path. RIP sends its entire routing database out every 30 seconds. When routing tables were small, many years ago, RIP worked fine. With larger tables, the traffic bursts and the resulting recomputing by other routers in the network causes routers to run at almost 100 percent CPU all the time.

Cables

Cables will be mentioned throughout the book, so we will review the major types here.

Copper cables

Copper cables have been around for a very long time. Originally, network devices were connected using coax cable (the same cable used for television antennas). These days, there are a few standard cables that are used. These are the different RJ45 cables:

- **Cat 5** : This is a 100 MB capable cable, used for both 10 MB and 100 MB connections
- **Cat 5e**: This is a 1 GbE capable cable, but not suggested for 1 GbE networks (Cat 6 is better and the price difference is nominal)
- **Cat 6**: This is a 1 GbE capable cable, and it can be used for any speed, at or below 1 GbE, including 100 MB and 10 MB

Fiber/hot pluggable cables

The following is the list of fiber/hot pluggable cables and ports:

- **Small Form-factor Pluggable (SFP):**
  - **SFP**: This is capable of up to 1 GbE connections
  - **SFP+**: This is of the same size as SFP, and is capable of up to 10 Gb connections
  - **SFP28**: This is of the same size as SFP, capable of up to 25 Gb connections
  - **Quad Small Form-factor Pluggable (QSFP)**: This is a bit wider than SFP, but capable of multiple GbE connections
  - **QSFP+**: This is of the same size as QSFP, and is capable of 40 GbE as 4x10GbE on the same cable
  - **QSFP28**: This is of the same size as the QSFP, capable of 100 GbE
- **Direct Attach Cable (DAC)**: Has a built in SFP or QSFP type connector and goes directly into the port cage on the switch.
- **Fiber optic cable**: Needs a SFP or QSFP type connector in the port cage to connect into the switch. Some switches may have fixed fiber optic ports, but this is uncommon in current generation products.

Breakout cables

As routers and switches continue to become more dense, where the number of ports on the front of the device can no longer fit in the space, manufacturers have moved to what we call breakout cables. For example, if you have a switch that can handle 3.2 Tbps of traffic, you need to provide 3200 Gbps of port capacity. The easiest way to do that is to use 32 100 Gb ports, which will fit on the front of a 1 U device. You cannot fit 128 10 Gb ports without using either a breakout patch panel (which will then use another few RUs) or a breakout cable.

For a period of time in the 1990s, Cisco used RJ21 connectors to provide up to 96 Ethernet ports per slot:

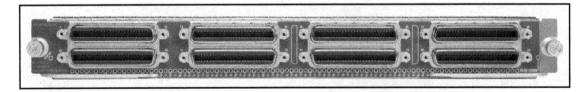

Network engineers would then create breakout cables to go from the RJ21 to RJ45.

These days, we have both DAC and fiber breakout cables. For example, here you can see a 1x4 breakout cable, providing 4x10 G or 25 G ports from a single 40 G or 100 G port:

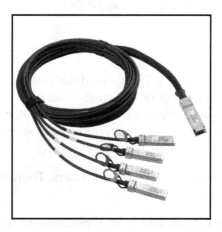

> If you build a LAN network that only includes switches that provide layer 2 connectivity, any devices you want to connect need to be in the same IP block. If you have a router in your network, it can route traffic between IP blocks.

What defines a modern network?

There are a litany of concepts that define a modern network, from simple principles to full feature sets.

In general, a next-generation data center design enables you to move to a widely distributed non-blocking fabric with uniform chipset, bandwidth, and buffering characteristics in a simple architecture.

In one example, to support these requirements, you would begin with a true three-tier Clos switching architecture with ToR, spine, and fabric layers to build a data center network. Each ToR would have access to multiple fabrics and have the ability to select a desired path based on application requirement or network availability.

Following the definition of a modern network from the introduction, here we lay out the general definition of the parts.

Modern network pieces

Here we will discuss the concepts that build an NGN.

SDN

SDNs can be defined in multiple ways. The general definition of a SDN is one which can be controlled as a singular unit instead of on a system-by-system basis. The control plane, which would normally be in the device and uses routing protocols, is replaced with a controller. SDNs can be built using many different technologies, including OpenFlow, overlay networks, and automation tools.

Within an SDN, you will have the concept of controllers. There are four controllers that we will talk about in this book:

- OpenDaylight and ONOS, which are OpenFlow-based open source controllers
- **Application Policy Infrastructure Controller** (**APIC**) from Cisco
- NSX from VMware

Next generation networking and hyperscale networks

As we mentioned in the introduction, 20 years ago, NGN hardware would have been the Cisco GSR (officially introduced in 1997) or the Juniper M40 (officially released in 1998). Large Cisco and Juniper customers would have been working with the companies to help come up with the specifications and determining how to deploy the devices (possibly Alpha or Beta versions) in their networks:

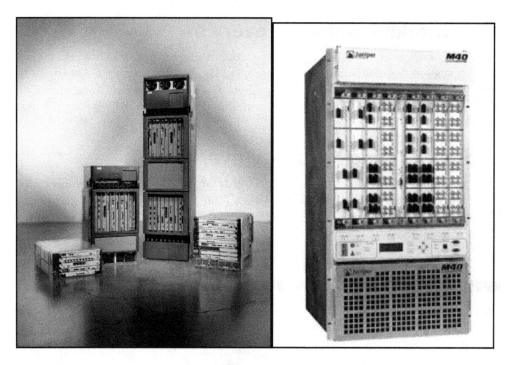

Today, we can look at the hyperscale networking companies to see what a modern network looks like. A hyperscale network is one where the data stored, transferred, and updated on the network grows exponentially. Technology such as 100 Gb Ethernet, SDN, open networking equipment, and software are being deployed by hyperscale companies.

Open networking hardware overview

Open hardware has been around for about 10 years, first in the consumer space and more recently in the enterprise space. Enterprise open networking hardware companies such as Quanta and Accton provide a significant amount of the hardware currently utilized in networks today. Companies such as Google and Facebook have been building their own hardware for many years. Facebook's routers such as the Wedge 100 and Backpack are available publicly for end users to utilize.

Some examples of open networking hardware are as follows:

- Dell S6000-ON: This is a 32x40 G switch with 32 QSFP+ ports on the front
- Quanta LY8: This is a 48x10 G + 6x40 G switch with 48 SFP+ ports and 6 QSFP+ ports
- Facebook Wedge 100: This is a 32x100 G switch with 32 QSFP28 ports on the front

Open networking software overview

To use open networking hardware, you need an operating system. The operating system manages the system devices such as fans, power, LEDs, and temperature. On top of the operating system, you will run a forwarding agent. Examples of forwarding agents are Indigo, the open source OpenFlow daemon, and Quagga, an open source routing agent.

Closed networking hardware overview

Cisco and Juniper are the leaders in the closed hardware and software space. Cisco produces switches such as the Nexus series (3000, 7000, and 9000) with 9000 programmable by ACI. Juniper provides the MX series (480, 960, and 2020) with 2020 being the highest end forwarding system they sell.

Closed networking software overview

Cisco has multiple NOSes including IOS, NX-OS, and IOS-XR. All Cisco NOSes are closed source and proprietary to the system that they run on. Cisco has what the industry call an *industry standard CLI*, which is emulated by many other companies.

Juniper ships a single NOS, Junos, which can install on multiple different systems. Junos is a closed source BSD-based NOS. The Junos CLI is significantly different from IOS and is more focused on engineers who program.

Network virtualization

Network virtualization, not to be confused with NFV, is the concept of recreating the hardware interfaces that exist in a traditional network in software. By creating a software counterpart to the hardware interfaces, you decouple the network forwarding from the hardware.

There are a few companies and software projects that allow the end user to enable network virtualization. The first one is NSX, which comes from the same team that developed **Open vSwitch** (**OVS**) called Nicira, which was acquired by VMware in 2012. Another project is Big Cloud Fabric by Big Switch Networks, which utilizes a heavily modified version of Indigo, an OpenFlow controller.

NFV

NFV can be summed up by the statement, *due to recent network focused advancements in PC hardware, any service able to be delivered on proprietary, application specific hardware should be able to be done on a virtual machine*, essentially, on routers, firewalls, load balancers, and other network devices, all running virtually on commodity hardware.

Traffic engineering

Traffic engineering is a method of optimizing the performance of a telecommunications network by dynamically analyzing, predicting, and regulating the behavior of data transmitted over that network.

The history of open hardware and software

While **Open-source software (OSS)** has been around for decades, the concept of open networking hardware has not. By combining OSS with open networking hardware, end users are able to create their own network devices that provide the connectivity and services that are necessary for them.

One of the first companies to come out with open networking hardware was Quanta Computer. In 2009, Pronto started to provide open networking switches including the LB4G and LB9(A). These switches were used by the OpenFlow team at Stanford to develop OpenFlow on hardware. Sold under the Pronto Networks name (now, Pica8), these switches were used by companies such as Google for their SDN projects.

In 2011, Facebook started the **Open Compute Project (OCP)**. The goal of the OCP was to provide a place where companies could share hardware and software designs. These designs are used by multiple hardware manufacturers to build OCP specification hardware. In 2013, the OCP introduced the networking project, where networking vendors could submit open hardware designs for network switches.

Companies such as Big Switch Networks, Cumulus Networks, and Pluribus Networks utilize open switching hardware built by companies such as Accton, Dell, and Quanta to create fully open and malleable networks. OSS projects such as Open Network Linux, OpenSwitch, and OS10 provide a open software base for these devices on which end users can build their own tools.

One of the most important software tools is **Open Network Install Environment (ONIE)**, which is a small Linux image that allows end users to install a NOS onto a network device such as a switch.

Some examples of open source networking software are as follows:

- Facebook's FBOSS, a Thrift-based daemon that manages the forwarding of the switch by interacting with Broadcom's OpenNSL. FBOSS has no routing capabilities of its own and requires all information to be provided via a configuration file and Thrift API calls.
- Microsoft's **Software for Open Networking in the Cloud** (**SONiC**) uses a Quagga-based routing daemon talking to **Switch Abstraction Interface** (**SAI**) and runs on a few open hardware switches including the Dell S6000-ON and the Mellanox SN2700.
- Google have also designed their own switches since 2004, but have not released the designs or software information. In 2012, one of their switches was accidentally shipped to the wrong location and appeared on the internet.

Hardware providers

Accton has been quite active in the open hardware space, providing a multitude of designs, including some designed by Facebook, such as the Wedge. The current generation Facebook Wedge is the Wedge 100, providing 32 ports of 100 G. Accton also has its own switches, such as the AS7716, that provide 32 ports of 100 G:

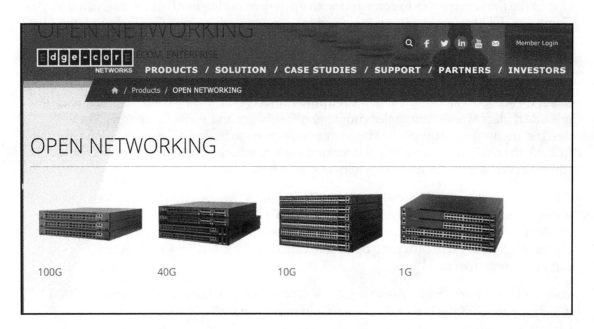

Most open networking hardware designs are based around switching ASICs from Broadcom, but over the past few years, other companies such as Barefoot Networks, Cavium, and Mellanox have brought out more open designs. Barefoot is a good example of a fully open design, where they utilize a specific language, called P4, to program the forwarding hardware.

The Facebook designed switches are focused on Facebook's own design needs. The Facebook Wedge 100 runs a standard Linux image with drivers for the Broadcom switching chips. On top of the software stack, Facebook uses an OSS project called FBOSS to control the switches via a Thrift API. This allows Facebook to manage their switches the same way they manage their servers.

Facebook contracted with both Accton and Quanta to build the Wedge 40. The Wedge 40 is built from commodity components and are reused from other Facebook systems. The CPU complex and **Board Management Controllers** (**BMC**) come from the Facebook servers.

Hyperscale networking

The next generation networking devices that have come from the needs of hyperscale networking companies have a few commonalities:

- In general, the configuration and operation of these devices have been designed to be automated or managed from a central controller
- Automation is done via tools that use everything from screen scraping to utilizing Thrift or REST APIs
- Most of these hyperscale-focused next generation networking devices have one or more parts that are traditionally found on servers, such as a BMC, powerful Intel processors, and large solid state storage drives

Hyperscale hardware

The equipment used in hyperscale networks can be from established vendors, such as Cisco and Juniper, or from open networking companies, such as Edgecore and Quanta. Dell is a special case as they offer both closed and open versions of their switching hardware, designated with a -ON at the end, for example, the S6000-ON and a 32x40G switch. Mellanox, which started as a storage network vendor, has been building open networking switches, including the SN2700, a 32x100 G switch, and the SN2100, a 16x100 G switch.

Many open networking designs come out of specific needs of the hyperscale companies and some even come from the hyperscale companies. Facebook have open sourced five switches, all designed to meet their needs:

- **Wedge 40**: This is a 16x40 G switch with a BMC—running FBOSS
- **6-pack**: This is a 128x40 G modular switch with multiple BMCs—running FBOSS
- **Wedge 100**: This is a 32x100 G switch with a BMC—running FBOSS
- **Backpack**: This is a 128x100 G modular switch with multiple BMCs—running SnapRoute
- **Voyager**: This is a open transponder for DWDM networks, which includes both 12x100 G Ethernet and 4x200 G DWDM ports—running an FBOSS-like daemon:

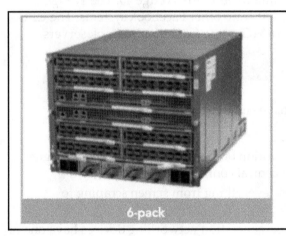
6-pack

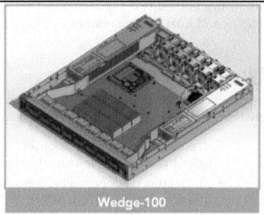
Wedge-100

Software

Software is the heart of any network: no matter how sophisticated hardware gets, software is necessary to utilize the hardware. Here we will discuss the software components behind open hardware initiatives.

ONIE

In order to use open hardware, there needs to be an installation environment. Currently, ONIE is the standard. ONIE was developed by Cumulus Networks in coordination with Big Switch Networks, and it provides a GRUB or U-Boot installable miniature Linux environment from which NOS can be installed on the system.

Cisco's Bootloader

The Bootloader is a small bootable software image that is flashed to Cisco hardware. The Bootloader initializes the system and brings up the devices necessary to load the main software, IOS.

OpenBMC

Open source projects such as OpenBMC have been released to provide the software to run on the BMC and system processor.

Forwarding agents

Networking companies such as RTBrick and SnapRoute have been formed to provide API manageable networking stacks. SnapRoute provides an entire forwarding infrastructure including L2/L3 and forwarding chip drivers. SnapRoute have written their project in Go, Google's language of choice.

Commercial products

Software-defined products such as Cisco's **Application Centric Infrastructure** (**ACI**) and VMware's NSX have come out of large companies such as Cisco and VMware along with products such as **Big Cloud Fabric** (**BCF**) from Big Switch Networks.

Open NOS companies such as Cumulus Networks and Pica8 have released software for open switches. Pica8 also provides a full solution, selling switches with PicOS installed. Pica8 originally provided switches under the Pronto name, but now sells them under the Pica8 name, for example, the P-5401—32x40 G switch.

Closed source NOS

Software from companies such as Cisco and Juniper are considered closed source as they do not include access to the source code. Cisco has multiple operating systems, including their original **Internetwork Operating System** (**IOS**), not to be confused with Apple's recent use for their iDevices.

IOS

IOS is a binary blob operating system that is loaded into memory on boot of Cisco devices. IOS is easy to upgrade since all of the configuration information is kept separate and the IOS filesystem is immutable. Installing a new IOS version simply requires that you upload it to the device and point the configuration to load it. IOS uses a CLI that is considered to be the *standard* interface and replicated by many other vendors.

Junos OS

Juniper Network Operating System (**Junos**), based on FreeBSD, has not changed significantly since its introduction in the mid-90s. While more complex than IOS, Junos won many customers with its ability to be used by power users.

Open source network operating systems

Once you have your hardware picked out, you need an NOS. An NOS is what runs on your switch and allows it to forward packets. Companies such as Cumulus Networks and Pica8 sell full NOSes with L2 and L3 forwarding capability. In the OSS world, there are a few choices, including **Open Network Linux** (**ONL**), OpenSwitch, and SONiC.

Open Network Linux (ONL)

ONL is a project started by Rob Sherwood, previously of Big Switch Networks and now at Facebook. The goal was to provide a simple, clean Linux-based open source network operating system. ONL provides a ONIE compatible installable NOS, on which the user can install their own forwarding agents. At the time of writing, ONL supported ~35 switches from Alpha Networks, Dell, DNI, Edgecore, Mellanox, Quanta, and others.

OpenSwitch

OpenSwitch is a project started by HP (now HPE) to provide a full NOS using Quagga as the base and creating a full layer 2 / layer 3 platform on top of a Linux base.

The project used a central database based on OVSDB and required all data to be exchanged through the database rather than directly between themselves. The design was complex and eventually supported ~3 switches directly, rebranded HP versions of Edgecore switches, and unofficially supported ~4 more that were ported by end user or vendors.

OpenSwitch started pivoting at the time of this book. The Quagga design with OVSDB was replaced with SnapRoute, an API-driven routing stack running on Dell's OS10 Open Edition, a Debian-based NOS.

SONiC

SONiC is a project that Microsoft started to run inside their own network on white-box switches. It uses Quagga for forwarding and Redis as a database to store information and exchange data between processes. SONiC runs on top of Debian 8 and can be run on Dell OS10 or ONL.

At the time of writing, SONiC supported more switches than OpenSwitch, including some Edgecore, Arista, and Mellanox switches.

Software forwarding agents

If you need to run a forwarding agent on a Linux-based NOS, there are a few options, of which most, other than Mellanox's SwitchDev implementation, have proprietary / closed source parts. Broadcom provides both OF-DPA and OpenNSL publicly as binary-only options for programming their ASICs. Cavium offers an SAI interface to their SDK, but it is not publicly available at the time of writing.

SwitchDev

To quote the Linux kernel documentation, *The Ethernet switch device driver model (switchdev) is an in-kernel driver model for switch devices which offload the forwarding (data) plane from the kernel*. Essentially, it is an open Netlink listener that allows for the offloading of forwarding information to hardware. It can also be used for soft switches such as OVS and offload network interface cards using SR-IOV.

From the open switching side, currently, only Mellanox supports SwitchDev for their 10/25/40/50/100G switches. Broadcom only supports its consumer-grade switches such as those in access points and home routers.

Indigo

Indigo is a OpenFlow-based forwarding agent that runs on the NOS to provide forwarding. Introduced in 2008 by Stanford University, Indigo is the base for Big Switch Networks OpenFlow daemon, the ON.Lab CORD project, and Indigo is integrated into OF-DPA, the Broadcom OpenFlow driver.

The concept of OpenFlow is simple, program forwarding tables in hardware and software switches using a standardized interface. We will cover OpenFlow in detail later in this book.

FBOSS

While specifically designed for the Facebook Wedge switches, FBOSS provides a Thrift-based API with integration into Broadcom's **Open Network Switch Layer** (**OpenNSL**). FBOSS allows for static configuration of interfaces and forwarding entries. FBOSS also has a Netlink listener available, which allows for the end user to run programs such as Quagga or FRR on the system.

SwitchD

SwitchD is the Cumulus Networks SDK programmer. It is available with the purchase of Cumulus Linux, a Linux-based NOS.

Open Route Cache (ORC)

ORC is a daemon provided for ONL. It is a very simple Netlink translator that talks directly to the Broadcom SDK. ORC only supports IPv4 and is meant to provide a guide on how to write your own forwarding platform.

Software controllers

There are two types of software controllers. The first type uses OpenFlow to manage the hardware in the network. OpenFlow is an open standard that is easily utilized to manage the forwarding of traffic. The second type uses a proprietary API to manage the hardware in the network. The API can be open or closed, but will not be generic.

An OpenFlow controller manages multiple networking devices by programming switches using the OpenFlow protocol. OpenFlow-based network devices run a OpenFlow daemon such as Indigo, which translates the OpenFlow commands into switch forwarding data.

There are branded and unbranded versions of OpenDaylight available. Brocade makes the **Brocade Virtual Controller** (**BVC**). The OpenDaylight foundation releases unbranded versions of the software. You can also obtain OpenDaylight from Cisco.

The following diagram shows a test setup for OpenDaylight using two switches:

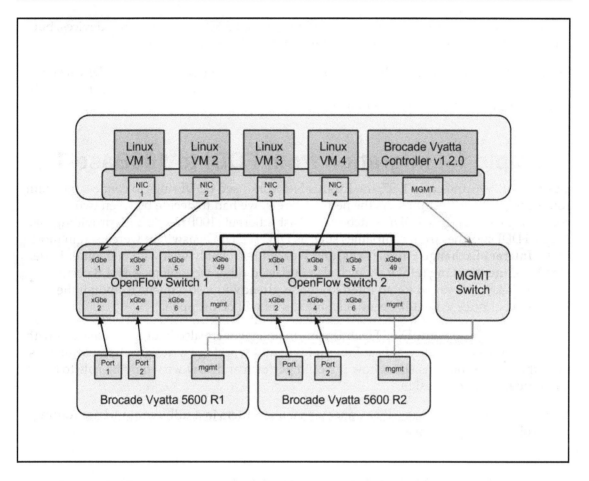

A good example of a open source, open API design is what the company called SnapRoute is doing with their product FlexSwitch. FlexSwitch uses a REST-based API to program the L2/L3 forwarding entries.

Next generation networking examples

In my 25 or so years of networking, I have dealt with a lot of different networking technologies, each iteration (supposedly) better than the last. Starting with Thinnet (10BASE2), moving through ARCNET, 10BASE-T, token ring, ATM to the Desktop, **Fiber Distributed Data Interface (FDDI)**, and onward. Generally, the technology improved for each system until it was swapped out. A good example is the change from a literal ring for token ring to a switching design, where devices hung off of a hub (as in 10BASE-T).

ATM to the Desktop was a novel idea, providing up to 25 Mbps to connected devices, but the complexity of configuring and managing it was not worth the gain.

Today, almost everything is Ethernet, as shown by the Facebook Voyager DWDM system, which uses Ethernet over both traditional SFP ports and the DWDM interfaces. Ethernet is simple, well supported, and easy to manage.

Example 1 – migration from FDDI to 100Base-T

During late 1996 and early 1997, the Exodus Network used FDDI rings to connect the main routers together at 100 Mbps. As the network grew, we had to decide between two competing technologies, FDDI switches and Fast Ethernet (100Base-T), both providing 100 Mbps. FDDI switches from companies such as DEC (FDDI Gigaswitch) were used in most of the **Internet Exchange Points** (**IXPs**) and worked reasonably well with one minor issue, **Head-of-Line Blocking** (**HoLB**), which also impacted other technologies. HoLB occurs when a packet is destined for an interface that is already full, so a queue is built; if the interface continues to be full, eventually, the queue will be dropped.

While we were testing the DEC FDDI Gigaswitches, we were also in deep discussions with Cisco about the availability of **Fast Ethernet** (**FE**) and working on designs. Because FE was new, there were concerns about how it would perform and how we would be able to build a redundant network design.

In the end, we decided to use FE, connect the main routers in a full mesh, and use routing protocols to manage failover.

Example 2 – NGN failure (LANE)

During the high-growth period at Exodus Communications, there was a request to connect a new data center to the original one and allow customers to put servers in both locations using the same address space. To do this, we chose **LAN Emulation** (**LANE**), which allows an ATM network to be used like a LAN. On paper, LANE looked like a great idea, the ability to extend the LAN so that customers could use the same IP space in two different locations. In reality, it was very different.

For hardware, we were using Cisco 5513 switches, which provided a combination of Ethernet and ATM ports.

There were multiple issues with this design:

- First, the customer is provided with an Ethernet interface, which runs over an ATM optical interface. Any error on the physical connection between switches or the ATM layer would cause errors on the Ethernet layer.
- Second, monitoring was very hard, when there were network issues, you had to look in multiple locations to determine where the errors were happening.

After a few weeks, we did a midnight swap, putting Cisco 7500 routers in to replace the 5500 switches and moving customers onto new blocks for the new data center.

Designing a modern network

When designing a new network, some of the following factors might be important to you:

- Simple, focused, yet non-blocking IP fabric
- Multistage parallel fabrics based on the Clos network concept
- Simple merchant silicon
- Distributed control plane with some centralized controls
- Wide multi-path (ECMP)
- Uniform chipset, bandwidth, and buffering
- 1:1 oversubscribed (non-blocking fabric)
- Minimizing the hardware necessary to carry east–west traffic
- Ability to support a large number of bare metal servers without adding an additional layer
- Limiting fabric to a five-stage Clos within the data center to minimize lookups and switching latency
- Support host attachment at 10 G, 25 G, 50 G, and 100G Ethernet
- Traffic management

In a modern network, one of the first decisions is whether you will use a centralized controller or not. If you use a centralized controller, you will be able to see and control the entire network from one location. If you do not use a centralized controller, you will need to either manage each system directly or via automation. There is a middle space where you can use some software-defined network pieces to manage parts of the network, such as an OpenFlow controller for the WAN or VMware NSX for your virtualized workloads.

Once you know what the general management goal is, the next decision is whether to use open, proprietary, or a combination of both open and proprietary networking equipment. Open networking equipment is a concept that has been around less than a decade and started when very large network operators decided that they wanted better control of the cost and features of the equipment in their networks. Google is a good example. In the following figure, you can see how Facebook used both their own hardware, 6-pack/Backpack, and legacy vendor hardware for their interoperability and performance testing:

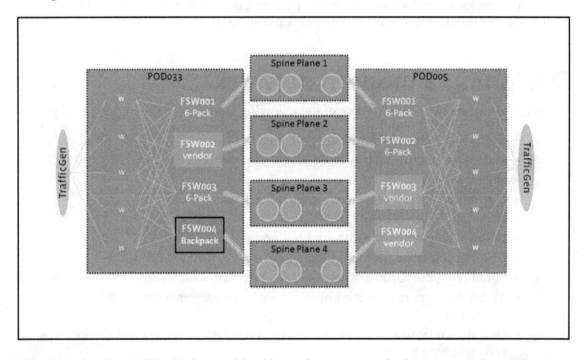

Google wanted to build a high-speed backbone, but were not looking to pay the prices that the incumbent proprietary vendors such as Cisco and Juniper wanted. Google set a price per port (1 G/10 G/40 G) that they wanted to hit and designed equipment around that. Later, companies such as Facebook decided to go in the same direction and contracted with commodity manufacturers to build network switches that met their needs.

Proprietary vendors can offer the same level of performance or better using their massive teams of engineers to design and optimize hardware. This distinction even applies on the software side, where companies such as VMware and Cisco have created SDN tools such as NSX and ACI.

With the large amount of networking gear available, designing and building a modern network can appear to be a complex concept. Designing a modern network requires research and a good understanding of networking equipment. While complex, the task is not hard if you follow the guidelines listed in this section.

These are a few of the stages of planning that need to be followed before the modern network design is started:

1. The first step is to understand the scope of the project (single site, multisite, multicontinent, and multiplanet).
2. The second step is to determine whether the project is a green field (new) or brown field deployment (how many of the sites already exist and will/will not be upgraded?).
3. The third step is to determine whether there will be any SDN, NGN, or open networking pieces.
4. Finally, it is key that the equipment to be used is assembled and tested to determine whether the equipment meets the needs of the network.

Scoping

The project scope is one of the most important pieces of information needed. The project scope can go from a single device in one location to hundreds or even thousands of devices across multiple continents. Understanding the project scope provides a guideline on which to base the network design and hardware/software needs.

If the network is being designed for internal use, then looking at other locations should give information about the best practices of the company the network is being designed for. If the network is being designed for an external company, then it is useful to ask for documentation, hardware lists, and even a tour of a current site so that the concept can be understood.

This is not meant to be an exhaustive list, but there are a few things that need to be understood when designing the network:

- Is the network all internal?
- Does the network have a DMZ?
- Does the network have multiple internet connections?
- Does the network have storage and compute separate or together?
- Does the network need to support iSCSI or other SAN protocols?

- Does the network use MPLS, SD-WAN, or other tunneling technologies?
- Does the network have multiple **Points of Presence** (**POP**), and how large is a POP?
- Does the network use containers? If so, does it have a container-specific network?

At the end of the book, you will find a generic check sheet to scope the project.

Greenfield and brownfield networks

A greenfield network is a site where there is no networking equipment currently. For a greenfield deployment, there are a lot of options, but the needs of the network musts be clearly understood. In a perfect situation, the site would be completely malleable, allowing for power, cooling, and infrastructure to be built out to meet the needs of the design. Since a perfect situation is not always possible, taking inventory of the infrastructure is necessary before a design can be committed.

At the end of the book, you will find a generic check sheet that provides an overview of what should be understood about the site.

Next generation hardware

If you plan to use any next generation hardware, you will need to do some research and show due diligence. Since next generation hardware generally means equipment that has not been out for very long (or may not be out in the public), there will be little to no public information or testing of the equipment. You will want to schedule a **Proof of Concept** (**PoC**) to be done with the hardware you expect to use.

If you are using open next generation hardware, you may be able to use reference customers to understand what designs are being used and what features.

NFV

While PC-based network devices have been available since the 80s, they were generally used by small companies and networking enthusiasts who didn't or couldn't afford to buy a commercial-based solution. In the last few years, many drivers have brought PC-based networking devices back into the limelight, including—Ethernet as the last mile, better network interface cards, and Intel's focus on networking processing in its last few generation of chips.

Today, many vendors are producing PC-based network devices with advancements in packet handling within Intel's processors, allowing processor cores to be re-programmed into network processors, and allowing PC-based network devices to push tens or even hundreds of Gbps.

Some of the values of the NFV concept are speed, agility, and cost reduction. By centralizing designs around commodity server hardware, network operators can do the following:

- Do a single PoP/site design based on commodity compute hardware:
    - Avoiding designs involving one-off installations of appliances that have different power, cooling, and space needs simplifies planning
- Utilize resources more effectively:
    - Virtualization allows providers to allocate only the necessary resources needed by each feature/function
- Deploy network functions without having to send engineers to each site:
    - Truck rolls are costly both from a time and money standpoint
- Achieve reductions in OpEX and CapEX
- Achieve reduction of system complexity

Traffic engineering

Traffic engineering and traffic shaping is the concept of detecting and prioritizing different types of network traffic. Once prioritized, different bandwidth allocations can be provided to the traffic. Prioritization can be strict or loose and as a set amount or a variable amount (percentage).

Traffic engineering can be done in a few different ways, including MPLS TE tunnels, **Virtual Circuits (VCs)**, and **Quality of Service (QoS)**.

Tools

There are many tools that we will discuss and utilize in this book, tools to monitor networks, tools to configure networks, and everything in between.

Network monitoring

Monitoring the network is highly important and has been the basis for quite a few great open-source tools such as Nagios, Monit, Sensu, and Zabbix.

Nagios is one of the older and most mature open source monitoring tools, providing a core infrastructure and a set of plugins for different devices:

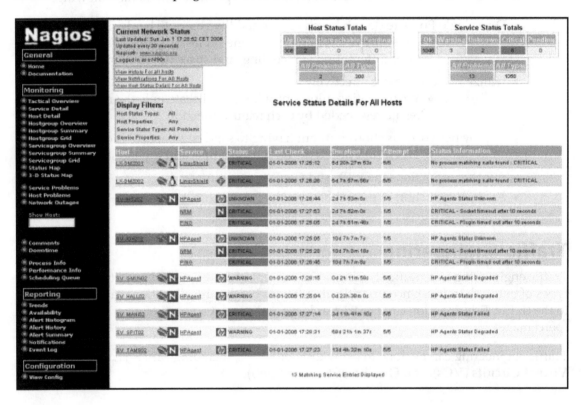

The generic Nagios display shows alerts and details about the network status.

Network configuration

The following tools will help you in network configuration.

RANCID

While we are working with the network, it will be useful to keep logs of changes in configurations. **Really Awesome New Cisco confIg Differ** (**RANCID**) is a free tool that can log in to many different types of systems, not just Cisco (though it started out that way).

 You can find more about RANCID at `http://www.shrubbery.net/rancid/`.

Postman

Postman is a program that works with APIs. It is available at `http://www.getpostman.com`. We will utilize Postman when dealing with REST-based APIs:

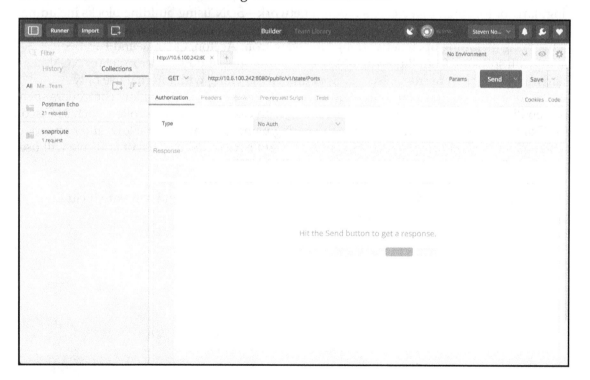

Git

Git is a protocol developed by Linus Torvalds in 2005 to have a better versioning system for the Linux kernel. Git will be used throughout the book for interactive exercises.

Summary

In this chapter, we discussed many different concepts that tie NGN together. These concepts will be discussed more in forthcoming chapters, so use this chapter as a reference if you need an explanation of any terms. Some takeaways from the chapter are as follows.

The term NGN refers to the latest and near term networking equipment and designs. We looked at networking concepts such as local, metro, and wide area networks, network controllers, routers, and switches as well as routing protocols such as BGP, IS-IS, OSPF, and RIP.

Now, what defines a modern network? There are many pieces, which are used either singularly or together, that create a modern network—SDN using building blocks including OpenFlow, Cisco ACI, and VMware NSX; next generation hardware and hyperscale networking including open networking hardware from Accton, Quanta, and Facebook along with software from Big Switch Networks, Cumulus, and Pica8; proprietary NGN hardware and software from Cisco, Juniper and Arista along with internal use only hardware from Google; open source software controllers such as OpenFlow controllers such as Floodlight, ONOS, and OpenDaylight, along with closed source controllers such as Cisco APIC and VMware NSX, NFV, traffic engineering using QoS, and OpenFlow; and network design planning including the scoping of the current network/site. A list of tools we will use in this book such as Git, Nagios, Postman, and RANCID.

In the next chapter, we will go deeper into networking hardware and software including, the Open Compute Project and its goals for hyperscale networks.

2
Networking Hardware and Software

Choosing the right networking hardware and software is key to the success of your project. Many companies choose to mix open and closed (proprietary) vendors in their network or use multiple proprietary or open vendors to avoid issues where the entire network can collapse due to a problem with software/hardware from one vendor.

If you recall from Chapter 1, *Open and Proprietary Next Generation Networks*, originally, routers were open as they were run on minicomputers. The first generation of switches or hubs (bridges) had no real features, so there was no need for configuration.

These days, switches are much more flexible, able to hold hundreds of thousands of forwarding entries, intelligent, and able to send traffic to the right ports rather than broadcasting it out across the entire network.

Companies that used to build hardware that was rebranded and sold under the names of Cisco, Juniper, HP, and others, are now building open hardware that is available directly to the end user with proprietary free software that is available as open source. However, companies such as Accton and Flextronics put their own branding on what we refer to as white-box switches. Other companies such as Lanner provide open hardware white-box solutions that anyone can rebrand.

In this chapter, we will cover the basics of open and closed networking hardware and software. When you are done with this chapter, you should have a good grasp of the following:

- The **Open Compute Project (OCP)**
    - Hardware designs submitted to the OCP
    - Software administered by the OCP

- The **Open Network Install Environment (ONIE)**
- Hardware from OCP member open vendors
- Hardware from proprietary vendors

Introducing the OCP

As we discussed in Chapter 1, *Open and Proprietary Next Generation Networks*, in 2011, Facebook started the OCP. They describe themselves as a collaborative community focused on redesigning hardware technology to efficiently support the growing demands on compute infrastructure. Essentially, entities contribute hardware designs for servers, storage, computing, rack infrastructure, and networking.

Back in 2009, Facebook was expanding its network at a rapid pace and was looking for the best way to standardize the building blocks for their network. Previously, companies such as Yahoo, Google, and Hotmail had been building their compute and storage infrastructure using generally available hardware from the consumer computer market. The goal of these designs was to maximize rack space usage and they often contained computer motherboards tied to rack shelves with their power supplies and hard drives attached openly:

Google rack in 1998

In the preceding image, you can see how tightly packed the boards were. Companies were stuffing two or more servers in a single RU, essentially, 1.75". These racks required special cooling infrastructure as they created a massive amount of heat. Over time, companies such as **Silicon Graphics International (SGI)** Corp. (formerly Rackable Systems, Inc.) came out with 1 RU servers that had close to the same computing power as the ones built by hyperscalers.

When I was working for Exodus Communications, it was common for companies who had hardware co-located in our facility to come in and replace parts and upgrade CPUs, memory, and hard drives, and put the old hardware to rest. It was a very inefficient and time-consuming way of dealing with hardware.

In 2011, when Facebook introduced the OCP to the world, they hosted a conference where there were many different vendors showing their open hardware designs. At that time, the OCP Networking subgroup did not exist, though some companies such as Intel and Quanta presented their networking projects at the OCP Summit.

While Intel was still dabbling in the market, they produced the FM6000 network switch and presented it at the 2013 OCP Summit. The Intel FM6000 reference switch was an OpenFlow-capable 640 Gbps switch produced for the open networking community. As the time of writing, Intel no longer produces full networking switches, but focuses on only parts.

When it was started, the OCP focused on servers and storage (hence the name). The first networking switch announced was the Facebook Wedge, a 16x40G (Wedge 40). The Wedge 40 was a switch that Facebook was using in its network as a replacement for the vendor (Cisco, Juniper) hardware. The first switch accepted was Accton/Edge-Core AS5712-54x. Other vendors such as Quanta and Interface Masters submitted their designs and started producing open networking switches.

Accepted open compute networking hardware

To be accepted to the OCP Networking Project, the hardware must meet certain requirements including having full hardware diagrams, and a luggage tag (a plastic pull out tab with information about the system), and go through a vetting process. As the time of writing, the following switches have been accepted:

Company	Model (if given)	Port configuration	Type of switch
Alpha Networks	SNX-60x0-486F	48-port 10 GbE SFP+ and 6-port 40 GbE QSFP+	Leaf switch
Alpha Networks	SNQ-60x0-320F	32-port 40 GbE QSFP+	Leaf/Spine switch

Alpha Networks	N/A	48x10GbT, 2x40 GbE QSFP+, 4x100 GbE QSFP28	Leaf switch
Alpha Networks	N/A	32x100 GbE QSFP28	Leaf/Spine Switch
Edgecore Networks	AS5712-54X	48-port 10 GbE SFP+ & 6-port 40GbE QSFP+	Leaf switch
Edgecore Networks	AS6712-32X	32-port 40 GbE QSFP+	Leaf/Spine switch
Edgecore Networks	AS7712-32X	32-port 100 GbE QSFP28	Leaf/Spine switch
Edgecore Networks	ORSA-1RU	Open Rack Switch Adapter	N/A
Inventec	DCS6072QS	48x10 GbE SFP+ and 6x40 GbE QSFP+	Leaf switch
Inventec	DCS7032Q28	32x100 GbE QSFP28	Leaf/Spine switch
Mellanox	MSX1410OCP	SwitchX-2 48x10 GbE SFP+ and 12x40 GbE QSFP+	Leaf switch
Mellanox	MSX1710OCP	SwitchX-2 36x40 GbE QSFP+	Leaf/Spine switch
Facebook	Wedge 40	16x40 GbE QSFP+	Leaf/Spine switch
Facebook	Wedge 100	32x100 GbE QSFP28	Spine switch

The following switches were pending:

Company	Model (if given)	Port Configuration	Type of switch
Edgecore Networks	AS7512-32x	32x100 GbE QSFP28 (Cavium based)	Spine switch
Edgecore Networks	OMP 256/512	256 and 512 port 100 GbE QSFP28	Spine switch
Edgecore Networks	AS5900	54-port 10 GbE SFP+ and 6 port 100 GbE QSFP28	Leaf switch
Edgecore Networks	AS4610	30 or 54 port 1 GbE with/without POE	Access switch
Edgecore Networks	ECW7212-L	2x2 indoor wireless access point	Access point
Edgecore Networks	ECW7220-L	3x3 indoor wireless access point	Access point
Edgecore Networks	ECWO7220-L	3x3 indoor wireless access point	Access point
Agema	AG6248C-POE	48-port 1 GbE, 2x10 GbE	Access switch

Facebook	6-pack	128x40 GbE QSFP+	Leaf/Spine switch
Facebook	Backpack	128x100 GbE QSFP28	Spine switch
Nephos	NPS4806	48x10 GbE and 6x40GbE	Leaf switch
SKT	CNA-SSX2RC	N/A	N/A

As of this writing, you can see that there are 15 accepted and 12 pending switches and access points.

Open compute networking software projects

The OCP Networking Project also hosts a few software projects including ONIE, **Open Network Linux (ONL)**, SONiC, and SnapRoute.

Details of these software projects are:

- ONIE is a **Tiny Core Linux (TCL)** installation that provides the ability for the end user to manage the software installed on the switch. ONIE is a requirement to be considered as an OCP switch.
- ONL is a base NOS designed to run on network switches, based on Debian Linux.
- SONiC is a full NOS based on Debian Linux and running Quagga as the routing agent.
- SnapRoute is a routing agent that runs on top of ONL and other Linux-based NOS.

ONIE

As we discussed in Chapter 1, *Open and Proprietary Next Generation Networks*, ONIE is an installable Linux image that works on switches and allows new operating systems to be installed.

ONIE offers a few options once booted including the following:

- **ONIE: Install OS**
- **ONIE: Rescue**
- **ONIE: Uninstall OS**
- **ONIE: Update ONIE**
- **ONIE: Embed ONIE**

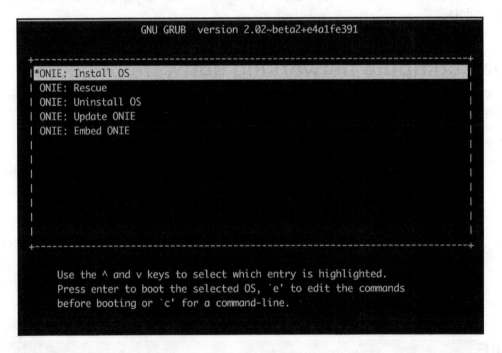

In install mode, ONIE will request images from an HTTP server in the same network. In rescue mode, you can run the `onie-nos-install` command to install an image from a web server or the `onie-self-update` command to upgrade ONIE. The main difference between rescue mode and the other options is that rescue mode will not attempt to grab an image from the network.

Consider this example of an ONIE upgrade via the rescue mode:

```
ONIE# onie-self-update http://local-http-server/onie-updater
```

Consider the example of ONIE NOS install via rescue mode:

```
ONIE# onie-nos-install http://local-http-server/NOS-installer
```

If you choose **ONIE: Uninstall OS**, ONIE will erase the entire disk other than the ONIE partitions and you will be left with ONIE only as a boot option. If you run **ONIE: Embed ONIE**, it will install ONIE to the local drive of the system; this is how you install ONIE from a USB or other external device.

ONL

ONL is a Linux distribution for bare-metal switches, that is, network forwarding devices built from commodity components. ONL is based on the Debian Linux release with limited tools installed and extra hardware support for switches.

ONL provides the base OS for many other projects from other open-source projects such as SnapRoute and CoRD. ONL does not provide any forwarding agents except where it runs FBOSS on the Facebook Wedge.

Broadcom-based switches running ONL can have an SDK, **Open Network Switch Library (OpenNSL)**, or **Openflow Data Plane Abstraction (OF-DPA)**, both by Broadcom, which we will discuss more in the next chapter, as their interface to the switching chip.

For any OCP submitted switches, ONL is a requirement. ONL currently runs on the Accton, Agema, Dell-EMC, Interface Masters, Lanner, Mellanox, Quanta, and Qwave switches.

SONiC

SONiC is a full NOS released by Microsoft. SONiC is based on Debian 8 running Quagga and is used in the Microsoft Azure network as part of the **Azure Cloud Switch (ACS)**.

The design of SONiC is similar to the OpenSwitch project, where there is a central database Redis, which talks to each of the daemons.

SONiC offers the following:

- **Border Gateway Protocol (BGP)**
- **Equal-cost multi-path (ECMP)**
- **Quality of Service (QoS)**
- **Priority Flow Control (PFC)** part of the IEEE 802.1Qbb specification
- **Weighted Random Early Discard (WRED)**

- **Class of Service (CoS)**
- **Simple Network Management Protocol (SNMP)**
- **Link Layer Discovery Protocol (LLDP)**, an open version of **Cisco Discovery Protocol (CDP)**
- **Network Time Protocol (NTP)**
- **Link Aggregation Group (LAG)**

Those of you with networking backgrounds will know that there is no traditional **Interior Gateway Protocol (IGP)** in the design such as **Intermediate System to Intermediate System (IS-IS)** or **Open Shortest Path First (OSPF)**. This is intentional as Microsoft uses iBGP as its IGP. Using only BGP is a common design across campus networks.

 IS-IS is a routing protocol designed to move information efficiently within a computer network, a group of physically connected computers, or similar devices. It accomplishes this by determining the best route for datagrams through a packet-switched network.

SnapRoute

SnapRoute is an API-based forwarding engine written in GO.

SnapRoute provides the following protocols:

- **Address Resolution Protocol (ARP)**
- **Bi-directional Forwarding Detection (BFD)**
- **Border Gateway Protocol (BGP)**
- **Dynamic Host Configuration Protocol Relay (DHCP Relay)**
- **Dynamic Host Configuration Protocol (DHCP)**
- **Open Shortest Path First (OSPF)**

- Routing Information Base (RIB)
- Tunneling protocols
- Virtual Router Redundancy Protocol (VRRP)

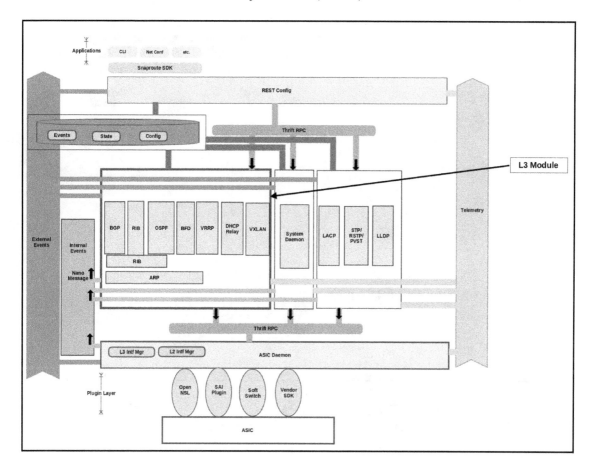

SnapRoute runs on top of ONL.

Consider this example REST API response from Postman, which we will cover in Chapter 5, *Using Postman for REST API Calls*:

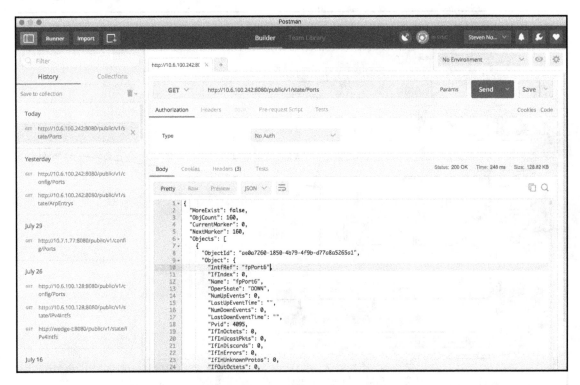

Following is the output of {GET}
http://10.6.100.242:8080/public/v1/state/Ports call:

```
"Objects": [
  {
    "ObjectId": "ae0a7260-1850-4b79-4f9b-d77a8a5265a1",
    "Object": {
      "IntfRef": "fpPort6",
      "IfIndex": 0,
      "Name": "fpPort6",
      "OperState": "DOWN",
      "NumUpEvents": 0,
      "LastUpEventTime": "",
      "NumDownEvents": 0,
      "LastDownEventTime": "",
      "Pvid": 4095,
```

```
    "IfInOctets": 0,
    "IfInUcastPkts": 0,
    "IfInDiscards": 0,
    "IfInErrors": 0,
    "IfInUnknownProtos": 0,
    "IfOutOctets": 0,
    "IfOutUcastPkts": 0,
    "IfOutDiscards": 0,
    "IfOutErrors": 0,
    "IfEtherUnderSizePktCnt": 0,
    "IfEtherOverSizePktCnt": 0,
    "IfEtherFragments": 0,
    "IfEtherCRCAlignError": 0,
    "IfEtherJabber": 0,
    "IfEtherPkts": 0,
    "IfEtherMCPkts": 0,
    "IfEtherBcastPkts": 0,
    "IfEtherPkts64OrLessOctets": 0,
    "IfEtherPkts65To127Octets": 0,
    "IfEtherPkts128To255Octets": 0,
    "IfEtherPkts256To511Octets": 0,
    "IfEtherPkts512To1023Octets": 0,
    "IfEtherPkts1024To1518Octets": 0,
    "ErrDisableReason": "",
    "PresentInHW": "YES",
    "ConfigMode": "Unconfigured",
    "PRBSRxErrCnt": 0
  }
 }
]
```

Here we can see that there is a port, Front Panel Port 6 (`fpPort6`), that is down and has not passed any traffic.

Network hardware designs from the OCP

Accton/Edgecore has released a large number of systems to the OCP including Facebook Wedges. In addition to the AS7712-32x, a 32x100 G switch based on the Broadcom Tomahawk chip, we will look at the Faceboook Wedge 100, a similar switch to the AS7712-32x, but adds a BMC and more LED colors.

Other vendors such as Quanta, Interface Masters, and Mellanox have also released open designs to the OCP.

Accton AS7712-32X

Accton/Edgecore AS7712-32x is a 32-port 100 GbE switch using QSFP28+ ports. The name translates as 7712 = model, 32 = number of ports, and x = fiber. A copper 1 GbE switch would be designated with a T, that is, 1 GbT (also known as IEEE 802.3ab) instead of an X.

The AS7712-32x uses a Broadcom Tomahawk switching chip providing 3.2 **Terabits per second** (**Tbps**). The AS7712-32x provides support for up to 32 × 100 GbE, 64 × 40/50 GbE, or even 128 × 25 GbE ports with an aggregate switching bandwidth of 3.2 Tbps.

The Tomahawk chip supports OpenFlow 1.3+ via OF-DPA and can handle up to 128,000 routes and 72,000 hosts.

Edge-Core AS7712-32X

Facebook/Accton Wedge 100

The Facebook Wedge 100 is built by Accton for Facebook. It is also available directly from Accton.

The Wedge has the following characteristics:

- The Wedge has a **Baseboard Management Controller** (**BMC**) that manages the fans, power, and other necessities to keep the switch running
- The Wedge has an Intel Bay Trail E3845 processor on its own board in the switch
- The Wedge has a Broadcom Tomahawk switch chip connected to 32 QSFP28s

- In total, the Wedge 100 has three different boards inside, two of which are field-replaceable

Facebook Wedge 100

Facebook's 6-pack and Backpack

Along with their 1 U fixed port switches, Facebook also uses two multi-slot chassis systems—the 6-pack, based on the Wedge 40, and the Backpack, based on the Wedge 100. The 6-pack is based on the Wedge 40 design and uses what consists of two Wedge 40s per physical line card and four line cards per chassis for 128 40 Gb ports. The fabric also has two Wedge 40s per physical card and there are two fabric cards for a total of 12 Wedge 40s in a 6-pack. Since there are only 6 physical cards, it is called the 6-pack.

The Backpack has the same design, but with the Wedge 100 boards and 100 Gb ports. Refer to the *Facebook's Backpack* image for a physical picture.

Hardware from Cisco and Dell

Both Cisco and Dell produce high-end switches for their customers. Both can utilize off-the-shelf forwarding chips such as Trident II and Tomahawk from Broadcom. Cisco also designs its own forwarding chips. In the case of the Nexus line of switches, the Nexus 3000 series uses commodity Broadcom forwarding chips, while the Nexus 9000 series uses specialty chips designed by Cisco that have been designed around having the functionality to handle ACI features. This is an important difference.

Cisco's APIC is able to interact with ACI switches to provide network wide control.

Cisco Nexus 3232C

The Cisco Nexus 3000 is a fixed port switch like the ones from Accton, which can provide 48 ports of 10 GbE or 32 ports of 100 GbE, depending on the model.

The Cisco Nexus 3232C has 32x100 GbE and looks quite similar to the Wedge 100 and Accton AS7712-32x. Since the Nexus 3232C is based on the Broadcom Tomahawk forwarding chip, it can handle up to 128,000 routes and 72,000 hosts.

Some of the important features are as follows:

- It provides layer 2 and 3 switching of up to 6.4 Tbps and more than 2,300 **Million packets per second (Mpps)**
- PHY-less design on all ports to optimize latency
- 32 fixed 100 GbE QSFP 28 ports
- It supports 10G/25G/40G/50G/100G in a single ToR platform
- It supports mobility and tenant isolation with VXLAN

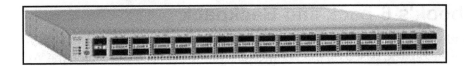

Cisco Nexus 3232C

Cisco Nexus 3172

The Cisco Nexus 3172 has 48 10 GbE ports with 6 40 GbE uplink. It is based on the Broadcom Trident II+ forwarding chip. Some of the important features are as follows:

- It provides layer 2 and 3 switching of up to 1.4 Tbps and more than 950 Mpps
- It supports mobility and tenant isolation with VXLAN (with a software upgrade)
- It optimizes latency with PHY-less design on all ports
- It supports 1/10/40 Gbps for maximum physical layer flexibility
- It offers up to 72 1/10 **Gigabit Ethernet (GE)** ports, or 48 1/10 GE plus six 40 GE ports in 1 RU

The 40 GbE ports can be configured as 4x10, making a total of 72 ports.

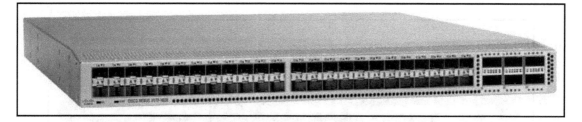

Cisco Nexus 3172

Cisco Nexus 9000

The Cisco Nexus 9504 is a 4-slot switch from Cisco that offers ACI functionality. It can hold up to 128 100 GbE ports and offers 15 Tbps of switching capacity. The Cisco Nexus 9504 switch offers 4 slots for networking cards, which are available in many different configurations including these:

- 32 x 100 GbE (QSFP28)
- 36 x 40 GbE (QSFP+)
- 48 x 1/10/25 GbE + 4 x 100 GbE

The Cisco Nexus 9504 runs NX-OS and can operate in either standalone mode or with ACI. It can also be configured using a REST/JSON interface.

The software licenses available for the Nexus 9000 series routers are as follows:

- Layer 2 only
- Layer 2 and Layer 3
- Span/Tap
- Cisco **Data Center Network Management** (DCNM)

One interesting thing about Cisco's NX-OS is that it contains a Linux boot loader and can be managed via the standard Linux GRUB system.

Cisco Nexus 9504

Another interesting thing is that the Cisco Nexus 9504 switch and Facebook's Backpack look very similar. At this point, there is a lot of convergence in the space.

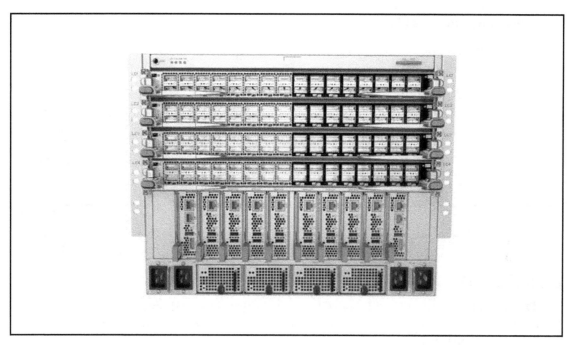

Facebook's Backpack

Dell Z9100-ON

In the networking space, Dell is an outlier as it produces both proprietary and open networking hardware.

Like the Dell S4048, the Dell Z9100 is available as an open networking switch—the Z9100-ON. It provides 32 ports of 100 GbE like the Edge-Core 7712 and the Cisco Nexus 3232C. It is an SDN-ready fixed form factor switch and is purpose-built for applications in high-performance data centers and modern computing environments.

The Z9100 runs Cumulus Linux as well as ONL and Dell OS9.

Dell Z9100

Dell Z9500

The Dell Z9500 is a 3 RU 132 QSFP (40 GbE) port switch that can handle up to 528 10 GbE interfaces using breakout cables. It is not an open networking switch and runs Dells OS9. It offers many of the same features as Cisco including full Layer 2 and Layer 3 support along with a programmable API.

Dell Z9500 has 10.5 Tbps of forwarding bandwidth and is able to forward all ports in a non-blocking fashion.

Dell Z9500

Summary

In this chapter, we discussed the multitude of open and closed hardware and software systems available to network architects. Many of these systems are very similar to each other. This is due to the fact that the industry is converging on designs based on the same hardware including forwarding chips from Broadcom, Cavium, and others.

The main decision from the design side is whether there will be open networking equipment in the design. You can build a NGN from completely proprietary equipment, so the inclusion of open networking equipment is optional, but in our mind it is a good idea.

We discussed the OCP, its goals, and members including Juniper Networks and now Cisco, who are both mostly in the proprietary networking space.

In the next chapter, we will explore OpenFlow and its use in networking.

3
Exploring OpenFlow

OpenFlow was created based on a better way to design and manage networks independent of different vendor equipment. Though OpenFlow seems to have appeared out of nowhere, OpenFlow is just one of the ways that we have historically tried to make computer networks more programmable using SDN.

In this chapter, we trace the history of programmable networks based on OpenFlow, how they work, and what the current state is. When done, you should have a good grasp of the following:

- Concepts around active networking and programmable networks
- The history of OpenFlow
- The different versions of OpenFlow and what is the importance of each
- Understanding OF-DPA, the open source OpenFlow agent from Broadcom
- Using an OpenFlow agent such as Indigo
- Open networking hardware from OCP networking vendors
- How controllers interact with OpenFlow agents

In `Chapter 1`, *Open and Proprietary Next Generation Networks*, we talked about the control plane and the data plane. The control plane is where the forwarding information is gathered and processed to create specific information for the data plane to use to forward packets.

Active and programmable network concepts

The generally accepted definition of an active network is one that modifies its behavior based on the packets crossing the devices. Active networks generally contain parts such as **Network Processor Units (NPUs)** or **Field Programmable Gate Arrays (FPGAs)** rather than **Application-Specific Integrated Circuit (ASIC)**.

While newer ASICs have some programmable capacity, they are still less malleable than FPGAs.

An NPU is a computer processor optimized for handling network data. As we discussed earlier, all of the initial routing devices on the internet did software forwarding, using a general-purpose **Computer Processing Unit (CPU)** which limited the throughput and speed of these devices. The NPU, similar to the CPU, will have a programmable path, or pipeline that can be modified in real-time to process network data. Network-specific ASICs, NPUs, and FPGAs brought forwarding to the hardware level.

An FPGA, as the name says, is a re-programmable application specific processor. An FPGA will have a programmable data plane, or pipeline that can be modified in real-time to process network data.

NPUs and FPGAs are what allowed SDN and OpenFlow to be brought into real-world networks. Having these chips in networking hardware allowed classic vendors to expand the features available to their customers. These chips also allowed for experimentation in the hardware data plane, previously only available in a software data plane.

The history of OpenFlow

The birth of OpenFlow is generally attributed to a program that came from within the Stanford computer science department entitled **Clean Slate**, referring to the concept of wiping a board to remove all of the current information and starting over. The limitations of the hardware/software at that time pushed the need for a new solution. Within this program, OpenFlow was born.

OpenFlow essentially replaces the complex control plane of a switch/router with an agent that listens to a central controller. The central controller does all of the heavy lifting to determine the best path(s) for packets to take and gives the agent a list of how the packets should be handled. The OpenFlow agent then interprets and translates the forwarding information for the hardware it is running on. An OpenFlow agent does not make any decisions locally, only translates the information from the OpenFlow controller for the local environment.

Before the emergence of OpenFlow, SDN was caught between the vision of fully programmable active networks and hardware/software that would enable deployment in live networks. OpenFlow struck a balance between these two goals by enabling more functions than earlier route controllers and building on existing commodity switch hardware due to the increasing use of merchant-silicon chipsets in commodity switches.

Because OpenFlow relied on the limited functionality of existing switches, OpenFlow was limited in features but immediately deployable, allowing the SDN movement to get a foothold in the network architecture space.

An overview of OpenFlow

A current OpenFlow switch has a table of rules to manage packets, where the rule matches on data in the packet header. The rule applies a list of actions, which are listed as follows:

- Drop the packet
- Flood the packet out of multiple interfaces
- Forward out of a specific interface
- Modify the packet header
- Push (punt) the packet to the controller

The rule increments a set of counters that track the number of bytes and packets that were processed by the rule. Lastly, the rule contains a priority, to allow the system to match the correct rule in case of a multiple match. When a packet is received that matches multiple rules, it is matched to the highest priority rule. With the introduction of multiple tables, the action of sending to another table was introduced. OpenFlow offered a few major values that helped push SDN forward; here are some notable ones:

- Programmable functions in the network to lower the barrier to innovation

  SDN introduced the concept of programmable networks as a way to lower the barrier to network innovation. The view that it is difficult to innovate in a production network and requests for increased programmability are commonly cited in the initial motivation for SDN. At the time, routers and switches were limited by the NOS that was provided with them. The NOS could not be modified to add/change features. At first, SDN was focused on programming the control plane, whereas the need was for data plane programmability. Work was being done in the data plane at the same time. Data plane programmability is important to emerging technologies such as **Network Function Virtualization (NFV)**.

- Network virtualization, and the ability to demultiplex to software programs based on packet headers

  Network virtualization was developed to support investigation into multiple programming models. The key components of an NFV platform are a base OS that manages shared resources; a set of containers, each of which defines a virtual machine for packet operations; and a set of network functions that work within a given container to provide an end-to-end service. Directing packets to a particular container depends on pattern matching on header fields and redirecting to the appropriate container.

- A unified architecture for central controller orchestration

  Although the vision was partially realized in active networking research, early designs stated the need for unifying the wide range of middlebox functions with a common, central framework. Although this vision may not have directly influenced the more recent work on NFV, various lessons from active networking research may prove useful as the application of SDN-based control and orchestration of middleboxes continues.

Though SDN showed the vision of active networks, the technologies did not see widespread deployment. Many factors affect the adoption of new technology. The lack of a *killer* application and the amount of work required to put OpenFlow to use in the network were two of the major ones. The community proffered various applications that could benefit from in-network processing, including information fusion, caching and content distribution, network management, and application-specific quality of service. Unfortunately, although performance benefits could be quantified in the lab, none of these application areas demonstrated a sufficiently compelling solution to a pressing need.

How OpenFlow works

OpenFlow uses a centralized controller that sends messages to one or more switches telling them how to handle packets. The controller may be getting information from multiple applications and sending it to the OpenFlow agent on the switch. The OpenFlow agent on the switch will interpret the commands and create API calls to configure the ASIC through the **Software Development Kit** (**SDK**). The SDK is the interface between the software and the hardware on the switch:

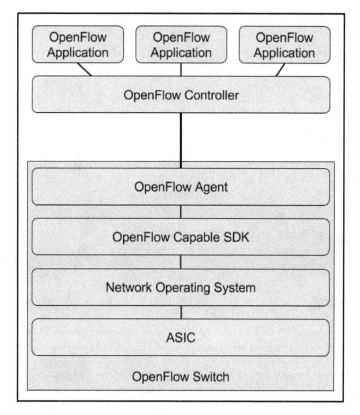

OpenFlow controller and switch

The growth of OpenFlow

The paradigm change driven by OpenFlow was the adoption of SDN in the industry compared to preceding concepts. OpenFlow appeared at the same time as merchant silicon vendors were opening up access to their software and hardware, including the following:

- Broadcom's open APIs, which allowed for open control of forwarding behaviors of their chipsets
- White-box switches, utilizing the Broadcom chipsets and reference designs to create their own less expensive hardware

OpenFlow started at version 0.8.9 and has moved to version 1.5. The first released version was 1.0 on December 31, 2009. All current OpenFlow capable switches support 1.0; many support OpenFlow 1.3. We will discuss versions 1.0 to 1.5, the current release.

OpenFlow 1.0

The first *production* version of OpenFlow, version 1.0, had a reasonable set of features, including the following:

- Multiple queues per port:
    - Allowed for minimum bandwidth guarantees (QoS)
- Flow cookies:
    - Flow cookies, like HTML cookies, allow for better tracking of flows
- Match on IP fields in ARP packets:
    - Allows for better control of packets
- Match on IP ToS/DSCP:
    - Being able to see the ToS/DSCP bit of packets allows the system to assign priority to traffic based on what originator of the traffic requested

While a good beginning, OpenFlow 1.0 was limited by a design constraint:

Because the hardware used in initial OpenFlow designs was not designed with OpenFlow in mind, the hardware was limited in how it could handle OpenFlow messages.

For example, switches running OpenFlow 1.0 cannot perform more than one action during the packet handling process. For every different flow, there needed to be a rule, for example, one per interface + MAC. Essentially, this means that if you have 6 interfaces and 100 MACs, you need 600 entries. Many OpenFlow capable switches only support a few thousand entries.

If you attempt to apply an **Access Control List** (**ACL**) to a port, the rules must be regenerated to contain the port, MAC, and ACL rule. So, if you add 10 ACLs, then you would need *600 * 10* or 6,000 entries. This problem scales very high:

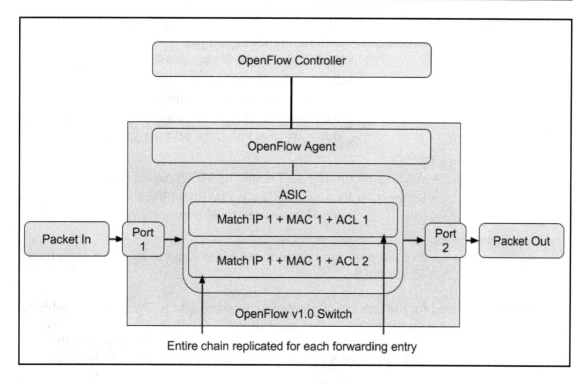

Entire chain replicated for each forwarding entry

This problem is solved with multiple tables. We will discuss this more in the OpenFlow 1.1 write-up, where tables are introduced.

OpenFlow 1.1

OpenFlow 1.1 added a few features that really helped push adoption, including multiple tables, groups, packet actions, and packet action sets:

- Multiple tables:
  - The biggest addition was the concept of tables. With tables, you could chain operations together, so instead of having a entry for every port + MAC + ACL, you could have one for each port, one for each MAC, and one for each ACL, then chain them together as needed.
  - Tables were able to manage the traffic path took through the switch using GOTO actions.
  - Packet actions could be combined into packet action sets.
  - Packet action sets are executed at the end of the pipeline while packet actions could be configured between tables.

- Groups:
    - Group tables with four types of groups:
        - **ALL**: This is used for multicast/broadcast
        - **Select**: This is used for multi-path
        - **Indirect**: This is used for simple failover
        - **Fast failover**: This allows for traffic to be easily sent out any active link if the primary link is down

- MPLS and VLANs:
    - Adding, modifying, and removing MPLS packet headers
    - Support for VLANs and QinQ (VLANs within VLANs)
        - VLANs are used by almost every corporate network

- Virtual ports:
    - Expand port number from a 16-bit to 32-bit to allow for more than 65,535 ports

Multiple tables allowed for the concept of pipelining to be brought to OpenFlow. Pipelining is generally used to explain the path a packet takes through a switch or routers forwarding chip. Pipelines are programmable and can be reprogrammed based on what packet the pipeline is processing. Pipelining is built by combining tables and packet actions/packet action sets.

With the addition of multiple tables in OpenFlow, every packet first goes through **Table 0**, which in turn makes the first decision on how to forward the packet:

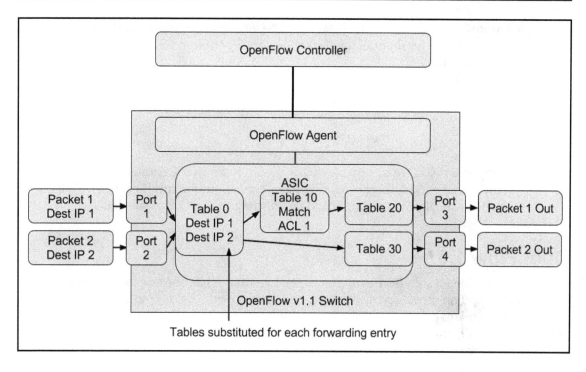

A packet coming into the system can be routed through multiple tables. In this case, **Table 0** determines that **Packet 1** needs to be sent to **Table 10**. Now, **Table 10** decides to send the packet to **Table 20** and **Table 20** sends the packet out **Port 3**. For **Packet 2**, it is sent directly to **Table 30**, which sends the packet out **Port 4**.

By default, the VLAN of 1 is used to represent none or default.

OpenFlow 1.2

OpenFlow 1.2 added some important features for advanced networks, such as IPv6 support, multiple controllers (active/failover), and extensible packets. The following is the list of some important features added in the OpenFlow 1.2 switch:

- IPv6 support
- Controller failover

- Extensible fields allow for metadata to be added to packets without setting a specific space for them in the packet design. OpenFlow 1.2 supports these extensible fields:
    - Match
    - Packet rewriting
    - Packet-in
    - Error messages

Extensible fields are a good way to deal with unknown amounts of metadata. In a standard IP packet, there would be parts carved out for specific data; with the extensible design, extra data could be attached to a packet as needed.

OpenFlow 1.3

OpenFlow 1.3 added a significant amount of features that it has become the standard version supported on most hardware, expanded on extensible fields, and provided a more flexible framework to express capabilities. **Capabilities** are a list of supported features announced by a OpenFlow capable device when the OpenFlow session is started. The capabilities are matched and the set with the least amount is used.

The main change is the clarity of the negotiation of table capabilities. Instead of being part of the table statistics structure, the capabilities have been moved to their own structure and have been encoded using the TLV format, which is more flexible. All of this allows for more tables, including next-table, table-miss flow entries, and experimenter.

The statistics framework (stats) has been renamed into the multiple part (multipart) framework as it is used for both statistics and capabilities. Description of ports has been moved into another new message that allows for a greater number of ports, along with moving the tables structure into its own multipart message.

The importance of this re-factor is the ability to now announce capabilities on their own within the handshake between two OpenFlow devices.

OpenFlow 1.4

OpenFlow 1.4 brought a few new key changes that are useful for companies that are looking for more redundancy and stability in their OpenFlow networks.

These are listed here:

- **Decision hierarchy**: This is a new bundle feature that adds transactional capabilities to rule set changes. This lets controllers group a set of actions and then either commit or rollback the entire group of actions in a single operation.
- **Eviction/vacancy events**: In earlier versions of the specification, if a flow table was full, new flows would not be inserted and an error would be sent to the controller. This version adds a vacancy feature that sends an early warning to the controller, in advance, to avoid filling up the table. The eviction feature removes entries of lower importance to free up space for new entries.
- **Multiple controllers**: This can monitor and control the same switch with notification to controller when group or meters are modified and when master/slave roles have changed.

OpenFlow 1.5

OpenFlow 1.5 added the ability to have inbound and outbound flow tables:

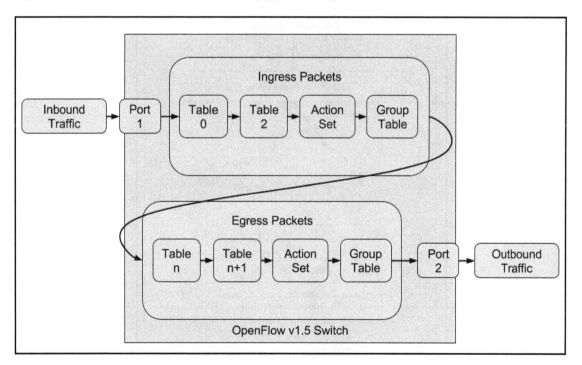

It also added flow monitoring, message bundling, and enhancements to eviction (introduced in version 1.4). **Message bundling** allows the controller to send multiple messages as one so that there is better synchronicity between OpenFlow switches.

Understanding OF-DPA – the open source OpenFlow agent from Broadcom

Broadcom's **OpenFlow Data Plane Abstraction** (**OF-DPA**) is an application software component that implements an adaptation layer between OpenFlow and the Broadcom Silicon SDK. OF-DPA enables scalable implementation of OpenFlow 1.3 on Broadcom switch devices.

OF-DPA was originally released to assist the networking community in building OpenFlow agents. The Broadcom SDK for switches is a licensed closed product while OF-DPA exposes APIs that can be utilized by OpenFlow agents:

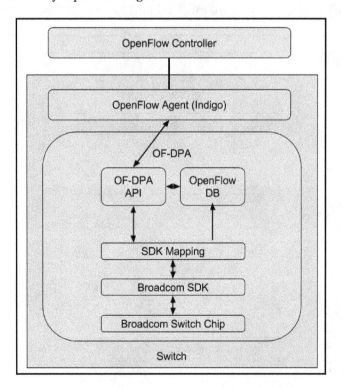

Some of the example API calls available are as follows:

- `ofdpaBcmCommand`: This executes a Broadcom command on the device and reports whether it was successful or failed (1 or 0)
- `ofdpaFlowAdd`: This adds a flow to the switching table
- `ofdpaFlowDelete`: This deletes a flow from the switching table
- `ofdpaFlowModify`: This modifies an existing flow table entry
- `ofdpaDropStatusAdd`: This drops an entry from the switching table
- `ofdpaDropStatusActionGet`: This checks the status of any requested drops
- `ofdpaDropStatusDelete`: This confirms that the delete has happened
- `ofdpaFlowByCookieGet`: This uses a OpenFlow cookie (introduced in version 1.0) to get data about a flow
- `ofdpaFlowByCookieDelete`: This deletes a flow from the table using its cookie

OF-DPA can be integrated with Indigo and other OpenFlow agents, which we will talk about next.

Using an OpenFlow agent such as Indigo

Indigo is provided with OF-DPA and is simple to run as it is a daemon that contacts and exchanges messages with an OpenFlow controller. The job of the OpenFlow agent is to take the information given by the OpenFlow controller and translate it for the local hardware. In the case of Indigo with OF-DPA, OF-DPA is providing the abstraction and Indigo is communicating with it based on the data received from the OpenFlow controller.

To see how simple Indigo is, you can run it from the command line and see the options:

Usage:

`ofagent [OPTION...]`: This runs the main OFAgent application.

Options:

- `-a, -agentdebuglvl=AGENTDEBUGLVL`: The verbosity of OFAgent debug messages
- `-l, -listen=IP:PORT Listen`
- `-t, -controller=IP:PORT Controller`
- `-?, -help`: Gives the help list

- -usage: Gives a short usage message
- -V, -version: Prints program version

The options are debug level, IP and port listening, controller IP and port, help, usage and version. That is all there is. Since Indigo is only translating information sent between the OpenFlow controller and the data plane, it does not need much, if any, extra configuration data.

OpenFlow capable OCP devices

Broadcom was the first chip vendor to embrace OpenFlow and release their OF-DPA package for their switching chips. Many of the Accton switches are based on forwarding chips from Broadcom and support OF-DPA.

Accton/Edgecore Broadcom based switches that are compatible with OpenFlow/OF-DPA are as follows:

- AS4600-54T (PowerPC)
- AS5710-54X (PowerPC)
- AS5712-54X (AMD64)
- AS5812-54X (AMD64)
- AS5812-54T (AMD64)
- AS6712-32X (AMD64)
- AS6812-32X (AMD64)
- AS7712-32X (AMD64)
- AS7716-32X (AMD64)

How controllers interact with OpenFlow agents

The general concept of controller and agent interaction is the following.

An OpenFlow controller is provided with information via many sources, including APIs, routing protocols, and information from the agent about the local devices connected to it. The OpenFlow controller then takes this information, aggregates it, and sends a generalized version of the information to the OpenFlow agents. The OpenFlow agent then translates the information for the local device it is running on and programs the forwarding table.

At the time of writing, there were a few major open source players in the OpenFlow controller space. The main thought-leading controllers were OpenDaylight and ONOS.

OpenDaylight

OpenDaylight was founded in part by Cisco and other large networking companies to provide a solution that was compatible with their products as to allow the consumer to continue to evaluate vendor products along with their open networking counterparts. Over time, OpenDaylight has been embraced by companies such as Brocade, which sells a commercial version of OpenDaylight called the Brocade SDN Controller.

Brocade SDN Controller

Formerly known as the Brocade Vyatta Controller, the Brocade SDN Controller is based on OpenDaylight and has a few extra features such as support for the 5600 series vRouters:

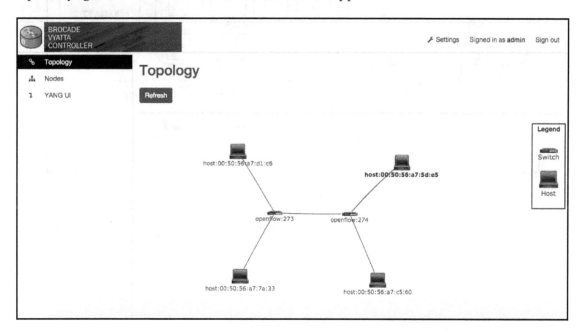

Brocade SDN Controller – simple topology

In the preceding screenshot, you can see that there are two OpenFlow switches (**273** and **274**) to which two hosts are connected to each for a total of four.

The following is a diagram of the setup used to produce the Brocade SDN Controller screenshots:

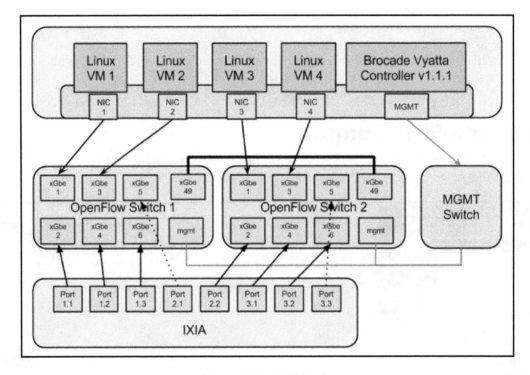

Testing setup for Brocade SDN Controller

In the preceding diagram, we have a PC running multiple VMs, four plain Linux VMs for connecting to the switches, and one VM for the Brocade Controller.

In the middle, there are two switches which are connected to the hosts, an IXIA tester, and a management switch for sending OpenFlow control messages:

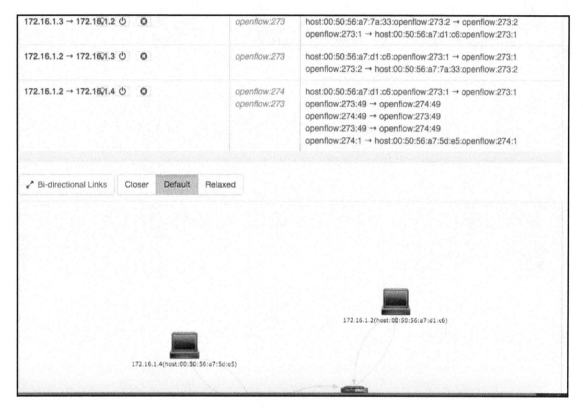

172.16.1.3 → 172.16.1.2 ⏻ ❌		*openflow:273*	host:00:50:56:a7:7a:33:openflow:273:2 → openflow:273:2 openflow:273:1 → host:00:50:56:a7:d1:c6:openflow:273:1
172.16.1.2 → 172.16.1.3 ⏻ ❌		*openflow:273*	host:00:50:56:a7:d1:c6:openflow:273:1 → openflow:273:1 openflow:273:2 → host:00:50:56:a7:7a:33:openflow:273:2
172.16.1.2 → 172.16.1.4 ⏻ ❌		*openflow:274* *openflow:273*	host:00:50:56:a7:d1:c6:openflow:273:1 → openflow:273:1 openflow:273:49 → openflow:274:49 openflow:274:49 → openflow:273:49 openflow:273:49 → openflow:274:49 openflow:274:1 → host:00:50:56:a7:5d:e5:openflow:274:1

Brocade SDN Controller – flow view

In the preceding diagram, you can see flows from switch **273** and **274** that connect the hosts.

Cisco Open SDN Controller

Cisco also produces a commercial version of OpenDaylight called the Cisco Open SDN Controller, which includes extra tools such as the Cisco OpenFlow Manager, Cisco Inventory Manager, and other Cisco-specific tools.

ONOS

ONOS was conceived and produced by ON.Lab with support from AT&T and NTT. ONOS later became a project of the **Linux Foundation** (**LF**) where it lives today. ONOS is meant to operate as a cluster, which is different than OpenDaylight which was designed to be run as a single system:

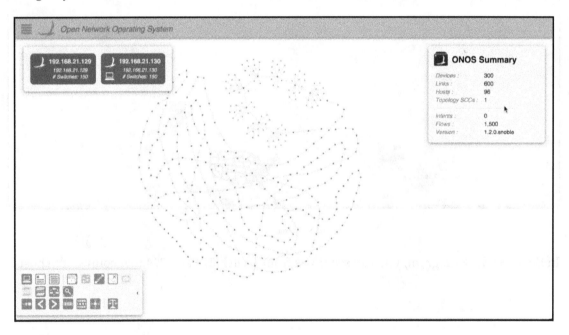

ONOS controller

The ONOS controller differs from OpenDaylight in how it handles clustering multiple controllers. In the preceding figure, you can see that there are 300 devices, spread across two controllers, 150 each.

Summary

In this chapter, we talked about programmable networks, more specifically, how OpenFlow works, the different OpenFlow controllers available, and the hardware that can use OpenFlow.

OpenFlow was conceived at Stanford in their Clean Slate lab as a way to overcome the limitations of current networking and allow for programmable (SDN) networks. The OpenFlow standards original release version was 0.8.9 and has moved to 1.5 at this time.

OpenFlow version 1.0 was functional but only utilized one table, partly due to the limitations of the hardware at the time. In OpenFlow 1.1 multiple tables were introduced, helping to push OpenFlow further into mainstream networking. Today most vendors are standardized on OpenFlow version 1.3, a few support 1.4 but are backwards compatible.

In the next chapter, we will discuss REST and Thrift-based APIs.

4
Using REST and Thrift APIs to Manage Switches

In Chapter 1, *Open and Proprietary Next Generation Networks*, we talked about both Facebook (FBOSS) and SnapRoute routing/switching applications, both managed by **Application Program Interfaces** (**APIs**). FBOSS uses Apache Thrift directly, while SnapRoute uses a RESTful interface and Apache Thrift internally.

The use of APIs provides you with easier management and automation of network devices. The concept is similar to OpenFlow in that you can use a central server to manage multiple devices instead of working on them one by one via a **Command-line Interface** (**CLI**) or a web interface.

Apache Thrift was originally developed by Facebook and became open source in 2007. Thrift has been under the stewardship of the Apache Foundation since 2008 and became an Apache Foundation Top Level Project in 2010. Thrift provides an abstraction interface to the user that can talk to multiple different languages in the background.

REST was created between 1996-1999 and introduced in 2000 as the basis for HTTP 1.1 **Universal Resource Identifiers** (**URIs**).

REST is an API that provides a consistent user experience across different systems by utilizing standardized operations, such as:

- GET: This is the command sent via a web/REST client when it is asking for a web page, web object, or RESTful data
- PUT: This is the command sent via a web/REST client when it is attempting to push data up to the web server
- PATCH: This is the command sent via a web/REST client when it is attempting to change data that already exists in the system

Prior to APIs, the only way to program networking devices remotely was to use **Simple Network Management Protocol (SNMP)** to read and write values or to screen scrape/automate the CLI. SNMPv1 was introduced in 1988 and designed around the precommercial internet. SNMPv2 came out in 1991 and introduced a level of security to SNMP.

In this chapter, we will discuss REST-based, Thrift-based, and general APIs, which are used to manage networking devices. When done, you should have a good grasp of the following:

- APIs and their use in networking
- **Representational State Transfer (REST)**, that is, RESTful APIs:
    - How to use RESTful APIs in Postman to manage SnapRoute
- Apache Thrift clients and servers:
    - Networking tools from Facebook that utilize Thrift
    - How to manage Facebook's FBOSS software via Thrift

API concepts

APIs themselves predate modern networks and computing but only became useful in networking around the year 2000 when REST was introduced. Since REST has been around longer than Thrift, we will discuss it first.

REST

REST, like other networking APIs, is available both on the local system and remotely. REST is designed to be:

- **Scalable**: RESTful applications must be scalable by utilizing some or all of the following concepts:
    - **Simplifying components**: A simple component will scale better than a complex one; complex components should be broken down into multiple simpler ones
    - **Decentralization**: This could be done by distributing processing across multiple components
    - **Frequency of operations**: The more the interactions that happen between the client and server, the more it impacts the performance of the application

- **High performance**: There are a few different ways in which performance can be measured:
    - **Network performance**: The application must be adaptable to the style and size of the data it is carrying to not overburden the application
    - **Perceived performance**: The application must minimize latency by deciding whether to compress data on the fly, create latency on the server side, or stream all of the data that may cause latency on the client side
- **Modifiable/evolvable**: The application must be evolvable, extensible, customizable, configurable, and reusable
- **Portable**: The application must be portable and return both the information and the structure
- **Visible**: The application must be visible to other applications
- **Reliable**: The application must return data in the format expected as designed within the constraints of the REST design
- **Simple**: By design, all REST implementations must use a uniform interface.

REST has six guiding constraints, all of which must be met for an application to be RESTful:

- **Client-server**: The needs of the user application are separate from the server application. The server and client may store data as they see fit but must transmit data in the requested format.
- **Stateless**: The application must be stateless as the server should not retain any client data from previous interactions with the same client.
- **Cacheable**: The data must define whether it is cacheable or not and the amount of time it can be cached.
- **Layerable**: You must be able to feed the application making the request from the server directly or any intermediary nodes that may have cached the required information without needing to be told so.
- **Code-on-demand**: The server can optionally provide code, such as compiled JavaScript or other programs, to be utilized by the client to extend the functionality of the client.
- **Uniform interface**: Once a developer becomes familiar with one of your APIs, they should be able to follow a similar approach for other APIs.

A uniform interface, as described by REST, must do the following:

- **Identification of resources**: When sending data, the data must be portable and sent in the manner the client requests, if available
- **Manipulation of data by client**: The client must have enough information to be able to modify or delete data
- **Self-descriptive**: Each message must contain the information necessary to process the message, for example, which parser (JSON/XML/so on) to utilize
- **Hypermedia as the engine of the application state**: A REST client after making a request to a URI should be able to utilize links provided by the server to discover the necessary information to fulfill its request

REST utilizes standard operations, such as:

- PUT: Sends data to be programmed to the REST agent, replacing or modifying the current data
- GET: Requests either a list of URIs or specific data necessary from an agent
- POST: Creates a new entry in the dataset or within a dataset
- DELETE: Deletes an entry in the dataset or within a dataset

In this book, we will focus on the SnapRoute RESTful API.

Apache Thrift

Apache Thrift (or Facebook Thrift as some refer to it) aims to provide scalable services across different programming languages. Thrift combines a generation engine for code with a software stack to create services that work effectively and efficiently between multiple programming languages, including:

- **C++**: A high-level programming language that is feature-full and object-oriented
- **Python**: A high-level general-purpose programming language
- **Java**: A multi-architecture programming language that allows you to run the same program on multiple different types of computers
- **Ruby**: An object-oriented language patterned after Perl and LISP
- **JavaScript**: A remotely interpreted programming language mostly utilized by web servers and websites

The goal of Thrift was to create a simple interface that could work with any programming language; to this end, the following goals are defined:

- **Simple**: The code should be simple, readable, and free of unnecessary dependencies
- **Consistent**: Language-specific code is kept in extensions, not included in the core
- **Transparent**: It should utilize as many commonalities between programming languages as possible
- **High performance**: Performance is more important than beauty; the code should be functional but not always beautiful

In comparison to REST, Thrift has an **Interface Definition Language** (**IDL**), which is programming-language-independent and is publish-subscribe instead of client-server. The publish-subscribe method is the concept where the client subscribes to the server to get the data. The client may only receive some of the data published based on filtering. Neither the client nor the server knows who each other are; it just knows the type of data to expect.

In this book, we will focus on Thrift and how it interfaces with the **Facebook Open Switch System** (**FBOSS**).

SnapRoute – a RESTful API programmable routing stack

SnapRoute is a newly formed company focused on providing an easily automated and functional routing platform. It was built by a group of engineers who had worked on Apple's network. Here we will dive into how an API programmable routing stack works.

As it uses a RESTful API, the commands sent to the switch are done using either POST, GET, OPTIONS, PATCH, or DELETE.

SnapRoute refers to ports on a switch as fpPortX, where X is the number of the **front panel** (**fp**) ports. If the port can be broken out (for example, 10 Gx4 for 40 G or 25 Gx4 for 100 G), then there will be a delineator fpPortXsY, where the port number is X and the breakout is referred to as Y. So fpPort1s1 would be the front panel port 1, which is the breakout link 1.

The following diagram shows the general software layout of a switch running SnapRoute's FlexSwitch. We have not included the operating system or any other programs or drivers necessary for the device to operate:

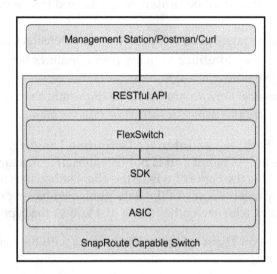

In order to send the output of commands to SnapRoute's FlexSwitch, use a Python module that formats JSON for better readability. If you don't use something to parse the data, the data will be somewhat readable but hard to understand. For example, if you want to see all the interfaces on the box, send this command:

```
curl -X GET --header 'Content-Type: application/json' --header 'Accept:
application/json' 'http://localhost:8080/public/v1/config/Ports'
```

Without a parser, you will see something similar to the following output, which is very hard to decipher:

```
{"ObjectId":"6ec727d1-c2c8-44dc-77fd-
d9b1fd6dce4c","Object":{"IntfRef":"fpPort1","IfIndex":145,"Name":"fpPort1",
"OperState":"DOWN","NumUpEvents":0,"LastUpEventTime":"","NumDownEvents":0}}
```

If we run the command again, using the Python-based `json.tool` parser, we get:

```
curl -X GET --header 'Content-Type: application/json' --header 'Accept:
application/json' 'http://localhost:8080/public/v1/config/Ports' | python -
m json.tool

{
  "CurrentMarker": 0,
  "MoreExist": false,
  "NextMarker": 0,
```

```
"ObjCount": 160,
"Objects": [
{
"Object": {
"AdminState": "DOWN",
"Autoneg": "OFF",
"BreakOutMode": "1x100",
"Description": "",
"Duplex": "Full Duplex",
"EnableFEC": false,
"IfIndex": 145,
"IntfRef": "fpPort1",
"LoopbackMode": "",
"MacAddr": "00:90:fb:55:e5:11",
"MediaType": "Media Type",
"Mtu": 9412,
"PRBSPolynomial": "",
"PRBSRxEnable": false,
"PRBSTxEnable": false,
"PhyIntfType": "KR4",
"Speed": 100000
},
"ObjectId": "6ec727d1-c2c8-44dc-77fd-d9b1fd6dce4c"
},
{
"Object": {
"AdminState": "DOWN",
"Autoneg": "OFF",
"BreakOutMode": "1x100",
"Description": "",
"Duplex": "Full Duplex",
"EnableFEC": false,
"IfIndex": 140,
"IntfRef": "fpPort2",
"LoopbackMode": "",
"MacAddr": "00:90:fb:55:e5:11",
"MediaType": "Media Type",
"Mtu": 9412,
"PRBSPolynomial": "",
"PRBSRxEnable": false,
"PRBSTxEnable": false,
"PhyIntfType": "KR4",
"Speed": 100000
},
"ObjectId": "8029f48f-5b1b-492f-73b7-dc879e386508"
},
```

The preceding information is much clearer.

Taking it further, to get information about a specific port, say `fpPort1`, send:

```
curl -X GET --header 'Content-Type: application/json' --header 'Accept:
application/json' -d '{"IntfRef":"fpPort1"}'
'http://localhost:8080/public/v1/config/Port' | python -m json.tool

{
 "Object": {
 "AdminState": "DOWN",
 "Autoneg": "OFF",
 "BreakOutMode": "1x100",
 ... duplicate content omitted (see above output)
 "Speed": 100000
 },
 "ObjectId": "6ec727d1-c2c8-44dc-77fd-d9b1fd6dce4c"
}
```

Some of the pieces of information you receive are as follows:

- The port speed is 100 Gbps
- The port breakout mode is 1x100 Gbps (that is, it is not broken out)

In the preceding code, note that we are including the filter:

```
{"IntfRef":"fpPort1"}
```

This says we are referring to the interface with the name `fpPort1` or front panel port 1.

To enable `fpPort1`, send:

```
curl -X PATCH --header 'Content-Type: application/json' --header 'Accept:
application/json' -d '{"IntfRef":"fpPort1","AdminState":"UP"}'
'http://localhost:8080/public/v1/config/Port' | python -m json.tool

{
 "Access-Control-Allow-Headers": "Origin, X-Requested-With, Content-Type,
 Accept",
 "Access-Control-Allow-Methods": "POST, GET, OPTIONS, PATCH, DELETE",
 "Access-Control-Allow-Origin": "*",
 "Access-Control-Max_age": "86400",
 "ObjectId": "6ec727d1-c2c8-44dc-77fd-d9b1fd6dce4c",
 "Result": "Success"
}
```

Refer to the following code:

```
{"IntfRef":"fpPort1","AdminState":"UP"}
```

This is the main piece of information; we are asking the system to turn front panel port 1 up.

This tells us that the call was successful:

```
"Result": "Success"
```

Now we can query the port again and see that it is now `"AdminState": "UP"`:

```
curl -X GET --header 'Content-Type: application/json' --header 'Accept:
application/json' -d '{"IntfRef":"fpPort1"}'
'http://localhost:8080/public/v1/config/Port' | python -m json.tool

{
  "Object": {
  "AdminState": "UP",
  "Autoneg": "OFF",
  "BreakOutMode": "1x100",
  "Description": "",
  "Duplex": "Full Duplex",
  "EnableFEC": false,
  "IfIndex": 145,
  "IntfRef": "fpPort1",
  "LoopbackMode": "",
  "MacAddr": "00:90:fb:55:e5:11",
  "MediaType": "Media Type",
  "Mtu": 9412,
  "PRBSPolynomial": "",
  "PRBSRxEnable": false,
  "PRBSTxEnable": false,
  "PhyIntfType": "KR4",
  "Speed": 100000
  },
  "ObjectId": "6ec727d1-c2c8-44dc-77fd-d9b1fd6dce4c"
}
```

To configure the speed of the port, you use the same command but substitute Speed with extra data:

Before:

```
curl -X GET "http://10.7.1.78:8080/public/v1/config/Port?IntfRef=fpPort2" |
python -m json.tool

  "Object": {
  "AdminState": "DOWN",
  "Autoneg": "OFF",
  "BreakOutMode": "1x100",
```

```
"Description": "",
"Duplex": "Full Duplex",
"EnableFEC": false,
"IfIndex": 140,
"IntfRef": "fpPort2",
"LoopbackMode": "",
"MacAddr": "00:90:fb:55:e5:11",
"MediaType": "Media Type",
"Mtu": 9412,
"PRBSPolynomial": "",
"PRBSRxEnable": false,
"PRBSTxEnable": false,
"PhyIntfType": "KR4",
"Speed": 100000
},
"ObjectId": "8029f48f-5b1b-492f-73b7-dc879e386508"
}
```

In the preceding code, you can see that the speed is 100 Gbps or 100 GbE. Now refer to the following code:

```
curl -X PATCH --header 'Content-Type: application/json' --header 'Accept:
application/json' -d '{"IntfRef":"fpPort2","Speed":40000}'
'http://localhost:8080/public/v1/config/Port'| python -m json.tool

"Access-Control-Allow-Headers": "Origin, X-Requested-With, Content-Type,
Accept",
"Access-Control-Allow-Methods": "POST, GET, OPTIONS, PATCH, DELETE",
"Access-Control-Allow-Origin": "*",
"Access-Control-Max_age": "86400",
"ObjectId": "8029f48f-5b1b-492f-73b7-dc879e386508",
"Result": "Success"
}
```

Here, we sent a command to change the speed to 40 Gbps or 40 GbE.

One thing to note is that integers do not have quotes ("") around them in the RESTful command, whereas strings do:

```
{"IntfRef":"fpPort2","Speed":40000}
```

To confirm the change, query the interface again:

```
curl -X GET "http://localhost:8080/public/v1/config/Port?IntfRef=fpPort2" |
python -m json.tool

"Object": {
"AdminState": "DOWN",
```

```
"Autoneg": "OFF",
"BreakOutMode": "1x100",
"Description": "",
"Duplex": "Full Duplex",
"EnableFEC": false,
"IfIndex": 140,
"IntfRef": "fpPort2",
"LoopbackMode": "",
"MacAddr": "00:90:fb:55:e5:11",
"MediaType": "Media Type",
"Mtu": 9412,
"PRBSPolynomial": "",
"PRBSRxEnable": false,
"PRBSTxEnable": false,
"PhyIntfType": "KR4",
"Speed": 40000
},
"ObjectId": "8029f48f-5b1b-492f-73b7-dc879e386508"
}
```

In the Postman API development program, which we will discuss in depth in `Chapter 5`, *Using Postman for REST API Calls*, we can send the same commands via a graphical interface, which will return the same data as we saw via `curl`. For example, we send the following:

```
{GET} http://snaproute.router.ip:8080/public/v1/config/Ports
```

We see the same output as we do with the `curl` command.

Configuring an interface

Using `curl`, you can easily configure an IP address on `fpPort1`:

```
curl -X POST --header 'Content-Type: application/json' --header 'Accept:
application/json' -d '{"IntfRef":"fpPort1","IpAddr":"100.10.100.1/24"}'
'http://localhost:8080/public/v1/config/IPv4Intf'

{
 "Access-Control-Allow-Headers": "Origin, X-Requested-With, Content-Type,
  Accept",
 "Access-Control-Allow-Methods": "POST, GET, OPTIONS, PATCH, DELETE",
 "Access-Control-Allow-Origin": "*",
 "Access-Control-Max_age": "86400",
 "ObjectId": "a5856728-ab49-47b4-4ad4-de6a5e5a1ed3",
 "Result":"Success"
}
```

To confirm that the interface was properly set up, you can confirm its functionality via `ping`:

```
# ping 100.10.100.2
PING 100.10.100.2 (100.10.100.2) 56(84) bytes of data.
64 bytes from 100.10.100.2: icmp_seq=1 ttl=64 time=0.432 ms
64 bytes from 100.10.100.2: icmp_seq=2 ttl=64 time=0.338 ms
```

You can also look at the ARP table:

```
curl -X GET --header 'Content-Type: application/json'
'http://localhost:8080/public/v1/state/ArpEntrys' | python -m json.tool
{
 "CurrentMarker": 0,
 "MoreExist": false,
 "NextMarker": 0,
 "ObjCount": 1,
 "Objects": [
 {
 "Object": {
 "ExpiryTimeLeft": "8m23.814811246s",
 "Intf": "fpPort1",
 "IpAddr": "100.10.100.2",
 "MacAddr": "00:90:fb:59:3e:b7",
 "Vlan": "Internal Vlan"
 },
 "ObjectId": ""
 }
 ]
}
```

Thrift

FBOSS is a Thrift API controlled forwarding agent from Facebook. In March of 2015, Facebook announced their first hardware switch, called the Wedge, and the network agent that ran on it, called FBOSS. On bringing up, FBOSS is configured statically. A Thrift-based API is used to add/modify/delete routes:

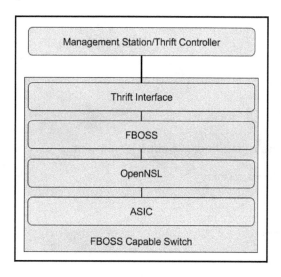

Overview of FBOSS software stack

In the preceding diagram, you can see that an FBOSS switch is very similar to a FlexSwitch-enabled one and the one based on OpenFlow. In general, all switch network operating systems will have the same flow:

- A configuration interface
- A forwarding stack
- SDK integration

FBOSS includes a Python script called `fboss_route.py`, which is used to configure the FBOSS agent directly. Our examples will use this:

```
fboss_route.py
usage: fboss_route.py [-h] [--port PORT] [--client CLIENT] [--host HOST]
{flush,add,delete,list_intf,list_routes,list_optics,list_ports,list_vlans,l
ist_arps,list_ndps,enable_port,disable_port}
  ...
fboss_route.py: error: too few arguments
```

Here is the help information from the `fboss_route.py` script; you can see that you have options to:

- Add/delete/flush route entries
- List interfaces
- List routes
- List optics
- List ports
- List VLANs
- List ARPs
- List NDPs
- Enable and disable ports

If we run the `list_vlans` command, we get the following:

```
# fboss_route.py list_vlans
===== Vlan 1000 ====
169.254.0.10
2001:00db:1111:1150:0000:0000:0000:000a
===== Vlan 1001 ====
172.31.1.1
===== Vlan 1002 ====
172.31.2.1
===== Vlan 1003 ====
172.31.3.1
===== Vlan 1004 ====
172.31.4.1
===== Vlan 1005 ====
172.31.5.1
===== Vlan 1006 ====
172.31.6.1
===== Vlan 3001 ====
10.11.0.111
2001:00db:3333:0e01:1000:0000:0000:00aa
===== Vlan 3002 ====
10.11.8.111
2001:00db:3334:0e01:1000:0000:0000:00aa
===== Vlan 3003 ====
10.11.16.111
2001:00db:3335:0e01:1000:0000:0000:00aa
===== Vlan 3004 ====
10.11.24.111
2001:00db:3336:0e01:1000:0000:0000:00aa
```

Running the list interface commands gives similar data, showing the L3 interface (VLAN) with the IP address you see in the preceding code:

```
# fboss_route.py list_intf
L3 Interface 1000: 169.254.0.10/16, 2001:db:1111:1150::a/64
(2e:60:0c:59:ab:4e)
L3 Interface 1001: 172.31.1.1/24 (2e:60:0c:59:ab:4e)
L3 Interface 1002: 172.31.2.1/24 (2e:60:0c:59:ab:4e)
L3 Interface 1003: 172.31.3.1/24 (2e:60:0c:59:ab:4e)
L3 Interface 1004: 172.31.4.1/24 (2e:60:0c:59:ab:4e)
L3 Interface 1005: 172.31.5.1/24 (2e:60:0c:59:ab:4e)
L3 Interface 1006: 172.31.6.1/24 (2e:60:0c:59:ab:4e)
L3 Interface 3001: 10.11.0.111/31, 2001:db:3333:e01:1000::aa/127
(2e:60:0c:59:ab:4e)
L3 Interface 3002: 10.11.8.111/31, 2001:db:3334:e01:1000::aa/127
(2e:60:0c:59:ab:4e)
L3 Interface 3003: 10.11.16.111/31, 2001:db:3335:e01:1000::aa/127
(2e:60:0c:59:ab:4e)
L3 Interface 3004: 10.11.24.111/31, 2001:db:3336:e01:1000::aa/127
(2e:60:0c:59:ab:4e)
```

If we list the ports, we can manipulate them:

```
# fboss_route.py list_ports
Port 1: [enabled=True, up=False, present=False]
Port 2: [enabled=True, up=False, present=False]
Port 3: [enabled=True, up=False, present=False]
Port 4: [enabled=True, up=False, present=False]
Port 5: [enabled=True, up=False, present=False]
```

To disable a port, simply send:

```
# fboss_route.py disable_port 1
Port 1 disabled
```

The system says port 1 is disabled; let's check:

```
# fboss_route.py list_ports
Port 1: [enabled=False, up=False, present=False]
Port 2: [enabled=True, up=False, present=False]
Port 3: [enabled=True, up=False, present=False]
Port 4: [enabled=True, up=False, present=False]
Port 5: [enabled=True, up=False, present=False]
```

If we want to add a route, we can do so using this:

```
# fboss_route.py list_routes
Route 10.11.0.110/31 --> 10.11.0.111
Route 10.11.8.110/31 --> 10.11.8.111
Route 10.11.16.110/31 --> 10.11.16.111
Route 10.11.24.110/31 --> 10.11.24.111
Route 169.254.0.0/16 --> 169.254.0.10
# fboss_route.py add 10.12.13.0/24 10.11.0.111
# fboss_route.py list_routes
Route 10.11.0.110/31 --> 10.11.0.111
Route 10.11.8.110/31 --> 10.11.8.111
Route 10.11.16.110/31 --> 10.11.16.111
Route 10.11.24.110/31 --> 10.11.24.111
Route 10.12.13.0/24 --> 10.11.0.111
Route 169.254.0.0/16 --> 169.254.0.10
```

To remove the route, do the same with delete instead of add:

```
# fboss_route.py delete 10.12.13.0/24
# fboss_route.py list_routes
Route 10.11.0.110/31 --> 10.11.0.111
Route 10.11.8.110/31 --> 10.11.8.111
Route 10.11.16.110/31 --> 10.11.16.111
Route 10.11.24.110/31 --> 10.11.24.111
Route 169.254.0.0/16 --> 169.254.0.10
```

You can also use the fboss_route.py script remotely by sending a host command:

```
# fboss_route.py --host 10.6.100.231 add 10.12.13.0/24 10.11.0.1
```

Summary

In this chapter, we talked about API-driven routing/switching applications. This concept allows you to have easier automation and management. Instead of programming systems box by box, you are now able to use a central server or application to manage multiple systems.

The main difference between Thrift and REST is that Thrift was designed to work as a frontend to multiple languages, such as Python, C, and C++. REST is a standard (RESTful) that allows companies to provide a well-defined HTML interface to programs.

For example, we used Facebook's FBOSS and SnapRoute's FlexSwitch.

FBOSS provides a Thrift interface that can be used for automation and is accessible via a Thrift server running on the Wedge and Wedge 100 switches. It provides both static and programmed configuration.

FlexSwitch is a RESTful API-driven routing protocol that gets all of its programming from the REST interface.

In the next chapter, we will talk about Postman, a tool for developing and testing APIs. We will demonstrate Postman working with FlexSwitch.

5
Using Postman for REST API calls

In this chapter, we will cover the Postman application, which we have touched on lightly in earlier chapters. When you are done with this chapter, you will have a good grasp of the following topics:

- What Postman is
- Installing Postman
- Using Postman
- Postman and SnapRoute

In `Chapter 4`, *Using REST and Thrift APIs to Manage Switches*, we talked about the SnapRoute routing application and its use of APIs. While exploring APIs, it is good to have tools other than just `curl` to gather data.

For example, the Postman tool, available at `https://www.getpostman.com`, is available as both a standalone application and as a plugin for most major browsers.

Postman advertises itself as a tool for building and testing APIs, and on this page, `https://www.getpostman.com/docs/install_native`, they state the following:

> *With Postman, you can construct requests quickly, save them for later use and analyze the responses sent by the API. Postman can dramatically cut down the time required to test and develop APIs. Postman adapts itself for individual developers, small teams or big organizations equally well.*

For our work with Postman, the notation we will use is the following:

- {GET} represents the **GET** pulldown choice in the Postman GUI.
- {PATCH} represents the **PATCH** pulldown choice in the Postman GUI.

To explain how Postman works, we will recreate the commands we used in the previous chapter to configure the SnapRoute FlexSwitch software.

Showing and modifying the configuration of SnapRoute's FlexSwitch via Postman

In the previous chapter, we sent the following hard-to-read and complex command via `curl`:

```
curl -X GET --header 'Content-Type: application/json' --header 'Accept:
application/json' 'http://localhost:8080/public/v1/config/Ports' | python -
m json.tool
```

```
{
   "CurrentMarker": 0,
   "MoreExist": false,
   "NextMarker": 0,
   "ObjCount": 160,
   "Objects": [
    {
      "Object": {
      "AdminState": "DOWN",
      "Autoneg": "OFF",
      "BreakOutMode": "1x100",
      "Description": "",
      "Duplex": "Full Duplex",
      "EnableFEC": false,
      "IfIndex": 145,
      "IntfRef": "fpPort1",
      "LoopbackMode": "",
      "MacAddr": "00:90:fb:55:e5:11",
      "MediaType": "Media Type",
      "Mtu": 9412,
      "PRBSPolynomial": "",
      "PRBSRxEnable": false,
```

```
      "PRBSTxEnable": false,
      "PhyIntfType": "KR4",
      "Speed": 100000
  },
 "ObjectId": "6ec727d1-c2c8-44dc-77fd-d9b1fd6dce4c"
 },
 {
  "Object":
  {
      "AdminState": "DOWN",
      "Autoneg": "OFF",
      "BreakOutMode": "1x100",
      "Description": "",
      "Duplex": "Full Duplex",
      "EnableFEC": false,
      "IfIndex": 140,
      "IntfRef": "fpPort2",
      "LoopbackMode": "",
      "MacAddr": "00:90:fb:55:e5:11",
      "MediaType": "Media Type",
      "Mtu": 9412,
      "PRBSPolynomial": "",
      "PRBSRxEnable": false,
      "PRBSTxEnable": false,
      "PhyIntfType": "KR4",
      "Speed": 100000
  },
 "ObjectId": "8029f48f-5b1b-492f-73b7-dc879e386508"
 },
```

This command is replicated using the following call in Postman:

```
{GET} http://snaproute.router.ip:8080/public/v1/config/Ports
```

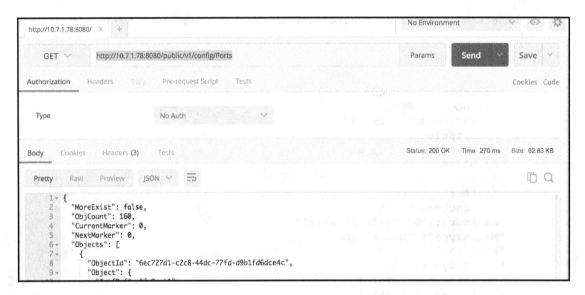

Using Postman to configure SnapRoute interfaces

If you want to query a specific port, such as front panel port 1 (fpPort1), you can add it to the command line:

```
{GET} http://snaproute.router.ip:8080/public/v1/state/Port/?IntfRef=fpPort1
```

The sequence of operations is as follows:

1. Choose **GET** from the Postman query pulldown.
2. Add `http://snaproute/public/v1/state/Port`, where `snaproute` is the IP or DNS name of your SnapRoute-powered switch and `public/v1/state/Port` is the common name for querying ports. Note the term `state` in the query.
3. Add the port you want to look at using `?IntfRef=fpPortX`, where X is the port you are looking for:

Querying the SnapRoute interface state using Postman

If we want to turn port `fpPort1` up, we follow these steps:

1. We send a **PATCH** REST command:

   `{PATCH} http://snaproute.router.ip:8080/public/v1/config/Port`

2. Here again we will use the Postman query pulldown and this time choose **PATCH**, which means to add/change information on the system.

3. We then put the generic `public/v1/config/Port` (note that we use `config` instead of `state`):

Here, the **Body** is set to **raw** with `{"IntRef":"fpPort1","AdminState":"UP"}` in the data section. Using raw data in RESTful calls is acceptable, but not preferred. As SnapRoute is a new company, these commands may change over time as they work with customers:

Turning interface fpPort1 up

If we want to query the IPv4 configuration for all of the interfaces, you can send the following GET command:

```
{GET} http://snaproute.router.ip:8080/public/v1/config/IPv4Intfs
```

To look at the ARP table, follow these steps:

1. We must first select the **GET** option and run the command:

    `{GET} http://snaproute.router.ip:8080/public/v1/state/ArpEntrys`

2. In this command, we will again use the **GET** selection in the Postman query pulldown.
3. We will put in the IP/DNS name for the `snaproute` box and the `public/v1/state/ArpEntrys` (note that we are back to using `state`, since we are querying information):

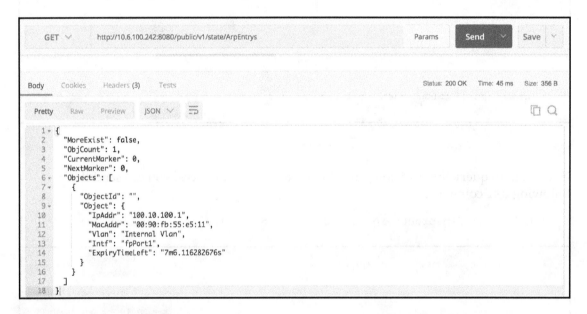

You will notice that the syntax is the similar when using `curl` or Postman.

One of the limitations of the SnapRoute API is its inability to take patch commands directly. For example, the RESTful call for turning an interface admin up should be this: `{PATCH}` `http://snaproute.router.ip:8080/public/v1/config/Port/?IntfRef=fpPort1&` `AdminState:UP`, rather than using the raw information in the body.

Summary

In this chapter, you learned how to install Postman, use it to configure, and get the configuration from a switch running SnapRoute's FlexSwitch software. You also learned how to program FlexSwitch using some of the extra features of Postman.

In the next chapter, we will be doing a deep dive into the OpenFlow protocol.

6
OpenFlow Deep Dive

In `Chapter 3`, *Exploring OpenFlow,*we covered how OpenFlow works and gave some general information about it. Here, we will cover OpenFlow in depth in a practical way, focusing mostly on usage. After reading this chapter, you will have a general knowledge of these:

- How and why OpenFlow was invented
- What issues OpenFlow solves
- How OpenFlow works internally
- How an OpenFlow agent and controller work together
- How to install and configure **OpenDaylight** (**ODL**) and ONOS

History of OpenFlow

As covered in `Chapter 3`, *Exploring OpenFlow,* OpenFlow came out of the need for a simple and straightforward way to program network devices such as switches. OpenFlow began at Stanford University and came to life as version 1.0. The key members of the Clean Slate program continue to contribute to the open networking space. Here is a small sample of the people involved and their current contributions.

Guru Parulkar, executive director of the Stanford Clean Slate program is now the executive director of the **Open Networking Foundation** (**ONF**) and the **Open Networking Lab** (**ON.Lab**), which recently merged. Guru started the **Open Networking Summit** (**ONS**), a yearly conference, focusing on open hardware and software. He is also heavily involved in ONOS, an OpenFlow controller and **Central Office Re-Designed** (**CORD**) .

Nick McKeown, currently the executive director of Barefoot Networks, a company that is building fully programmable, open network chips. Nick co-founded Nicira, a company purchased by VMware, which created NSX, which we will cover in this book.

Before OpenFlow

Prior to OpenFlow, in order to program a forwarding chip or ASIC on open hardware, you needed the skills necessary to use the **Software Development Kit** (**SDK**) provided by the company who produced the ASIC. The agreement necessary to get access to the SDK was and still is onerous. Many researchers, developers, and end users have trouble acquiring access rights to SDKs. Some developers especially, those dealing with open source software, are completely against the concept of being under NDA and contract.

All of this meant that developers and users had no access to program their switches in the way they wanted or needed. Some clever folks utilized the **Joint Test Action Group** (**JTAG**) standards along with readers/programmers to determine some of the inner workings of the systems. Once you knew how the system operated, you were able to modify registers, memories, and so on to *possibly* get the system to behave in the way you wanted.

As open hardware became more visible, a few companies were formed including Pica8, Cumulus Networks, Big Switch Networks, and others that focused on open hardware. Pica8 released PicOS, building on top of the SDK and providing OpenFlow capabilities.

After OpenFlow

The introduction of hardware that supported OpenFlow was a big turning point for open networking. End users were now able to develop and use applications that talked to an open API interface (that is, the commands that had to be sent to the switch were public).

OpenFlow used the fact that most switches used flow tables to process packets. Many features of these flow tables were similar across different vendors and created the initial OpenFlow specification. An OpenFlow-capable switch needed to have three properties:

- A flow table implementation
- A secure channel to connect to the OpenFlow controller
- An implementation of the OpenFlow protocol

OpenFlow also provided a guideline for a dedicated OpenFlow switch, which only speaks OpenFlow and simply forwards traffic between ports based on the information it gets from the controller.

While OpenFlow was developed in 2009, OpenFlow hardware and software did not become mainstream for a few years and open source implementations of forwarding chip drivers did not appear until 2014.

In 2012, I worked with SiliconANGLE to produce a report called *The State of OpenFlow 2012* available at `http://www.slideshare.net/siliconangle/ra-01151301finalv3`. In the report, we worked with multiple vendors who supported OpenFlow, including HP, IWNetworks, and Pica8. The goal of the report was to test whether OpenFlow was ready for the real world. At that time, 1,000 flow entries were considered a reasonable number, today it is much too low.

Some other interesting takeaways from the report are the fact that HP had its own proprietary additions to OpenFlow and that Pica8 was supporting OpenFlow in hybrid mode, which allowed OpenFlow to be enabled on a port-by-port basis.

The report came out before ODL and ONOS were realized in 2013 and 2014, respectively. So, all of the work was done using Floodlight as the SDN controller.

OpenFlow solved most of these issues. For example, with Broadcom forwarding chips supported by **OpenFlow Data Plane Abstraction (OF-DPA)**, the system API calls used by OpenFlow are public. In contrast, the ones in the SDK are under NDA and cannot be publicly disclosed. Broadcom has been relatively responsive about releasing Open API binaries that allow for the programming of their hardware. After releasing OF-DPA, they subsequently released **Open Network Switch Library (OpenNSL)**. When we discuss OpenFlow in reference to Broadcom chips, we will focus on OF-DPA.

OF-DPA

OF-DPA was introduced in early 2014 at the **Open Networking Summit (ONS)**. OF-DPA v1.0 supported OpenFlow version 1.3.1, which as discussed earlier provides multiple tables and other features needed to move OpenFlow forward.

OF-DPA is considered an Open API project, which publicly releases the header files for OF-DPA and a list of API calls that can be made. In comparison, the Broadcom SDK is completely hidden and all API calls are provided under NDA and cannot be exposed.

PicaOS

PicaOS is a NOS from Pica8 that supports both L2 switching and L3 routing. PicaOS uses XORP, a lightly active open source routing platform that is similar to **Free Range Routing (FRRouting)** (the Quagga/Zebra fork). Pica8 was spun out of Quanta computers, who had released the LB9, a switch that was used by many research organizations and universities. Furthermore, PicaOS also supports OpenFlow in both a full and a hybrid setting.

Open Network Linux

Open Network Linux (**ONL**) is a platform OS for open networking switches. It provides the necessary functionality to manage fans, power, SFPs, and other important low-level hardware. ONL is available with the **Open Route Cache(ORC)** daemon to provide network forwarding support to the system. ONL with ORC daemon can be used with routing protocol suites such as Bird and FRR. ONL can be used with forwarding agents such as FBOSS and SnapRoute.

What issues does OpenFlow solve?

One of the main benefits of OpenFlow is the ability to control devices from a central OpenFlow controller. Products such as Floodlight, ODL, and ONOS provide the frontend to the switches, allowing end users to program the switch(es). The central controller allows network admins to solve problems in new ways, such as SD-WAN, which can use OpenFlow as the mechanism to exchange network information between multiple sites.

Google learned from their B4 WAN project how valuable OpenFlow controllers could be. The B4 project carried inter-datacenter traffic, which grew as new products and features were added to Google's portfolio. Google was able to roll out new features via the controllers rather than the switching hardware, which lessened the frequency of updates to their switching hardware.

On a generic switch/router, either a static configuration or routing protocols control how traffic is forwarded. For example, on a Cisco switch running IOS, you would need to configure the port as shown here:

```
Switch# configure terminal
Enter configuration commands, one per line.  End with CNTL/Z.
Switch(config)# interface FastEthernet0/0
Switch(config-if)# ip address 10.10.2.1 255.255.255.0
Switch(config-if)# no shutdown
```

To allow for packet forwarding to other devices, you would need to configure static routing for their addresses. To do so, you must run the following command:

```
Switch(config)# ip route 10.0.0.1 255.255.255.255 FastEthernet0/0
```

This will add a route for `10.0.0.1/32` out interface `FastEthernet0/0`.

To reproduce the forwarding in OpenFlow, you must run the following command:

```
curl -X POST -d '{"nw_dst": "10.0.0.1/32", "actions":"output=2"}'
http://localhost:8080/wm/staticentrypusher/json
```

Internal workings of OpenFlow

The OpenFlow protocol is divided into four components:

- Configuration (language and utility)
- State machine
- Message layer
- System interface

Configuration

Configuration is divided into two parts, the configuration language and the configuration utility. The configuration language is designed with a straightforward interface to configure OpenFlow switches and OpenFlow controllers. The structure of the language is based on the types of information the switch or controller can handle.

For example, the configuration language for an OpenFlow 1.3 switch will contain type definitions for the supported internet protocols, IPv4 and IPv6. Type definitions can be combined to create stages. Examples of stages are initialization, authentication, and authorization.

State machine

The state machine defines the lower level behavior of the protocol such as capabilities, flow control, and negotiation. Capabilities are a list of features that the OpenFlow switch supports such as packet reassembly, setting, or reading the **Type of Service** (**ToS**) of packets (packet handling priorities).

Message layer

The message layer is the central component in OpenFlow, providing message handling and manipulation services. An example of a message is the *Hello* message, used during session setup to negotiate OpenFlow versions.

System interface

The system interface is what talks to the outside world. It contains the necessary keys, interfaces, and transport channels. An example of a system interface is the switch agent interface, which interacts with the switch to forward packets to and from the OpenFlow controller and the switch system kernel:

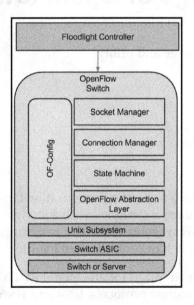

How an OpenFlow controller and agent work together

Without an OpenFlow controller, an OpenFlow-capable switch has no intelligence when it comes to forwarding traffic. Whether the controller runs locally on the switch, or on a server in the network, the controller is central to how OpenFlow works. Here, we will look at two simple examples: Floodlight and Indigo.

Floodlight

Floodlight is an open source OpenFlow controller that was initially released by Big Switch in 2011. It is a Java-based OpenFlow controller based on the Beacon OpenFlow controller written by David Erikson originally at Stanford and then further enhanced while he was working for Big Switch Networks.

Floodlight utilizes a RESTful API, which can be controlled via `curl`, Postman, or any other REST compliant tool.

Indigo

Indigo is an open source OpenFlow agent that runs on open networking switches. Indigo is the basis for Big Switch Networks, Switch Light, which is a combination of ONL and a commercial version of Indigo. Indigo is included with OF-DPA and hence is easy to get installed; if you have an OF-DPA for the system you are working on, you have Indigo.

Connecting Indigo and Floodlight together

For this exercise, we will use the **Indigo Virtual Switch** (**IVS**), which is a software-based high-performance OpenFlow switch that utilizes **Open vSwitch** (**OVS**). If you do not have access to a Linux machine to do the work, follow these directions to create a virtual machine under VirtualBox:

To install IVS, you can pull it down from Git:

1. Open Terminal on a Linux box and run the following command:

   ```
   git clone --recurse-submodules
   https://github.com/floodlight/ivs.git
   ```

   This will download Indigo Virtual Switch and all of its necessary parts. From there, you can enter the `ivs` directory and run `make` to build the switch. You should see something like this:

   ```
   $ git clone --recurse-submodules
   https://github.com/floodlight/ivs.git
   Cloning into 'ivs'...
   remote: Counting objects: 6881, done.
   remote: Compressing objects: 100% (2/2), done.
   remote: Total 6881 (delta 1), reused 1 (delta 1), pack-reused 6878
   Receiving objects: 100% (6881/6881), 1.55 MiB | 2.89 MiB/s, done.
   Resolving deltas: 100% (4241/4241), done.
   ```

```
Checking connectivity... done.
Submodule 'submodules/bigcode'
(git://github.com/floodlight/bigcode.git) registered for path
'submodules/bigcode'
Submodule 'submodules/indigo'
(git://github.com/floodlight/indigo.git) registered for path
'submodules/indigo'
Submodule 'submodules/infra'
(git://github.com/floodlight/infra.git) registered for path
'submodules/infra'
Submodule 'submodules/loxigen-artifacts'
(git://github.com/floodlight/loxigen-artifacts.git) registered for
path 'submodules/loxigen-artifacts'
Submodule 'submodules/luajit-2.0'
(git://github.com/floodlight/luajit-2.0.git) registered for path
'submodules/luajit-2.0'
Cloning into 'submodules/bigcode'...
remote: Counting objects: 3262, done.
remote: Total 3262 (delta 0), reused 0 (delta 0), pack-reused 3262
Receiving objects: 100% (3262/3262), 939.43 KiB | 296.00 KiB/s,
done.
Resolving deltas: 100% (1991/1991), done.
Checking connectivity... done.
Submodule path 'submodules/bigcode': checked out
'6d63049bc7a46facad4b9706c21fcae633cf5cac'
...
Cloning into 'submodules/luajit-2.0'...
remote: Counting objects: 12035, done.
remote: Compressing objects: 100% (2229/2229), done.
remote: Total 12035 (delta 9823), reused 12002 (delta 9801), pack-
reused 0
Receiving objects: 100% (12035/12035), 3.51 MiB | 2.29 MiB/s, done.
Resolving deltas: 100% (9823/9823), done.
Checking connectivity... done.
Submodule path 'submodules/luajit-2.0': checked out
'c2924c3e1d17ffe469a654233481d7be1248d7e0'
```

You can see that there are a lot of software repositories downloaded for IVS including loxigen and other necessary infrastructure. Now we will build the software.

2. If you see any submodule failures, you can do the following:

```
cd ivs
git submodule update --init
snoble@build$ cd ivs
snoble@build:~/ivs$ ls
build docker INTERNALS.md Makefile oftests README.md submodules
tests
debian init.mk LICENSE modules openvswitch rhel targets
snoble@build:~/ivs$ make
make -C targets/ivs
make[1]: Entering directory '/home/snoble/ivs/targets/ivs'
 Compiling[ release ]: IVSMain::cli.c
 Compiling[ release ]: IVSMain::main.c
 Creating Library: build/gcc-local/lib/IVSMain.a
 ....
make -C targets/ivs
make[1]: Entering directory '/home/snoble/ivs/targets/ivs'
make[2]: Entering directory
'/home/snoble/ivs/submodules/luajit-2.0/src'
make[2]: 'libluajit.a' is up to date.
make[2]: Leaving directory
'/home/snoble/ivs/submodules/luajit-2.0/src'
 Linking[release]: IVS::ivs
make[1]: Leaving directory '/home/snoble/ivs/targets/ivs'
make -C targets/ivs-ctl
make[1]: Entering directory '/home/snoble/ivs/targets/ivs-ctl'
 Compiling[ release ]: IVSCtlMain::main.c
 Creating Library: build/gcc-local/lib/IVSCtlMain.a
 Linking[release]: IVSCtl::ivs-ctl
make[1]: Leaving directory '/home/snoble/ivs/targets/ivs-ctl'
snoble@build:~/ivs$
```

3. Once it is done building, you will find the binaries here:

```
targets/ivs/build/gcc-local/bin/ivs
targets/ivs-ctl/build/gcc-local/bin/ivs-ctl
```

These can be run directly from the directory.

4. To connect IVS to your Floodlight server, you need to tell IVS where the OpenFlow server is:

```
snoble@build:~/ivs$ targets/ivs/build/gcc-local/bin/ivs --help
ivs: Indigo Virtual Switch
Usage: ivs [OPTION]...

 -v, --verbose Verbose logging
```

```
-t, --trace Very verbose logging
-c, --controller=IP:PORT Connect to a controller at startup
-l, --listen=IP:PORT Listen for dpctl connections
-i, --interface=INTERFACE Attach a network interface at startup
--pipeline=NAME Set the default forwarding pipeline (standard-1.0
or standard-1.3)
--dpid=DPID Set datapath ID (default autogenerated)
--syslog Log to syslog instead of stderr
--inband-vlan=VLAN Enable in-band management on the specified VLAN
--internal-port=NAME Create a port with the given name connected
to the datapath
--hitless Preserve kernel flows until controller pushes
configuration
-h,--help Display this help message and exit
--version Display version information and exit
```

5. So to run IVS, connect to the Floodlight server and put two interfaces under command, you would do the following:

```
sudo ivs -c 192.168.1.1 -i eth1 -i eth2
```

This tells the IVS to connect to a OpenFlow server at IP address `192.168.1.1` and use `eth1` and `eth2` as the interfaces that it controls:

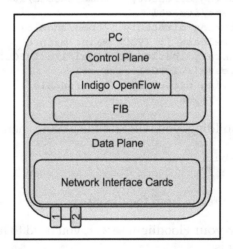

The preceding diagram shows what the PC running IVS configured as stated looks like.

Now that Floodlight and Indigo are connected, you can send some commands to the IVS via REST.

In the following example, the **Access Control Lists** (**ACLs**) on the switch are listed. Notice how similar the command is to how we integrated with FlexSwitch:

```
curl http://controller-ip:8080/wm/acl/rules/json | python -m json.tool
```

You can also delete all of the ACL entries:

```
curl http://controler-ip:8080/wm/acl/clear/json
```

About OpenDaylight

The ODL project was started in 2013 by a large number of networking companies including Arista Networks, Big Switch Networks, Brocade, Cisco, and others.

The goal of the ODL project was to build an open source OpenFlow controller, which would offer a more extensible platform than the currently available ones. ODL is built around a concept of the **Model-driven Service Abstraction Layer** (**MD-SAL**), which utilizes **Yet Another Next Generation** (**YANG**)—an interesting name for referring to this book:

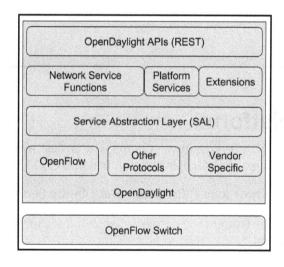

The preceding diagram depicts ODL as first designed. It was a simple controller with a REST API (REST is very common as we can see).

Installing OpenDaylight

To install ODL, you can use the public releases, which can be found at: `https://www.opend aylight.org/downloads`. Currently, the latest version is Carbon released on May 26, 2017. The documents are located at `http://docs.opendaylight.org/en/stable-boron/gettin g-started-guide/index.html`:

Installation platform

You can install ODL on UNIX or Windows systems. The easiest way to run ODL is in a UNIX virtual machine using a tool such as Oracle VirtualBox, VMware, or Fusion/Desktop.

Here we will step through how to use VirtualBox and Ubuntu Server:

1. Install VirtualBox from `https://www.virtualbox.org/wiki/Downloads` for your operating system.

2. Then, download the server `iso` for Ubuntu from `https://www.ubuntu.com/down load/server`. The current version is 16.04.2 **Long Term Support** (**LTS**):

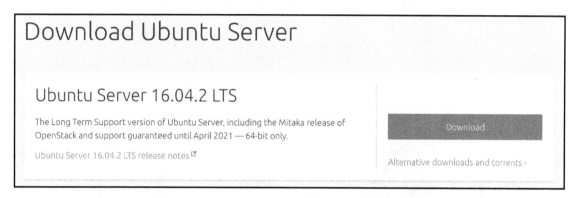

3. Once you have downloaded Ubuntu, you will create a new virtual machine with 4 GB of RAM and a 16 GB disk. Follow these steps during the install:
    1. Choose **Linux** and **Ubuntu (64-bit)** as the **Type** and **Version** of the operating system:

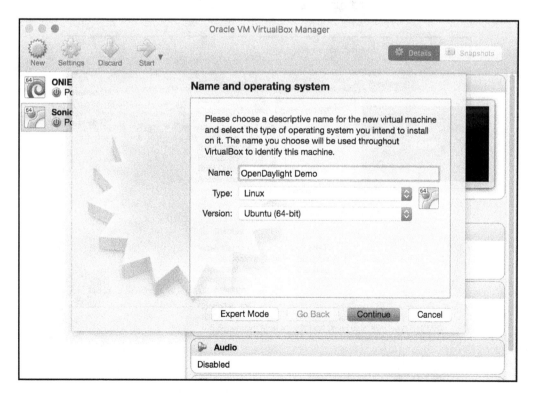

2. Increase the memory from 768 MB to 4096 MB (4 GB):

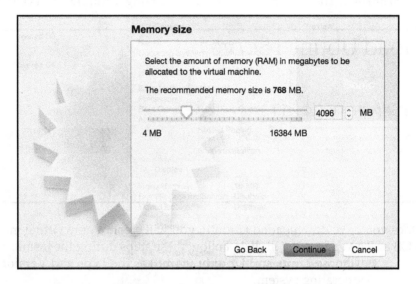

3. Set the hard drive size to 16GB:

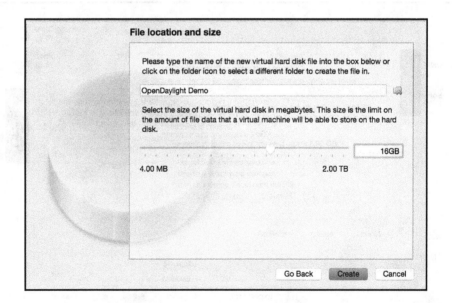

4. Once you boot the system, you will be presented with the following screen; choose **Install Ubuntu Server** and continue through the default choices until you get to the window that asks you to choose what programs to install:

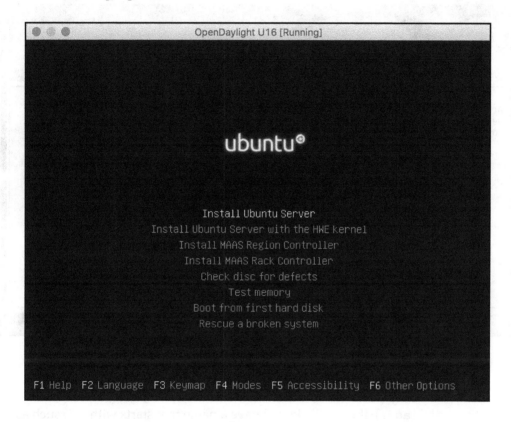

5. Choose **standard system utilities, OpenSSH server,** and **Manual package selection**:

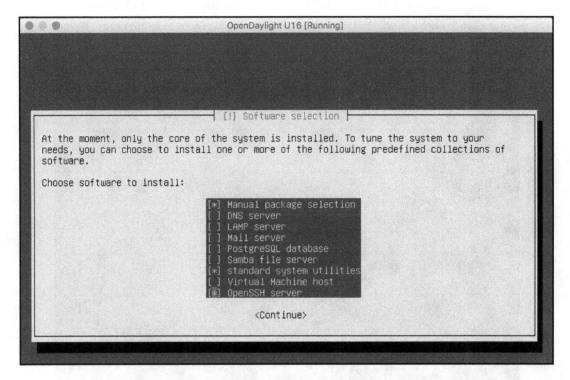

6. After this, the system will reboot and you will log in using the username and password you chose during the install. You will want to log in and take note of the name of the primary Ethernet interface (ip addr). It most likely will have a name that starts with enp such as enp0s3

7. Now you will need to power off the machine by typing this:

```
sudo poweroff
```

8. Now there are some steps that need to be done before you start the machine back up. You will need to add a second network adapter and configure it:

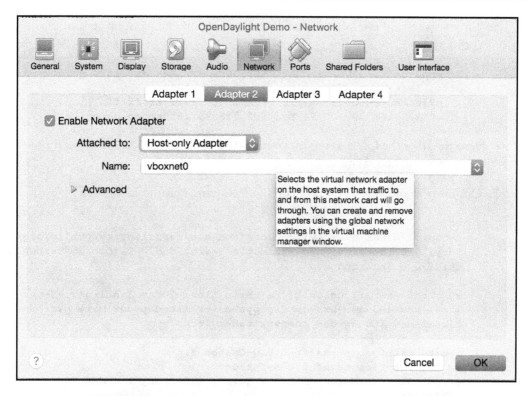

4. Once your install is done, turn the machine on and run the following command:

```
ifconfig -a
```

You should see one interface with an IP and one without. The one with the IP should be the same as the one you wrote down. In Ubuntu 16, they can have different names. For example, on my test machine the names are enps03 and enps08.

5. So to turn up the second Ethernet, I need to do the following:

```
sudo ifconfig enp0s8 up
sudo dhclient enp0s8
```

6. Now you should see a new IP address under the `ifconfig` or `ip addr` command:

```
3: enp0s8: <BROADCAST,MULTICAST,UP,LOWER_UP> mtu 1500 qdisc
pfifo_fast state UP group default qlen 1000
   link/ether 08:00:27:d9:10:f9 brd ff:ff:ff:ff:ff:ff
   inet 192.168.99.100/24 brd 192.168.99.255 scope global eth1
```

Here the IP of the ODL demo machine is `192.168.99.100`. You should now be able to access the machine using `ssh`.

7. Once on the machine, you will run the following commands:

```
wget
"https://nexus.opendaylight.org/content/repositories/public/org/ope
ndaylight/integration/distribution-karaf/0.6.0-Carbon/distribution-
karaf-0.6.0-Carbon.zip"

sudo apt install default-jre unzip libnl-3-dev libnl-genl-3-dev
libnl-route-3-dev pkg-config python-tz libpcap-dev make pkg-config
libssl-dev libcap-dev openvswitch-switch

unzip distribution-karaf-0.6.0-Carbon.zip
cd distribution-karaf-0.6.0-Carbon
export JAVA_HOME=/usr/lib/jvm/java-1.8.0-openjdk-amd64
./bin/karaf

snoble@odl:~/distribution-karaf-0.6.0-Carbon$ ./bin/karaf
Apache Karaf starting up. Press Enter to open the shell now...
100%
[=================================================================
======]

Karaf started in 5s. Bundle stats: 64 active, 64 total

OpenDaylight (in ASCII see picture).

Hit '<tab>' for a list of available commands
and '[cmd] --help' for help on a specific command.
Hit '<ctrl-d>' or type 'system:shutdown' or 'logout' to shutdown
OpenDaylight.

opendaylight-user@root>
```

You will get the following output:

```
Apache Karaf starting up. Press Enter to open the shell now...
100% [=================================================================]

Karaf started in 4s. Bundle stats: 64 active, 64 total




Hit '<tab>' for a list of available commands
and '[cmd] --help' for help on a specific command.
Hit '<ctrl-d>' or type 'system:shutdown' or 'logout' to shutdown OpenDaylight.

opendaylight-user@root>
```

8. Now that we have the OpenDaylight prompt, we can start looking at what is installed:

```
opendaylight-user@root> feature:list -i
Name | Version | Installed | Repository | Description
-------------------------------------------------------------------------
----------------------------------------
standard | 3.0.7 | x | standard-3.0.7 | Karaf standard feature
config | 3.0.7 | x | standard-3.0.7 | Provide OSGi ConfigAdmin
support
region | 3.0.7 | x | standard-3.0.7 | Provide Region Support
package | 3.0.7 | x | standard-3.0.7 | Package commands and mbeans
kar | 3.0.7 | x | standard-3.0.7 | Provide KAR (KARaf archive)
support
ssh | 3.0.7 | x | standard-3.0.7 | Provide a SSHd server on Karaf
management | 3.0.7 | x | standard-3.0.7 | Provide a JMX MBeanServer
and a set of MBeans in K
```

9. By default, ODL has only a minimal number of packages installed. It doesn't have the OpenFlow plugin or web GUI installed by default, so let's fix that:

```
opendaylight-user@root>feature:install odl-restconf odl-l2switch-
switch odl-mdsal-apidocs odl-dlux-core
opendaylight-user@root>feature:list -i
Name | Version | Installed | Repository | Description
--------------------------------------------------------
standard | 3.0.7 | x | standard-3.0.7 | Karaf standard feature
...
odl-config-api | 0.5.2-Boron-SR2 | x | odl-config-0.5.2-Boron-SR2 |
OpenDaylight :: Config :: API
odl-config-netty-config-api | 0.5.2-Boron-SR2 | x | odl-
config-0.5.2-Boron-SR2 | OpenDaylight :: Config :: Netty Config API
odl-config-core | 0.5.2-Boron-SR2 | x | odl-config-0.5.2-Boron-SR2
| OpenDaylight :: Config :: Core
odl-config-manager | 0.5.2-Boron-SR2 | x | odl-config-0.5.2-Boron-
SR2 | OpenDaylight :: Config :: Manager
odl-yangtools-yang-data | 1.0.2-Boron-SR2 | x | odl-
yangtools-1.0.2-Boron-SR2 | OpenDaylight :: Yangtools :: Data
Binding
odl-yangtools-common | 1.0.2-Boron-SR2 | x | odl-yangtools-1.0.2-
Boron-SR2 | OpenDaylight :: Yangtools :: Common
odl-yangtools-yang-parser | 1.0.2-Boron-SR2 | x | odl-
yangtools-1.0.2-Boron-SR2 | OpenDaylight :: Yangtools :: YANG
Parser
odl-openflowplugin-flow-services | 0.3.2-Boron-SR2 | x |
openflowplugin-0.3.2-Boron-SR2 | OpenDaylight :: Openflow Plugin ::
Flow Services
odl-openflowplugin-southbound | 0.3.2-Boron-SR2 | x |
openflowplugin-0.3.2-Boron-SR2 | OpenDaylight :: Openflow Plugin ::
Li southbound A
odl-openflowplugin-nsf-model | 0.3.2-Boron-SR2 | x |
openflowplugin-0.3.2-Boron-SR2 | OpenDaylight :: OpenflowPlugin ::
NSF :: Model
odl-openflowplugin-app-config-pusher | 0.3.2-Boron-SR2 | x |
openflowplugin-0.3.2-Boron-SR2 | OpenDaylight :: Openflow Plugin ::
Application - d
odl-openflowplugin-app-topology | 0.3.2-Boron-SR2 | x |
openflowplugin-0.3.2-Boron-SR2 | OpenDaylight :: Openflow Plugin ::
Application - t
odl-openflowplugin-app-forwardingrules-manager | 0.3.2-Boron-SR2 |
x | openflowplugin-0.3.2-Boron-SR2 | OpenDaylight :: Openflow
Plugin :: Application - F
odl-dlux-core | 0.4.2-Boron-SR2 | x | odl-dlux-0.4.2-Boron-SR2 |
Opendaylight dlux minimal feature
odl-l2switch-switch | 0.4.2-Boron-SR2 | x | l2switch-0.4.2-Boron-
SR2 | OpenDaylight :: L2Switch :: Switch
```

```
odl-l2switch-hosttracker | 0.4.2-Boron-SR2 | x | l2switch-0.4.2-
Boron-SR2 | OpenDaylight :: L2Switch :: HostTracker
odl-l2switch-addresstracker | 0.4.2-Boron-SR2 | x | l2switch-0.4.2-
Boron-SR2 | OpenDaylight :: L2Switch :: AddressTracker
odl-l2switch-arphandler | 0.4.2-Boron-SR2 | x | l2switch-0.4.2-
Boron-SR2 | OpenDaylight :: L2Switch :: ArpHandler
odl-l2switch-loopremover | 0.4.2-Boron-SR2 | x | l2switch-0.4.2-
Boron-SR2 | OpenDaylight :: L2Switch :: LoopRemover
odl-l2switch-packethandler | 0.4.2-Boron-SR2 | x | l2switch-0.4.2-
Boron-SR2 | OpenDaylight :: L2Switch :: PacketHandler
odl-openflowjava-protocol | 0.8.2-Boron-SR2 | x | odl-
openflowjava-0.8.2-Boron-SR2 | OpenDaylight :: Openflow Java ::
Protocol
```

Note how many more applications are installed. These are the applications necessary to make OpenFlow work. The important packages are as follows:

- `odl-l2switch-*`: These packages provide a layer 2 learning switch
- `odl-openflowplugin-*`: These packages provide the OpenFlow functionality
- `odl-dlux-*`: These packages provide the web UI (called DLUX)
- `odl-yangtools-*`: These packages provide the system with a YANG interpreter

10. Now use OVS to connect to the controller:

```
sudo ovs-vsctl add-br openflow
sudo ovs-vsctl set-controller openflow tcp:127.0.0.1:6653
```

This creates an interface on the OpenDaylight box named `openflow` and connects it to the OpenFlow port `6653` of OpenDaylight:

```
snoble@odl:~/ivs$ sudo ovs-vsctl list controller
_uuid : 90d84bdb-de30-436f-b0b1-c7171e0d58af
connection_mode : []
controller_burst_limit: []
controller_rate_limit: []
enable_async_messages: []
external_ids : {}
inactivity_probe : []
is_connected : true
local_gateway : []
local_ip : []
local_netmask : []
```

```
max_backoff : []
other_config : {}
role : master
status : {sec_since_connect="599", state=ACTIVE}
target : "tcp:127.0.0.1:6653"

snoble@odl:~/ivs$ sudo ovs-vsctl show
70ccc243-1f5d-4737-97e7-955dc6ecb9ef
Bridge openflow
Controller "tcp:127.0.0.1:6653"
is_connected: true
Port openflow
Interface openflow
type: internal
ovs_version: "2.5.0"
```

11. You should see something like this on the OpenDaylight DLUX UI:

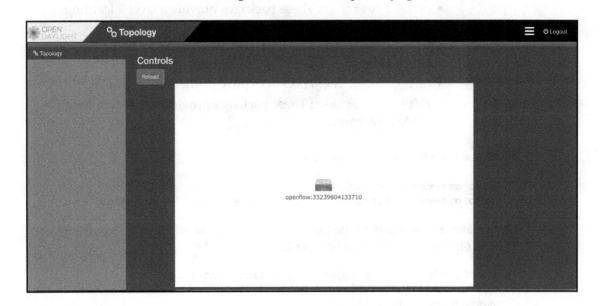

ONOS

The **Open Network Operating System (ONOS)** is a **Software-defined Networking (SDN)** platform that provides an OpenFlow controller and integrates with OF-DPA and Indigo.

Installing and configuring ONOS

Using the same Ubuntu box from our ODL and IVS demos, we will stop Karaf and install ONOS.

Similar directions can be found at `https://wiki.onosproject.org/display/ONOS/Installing+on+a+single+machine`. First we need to add the java repository to our Linux machine, this is necessary to get the latest version of Java and to update if a security patch is released.

```
sudo add-apt-repository ppa:webupd8team/java -y
sudo apt-get update
sudo apt-get install oracle-java8-installer oracle-java8-set-default maven -y
```

We can now proceed to download and install ONOS. The first step is to acquire a copy of ONOS, which we can accomplish using the web get tool (`wget`). The first two steps will download and install ONOS, the next steps show logging in and what ONOS should look like if devices are connected:

1. We will download ONOS into the `/opt` directory and expand it:

   ```
   cd /opt
   sudo wget -c
   http://downloads.onosproject.org/release/onos-1.7.1.tar.gz
   sudo tar xzf onos-1.7.1.tar.gz
   sudo mv onos-1.7.1 onos
   ```

2. Then run ONOS:

   ```
   snoble@odl:/opt$ /opt/onos/bin/onos-service start
   karaf: JAVA_HOME not set; results may vary
   Welcome to Open Network Operating System (ONOS)!
   ```

   ```
   Documentation: wiki.onosproject.org
   ```

```
Tutorials: tutorials.onosproject.org
Mailing lists: lists.onosproject.org

Come help out! Find out how at: contribute.onosproject.org

Hit '<tab>' for a list of available commands
and '[cmd] --help' for help on a specific command.
Hit '<ctrl-d>' or type 'system:shutdown' or 'logout' to shutdown
ONOS.

onos>
```

3. At this point, ONOS is running on the server and you can log in by going to the following link: `http://192.168.99.101:8181/onos/ui/login.html` (replace the IP with the IP of your server).

4. Now log in with the `onos` username and `rocks` password:

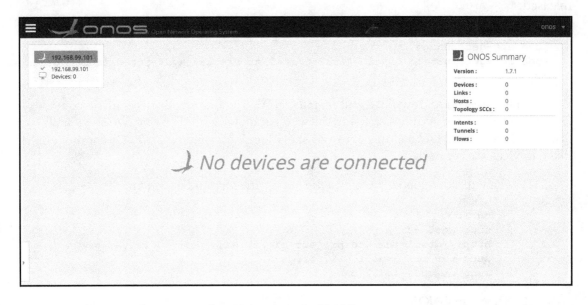

The preceding screenshot is the default ONOS screen.

5. The following is a screenshot from some earlier testing I did with ONOS, showing two Pica8 switches connected with a few hosts and ONOS running in multi-instance mode:

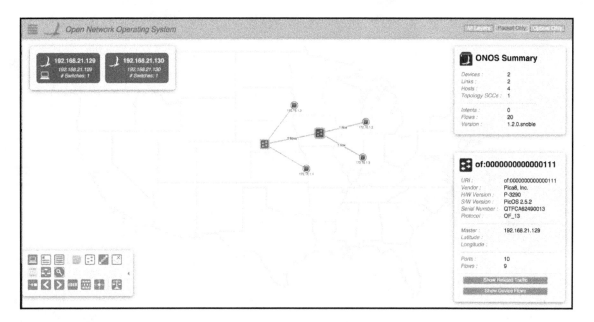

Summary

In this chapter, you learned about the history of OpenFlow, why it was invented, and what issues it solves. We looked at how OpenFlow works internally and how an OpenFlow agent and controller work together. Finally, we set up ODL and ONOS.

In the next chapter, we will look at VMware NSX.

7
VMware NSX

VMware's NSX is a network virtualization platform. Network virtualization replaced data plane functions, such as routers, switches, firewalls, ports, and other physical network hardware constructs in software. Replacing physical hardware with software versions creates the **Software-defined Networking** (**SDN**) part of what is referred to as a **Software-defined Data Center** (**SDDC**). These constructs are then used to create replacements or new devices in the network. VMware acquired Nicra in 2012, and Nicra's **Network Virtualization Platform** (**NVP**), together with **VMware's Cloud, Network, and Security** (**vCNS**), and vSwitch created NSX.

In this chapter, we will cover VMware's NSX.

When done, you should have a good grasp of the following:

- The origins of NSX
- How NSX differs from OVS and ACI
- How to design a network using NSX
- How to install NSX
- How to configure NSX

NSX

Now, let's begin with the NSX product. It consists of two parts—the NSX Manager and the NSX Controller.

NSX Manager

NSX Manager is the central management pane for all NSX-related objects within the data center. It provides multiple interfaces, including a **User Interface** (**UI**) and an **Application Program Interface** (**API**). It is also responsible for installing the **vSphere Installation Bundle** (**VIB**).

The VIBs included with NSX are as follows:

- **VXLAN**: Provides VXLAN support to vSphere
- **Distributed routing**: Allows routing between VMs without leaving the NSX network
- **Distributed firewall**: A kernel-level firewall that can be offloaded onto a smart **Network Interface Card** (**NIC**)

NSX Controller

NSX Controller is the central manager for NSX virtual networks and overlay technologies. All information about logical switches, connected devices such as virtual machines, and hosts is managed by the NSX Controller.

The history of virtualization

Virtualization originally showed up in servers, where VMware provided software to virtualize servers and storage so that multiple servers could be run on a single hardware device. Each server had its own shared or dedicated CPU, memory, and disk resources. As the concept of SDN came along, the need for virtualized networks arrived. In the beginning, network virtualization was local to the network adapters in the server, allowing multiple virtual servers to share the same network connection.

While, initially, simple network virtualization was useful, the need for more powerful features came along. These features, such as firewalls, hardware pass-through, and others, pushed the industry to create better hardware with features such as SR-IOV, which is the ability to utilize hardware features on network cards on multiple virtual machines, essentially virtual functions.

Where VMware came in

In the late 2000s, VMware introduced their vCNS product that combined with their vSwitch to create a full stack solution for SDDC. At the same time, Nicira was developing the NVP product. When VMware acquired Nicira in 2012, the combined R&D teams from both the companies were able to release NSX in about a year.

The difference between NSX, ACI, and OVS

Both VMware NSX and Cisco **Application Centric Infrastructure** (**ACI**) provide application-based network virtualization, with NSX focused on fully virtualized infrastructure and ACI focused on hardware. OVS also provides network virtualization, but it does not have the controller-based operation that ACI has with **Application Policy Infrastructure Controller** (**APIC**) and the NSX Controller. The **Open Virtual Network** (**OVN**) project creates a controller for OVS that focuses on layers 2-4, adding security groups and ACLs to OVS.

We will talk more about ACI in the next chapter.

How to design a network using NSX

The approach to designing a network around NSX is similar to designing any network; you look at your L1-L7 needs and determine what hardware/software combination would fulfill your needs. For this design, we will limit the design needs to the features available in NSX and the hardware it supports.

The first part of the design will be the physical network, that is, the cables and hardware that connect the servers together and to the network. For NSX, the underlying hardware does not matter as long as it can provide L2/L3 connectivity between the servers running the hypervisor, and therefore, the virtualized workloads. While there is integration with physical servers via hardware that supports VXLAN, to fully utilize all of the features that NSX provides the applications need to run as virtualized workloads.

NSX is a virtualization platform that runs on VMware's vSphere product, with ESXi as the hypervisor and distributed vSwitch as the networking platform. NSX provides orchestration across layers 2 through 7 of the networking stack. It uses overlay networking to create virtual networks across physically routed networks.

For network switches, any switch that supports VXLAN can be utilized with NSX. Some **Network Operating System** (**NOS**) providers provide direct integration with NSX. Both Big Switch and Cumulus Networks offer a hybrid solution with NSX. In the case of Big Switch, the Big Cloud Fabric solution provides physical network orchestration and interoperability with NSX VTEP. Cumulus Networks provide VXLAN support, and the network is managed by NSX. Refer to the following diagram:

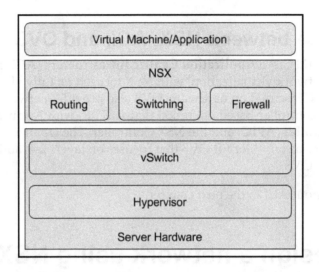

In this diagram, we see a generic view of NSX that runs above VMware's vSwitch and provides micro segmentation with features such as routing, switching, firewall/filtering, and load balancing. For this design, we are going to use open networking hardware in a leaf-spine design.

Review of the leaf-spine design

In a leaf-spine network design, there are leaf switches (the switches that connect to the servers). These are sometimes called **Top of Rack** (**ToR**) switches, connected to a set of spines (switches that connect leaves together), and sometimes called **End of Rack** (**EoR**) switches:

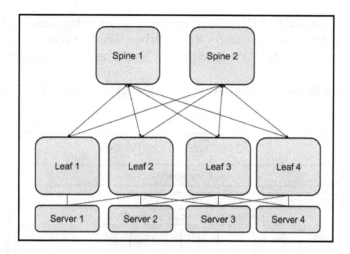

We will use a Clos-based leaf-spine to construct our NSX network design, as shown in the preceding diagram. We will use **VXLAN Tunnel Endpoints (VTEP)** to provide a single virtual switch to NSX.

The physical design will look as illustrated in the preceding diagram with the addition of virtual servers and a controller for the underlay. Now refer to the following diagram:

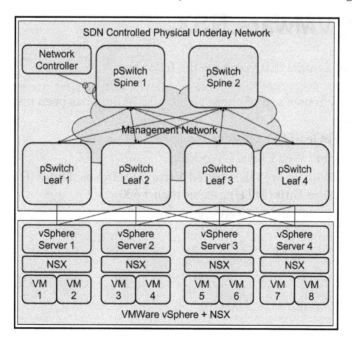

In this diagram, you can see an SDN-managed physical underlay network that uses a separate management network to control the switches. On the network, we are running VMware vSphere on bare-metal servers with NSX handling the networking.

To NSX and the VMs, the network looks like a single logical network, as shown in the following diagram:

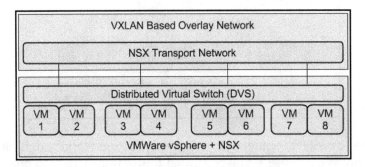

Now that we have an idea of how the network will look, we can acquire the hardware and start setting up VMware NSX.

Installing VMware NSX

For this process, we assume that you have the following:

- VMware vCenter and vSphere version 5.5 or later has been installed on the server hardware
- You have at least two clusters
- Your vSphere Web Client is working
- All your switches are **Distributed Virtual Switches** (**DvSwitch**) with **Maximum Transmission Unit** (**MTU**) greater than 1,600
- Functional DNS and NTP configuration

The suggested minimum NSX setup is as follows:

- One NSX Manager per vCenter server
- Three NSX Controllers

For our setup, we will have four ESXi host servers and run an NSX edge on each one of them.

The minimum suggested hardware requirements for the preceding installation are as follows:

- 30 GB memory
- 20 vCPU
- 122 GB disk

NSX also requires some ports to be open, including the following:

- TCP
    - **Port 22**: SSH by default (this port is not enabled on the server)
    - **Port 80**: Communication between NSX Manager and NSX hosts
    - **Port 443**: Secure communication for APIs and OVA distribution
    - **Port 1234**: Communication between ESXi hosts and NSX Controllers
    - **Port 5671**: RabbitMQ

Once you have acquired the correct resources and modified the filters to allow the ports we just discussed, you can start the installation.

Installation steps

To install NSX, perform the following steps:

1. The first step is to install and deploy the NSX Manager from the supplied **Open Virtual Format (OVF)**. This file is supplied by VMware in the NSX package.
2. Log in to the vSphere Web Client:

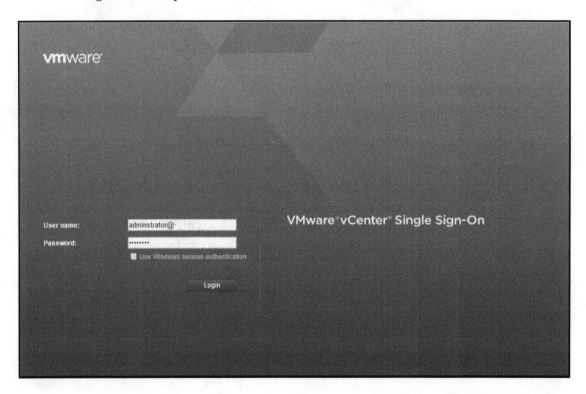

3. Click on **vCenter** and then click on **Hosts**.

4. *Alt* + click on the ESXi Server that you want to install NSX Manager on and then choose **Deploy OVF Template...**:

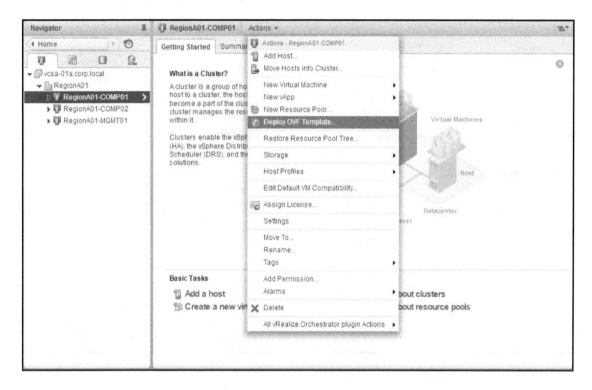

5. Review the details, accept the **End User License Agreement (EULA)**, and select where to install NSX.

6. Set the normal user CLI password and the admin user password:

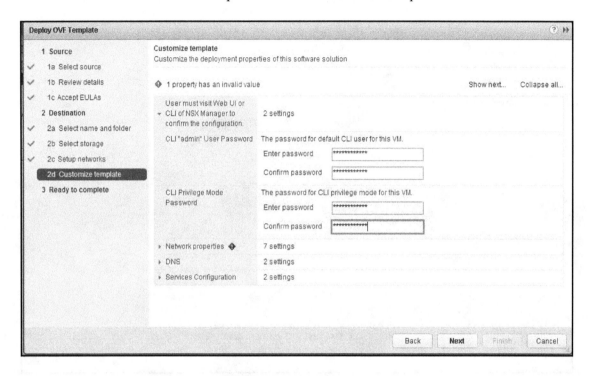

7. Once the NSX Manager is deployed, log in to it:

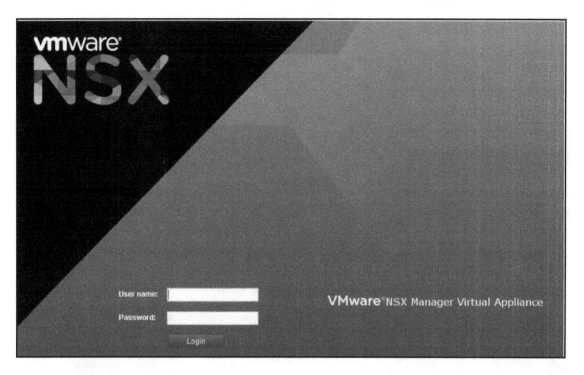

8. Once you log in, you need to register the NSX Manager with the vCenter server.
9. Use the vSphere web interface to deploy NSX Controllers.
10. Once the NSX Controllers are installed, use the NSX Manager to install VIBs on ESXi hosts.
11. Now that everything is installed, you can start defining the virtual firewall, routing, and other NSX features.

Working with NSX

Now that you have installed NSX, you can go back to the vSphere Web Client and manage the network. In this section, we will add an AD server using LDAP. Here are the steps to do this:

1. The first step is to choose **Networking & Security** from the sidebar:

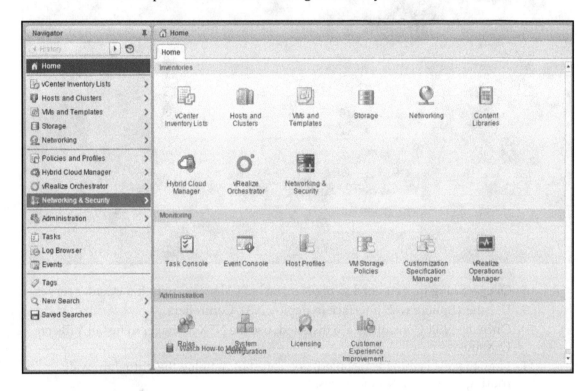

2. This will put you on the NSX control pane:

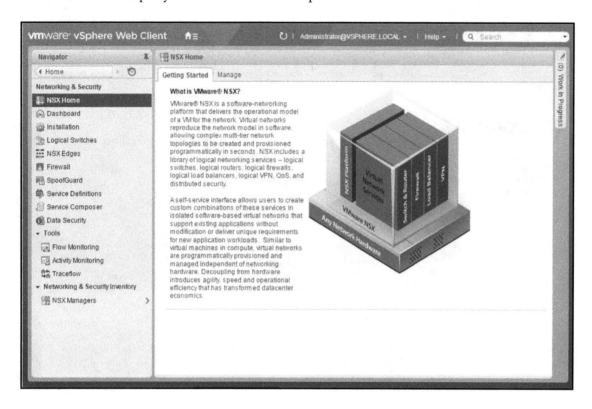

3. Check the installation to confirm that all the controller nodes are visible:

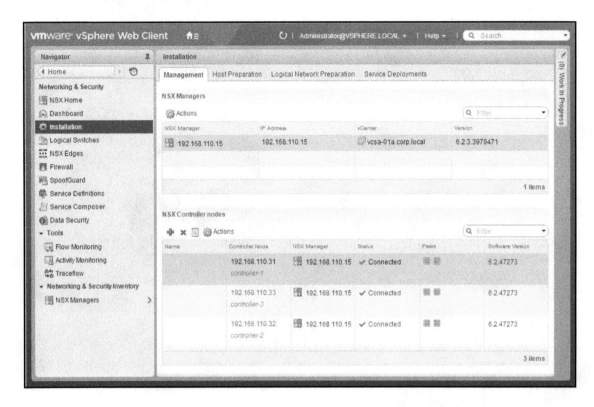

4. Now we will add the LDAP authentication server and configure NSX so that it can utilize users in the firewall settings. First, we will select the NSX Manager seen in the preceding screenshot:

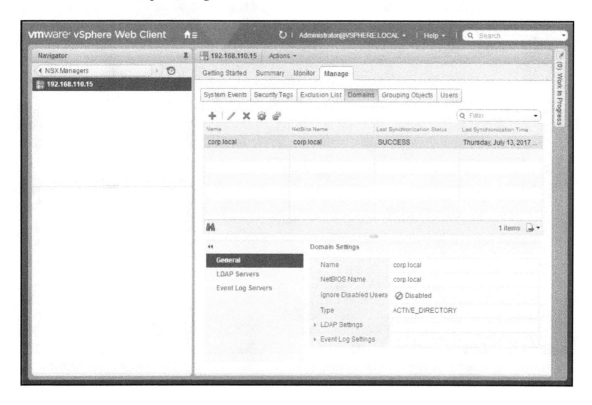

5. Now we need to set the LDAP **Server**, **Port**, **User Name**, and **Password**:

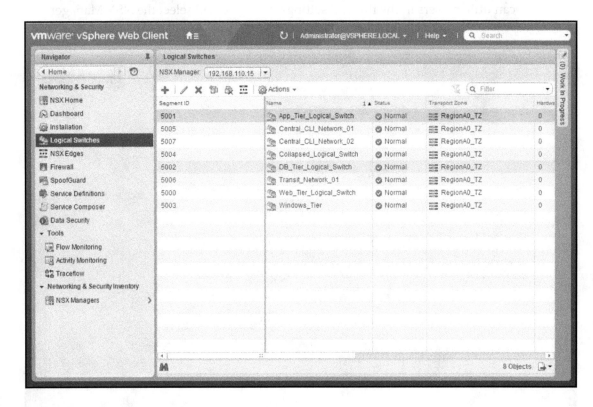

6. Confirm that the connection method (CIFS) and port number are correct, select use domain credentials if it is not already selected:

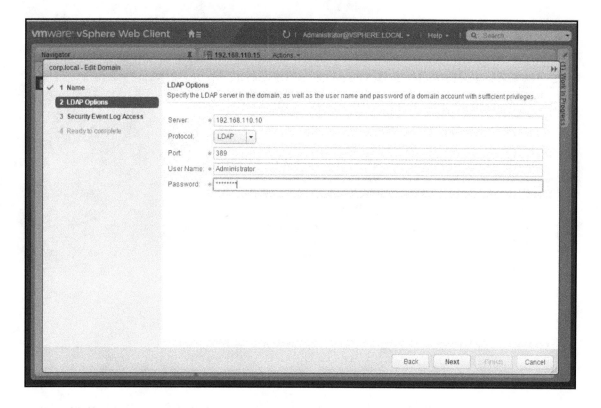

7. Check the information here, confirm that the AD information is correct, and select **Finish**:

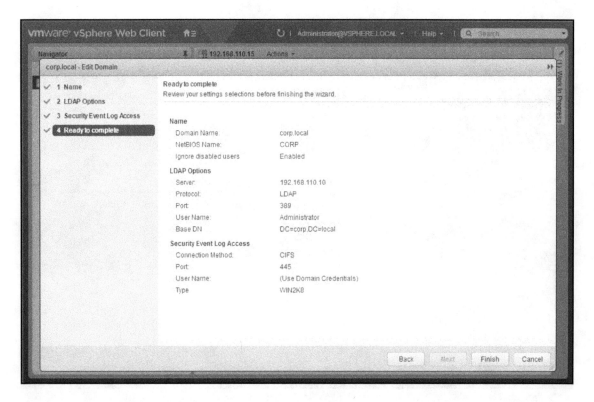

In Chapter 13, *Securing the Network*, we will talk about setting up a firewall rule using the AD credentials of a group of users.

A walkthrough of other NSX features

Now that we have completed configuring the basic features of NSX, let's look around and check the information found in the GUI:

In **Dashboard**, we will find the status of the deployed features, including the NSX Manager, three controller nodes, eight logical witches, and five hosts. If there are any errors, they will be noted here.

We also have the ability to look at the flows traversing the network. In this case, there is no traffic to look at. We can look at the top flows, top destinations, and top sources:

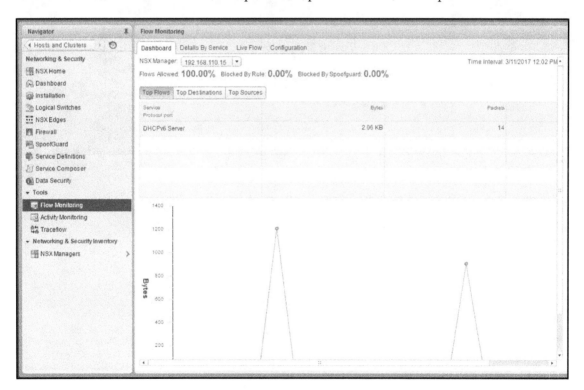

Under NSX Manager, we can monitor and manage system events, domains, users, and other NSX-related information:

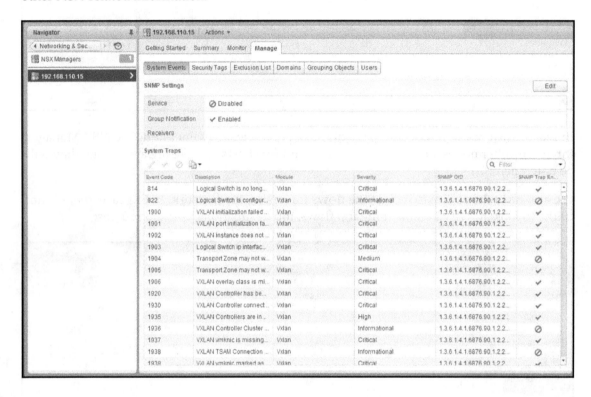

Under the **SpoofGuard** tab object, we can see the policies being used by the different vSphere devices:

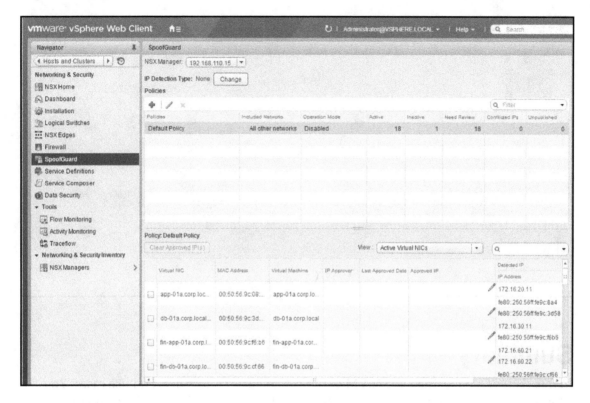

Finally, we can review how much hardware is necessary to run the setup of five hosts and 22 virtual machines with 35 networks and four data stores:

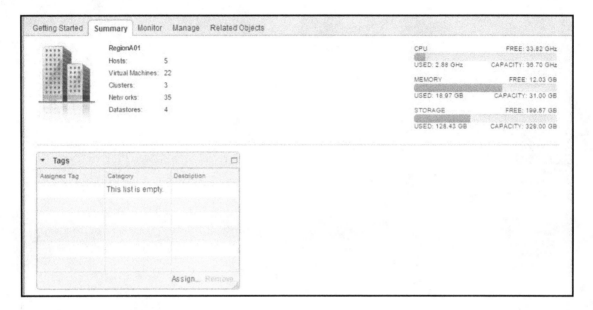

Summary

In this chapter, you learned about VMware NSX, its history, features, and use cases. You should now have a general understanding of what VMware NSX is and how you can integrate it into an existing or new SDDC.

In the next chapter, we will discuss Cisco ACI, another SDDC product.

8
Cisco ACI

Cisco's **Application Centric Infrastructure** (**ACI**) framework is an integrated solution of the Nexus 9000 switching/routing hardware and the **Application Policy Infrastructure Controller** (**APIC**) software. The solution is similar to VMware NSX and Big Switch Networks' Big Cloud Fabric.

In Chapter 7, *VMware NSX*, we discussed the differences between NSX and ACI. While there are many similarities, such as the use of an overlay network, VXLAN, and other technologies, ACI is still a hardware-focused system, whereas NSX is a software-based system. From a technical perspective, NSX can be integrated into ACI and provides complementary features.

ACI was created at Insieme Networks, a spin-in company that Cisco originally funded and then acquired. ACI is a straightforward concept where policies are applied to end users/groups instead of interfaces; these policies are called **Endpoint Groups** (**EPGs**).

At the 10,000 foot level, an ACI network looks just like a normal leaf-spine network. As you dig deeper, you see the overlay aspects provided by APIC and ACI.

In this chapter, we will cover Cisco ACI's hardware-based network virtualization platform.

When done, you should have a good grasp of the following:

- The origins of ACI
- The concept and use of EPGs
- The current scale limits of ACI
- How to design a network using ACI
- How to install ACI
- How to configure ACI using the GUI and CLI

ACI terminologies and concepts

ACI has a few concepts that need to be understood before getting into design and deployment.

Contracts

A contract in the ACI/APIC world is a combination of two pieces of information—a filter that tells the contract what to operate on and an action that states what to do when the filter is matched.

APIC configuration

The APIC configuration is created via either the GUI or CLI on the APIC controller. It is the central repository for network design information.

Policy model

The policy model manages the network fabric, including the physical hardware, users, services, and applications. It defines how the fabric manages features and their configurations.

Logical model

When APIC configures a network, it produces a logical model that references the physical model. The logical model holds information about the entire network, including hardware, software, interconnects, and hosts.

Concrete model

The concrete model is rendered by NX-OS on the switches based on the logical model. In the event the APIC controllers become unreachable, the system will continue to operate, but no changes can be made.

Tenants

The term tenant is often used for the end device, but in this case Cisco uses it to describe a group of policies that are used to manage access control across the entire fabric. A tenant can represent an end customer, organization, or a just a group of policies.

Cisco defines four types of tenant:

- **User tenant**: User tenants are based on end-user needs; policies created here tend to focus on end devices, such as web servers, database servers, and so on.
- **Common tenant**: The common tenant defines what services are available to all the tenants. It is managed by the fabric administrator.
- **Infrastructure tenant**: The infrastructure tenant defines the network services available to user tenants.
- **Management tenant**: The management tenant manages the in-band and out-of-band configuration of the switching nodes.

EPGs

An EPG is a policy that defines a group of devices that are treated similarly and provides a container around them.

The concept behind EPGs is that organizations have multiple servers/devices that utilize the same policies, such as filtering, port forwarding, and so on. To use them, users determine whether their current traditional networking design can be converted or whether they will need to modify the network design.

EPGs can be defined by multiple criteria, such as VLAN ID, IP address blocks, system type, and software version (when connected to a virtualized system that supports ACI integration).

EPGs can be linked together using Application Network Profiles, where permissions between groups of EPGs are defined:

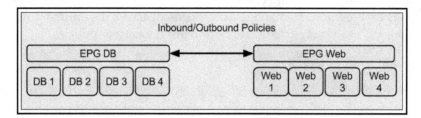

EPGs can be used in many ways, including replicating the behavior of traditional network constructs such as VLANs, IP subnets, VXLANs, VMware port groups, and others.

In cases where EPGs are used to replicate a current VLAN infrastructure, each VLAN is replaced by a single EPG and then all policies are applied to it directly:

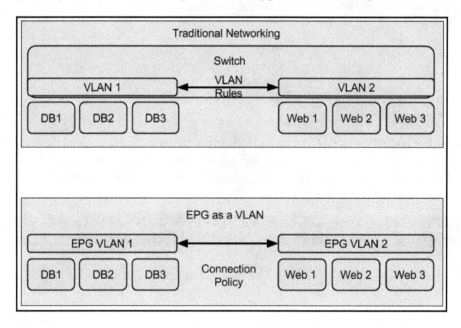

For IP subnets, the IP address space is used to define the devices contained within the EPG:

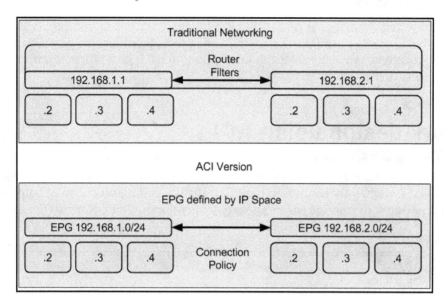

For other examples, the construct is the match within the EPG.

ACI modes

ACI can be configured in a few different ways, including the following:

- **L2 Fabric**: The L2 Fabric configuration or legacy mode has no routing or L3 concepts. Tenants are represented as a set of EPGs.
- **L3 Fabric**: The L3 Fabric configuration adds the L3 features available in ACI and the concept of tenants.
- **Stretched Fabric**: The Stretched Fabric design allows multiple fabrics (up to three) to be managed as a single fabric, even if the fabrics are in different locations.
- **Multipod**: This is a more fault-tolerant fabric utilizing multiple *pods* or fabric sets. Depending on the location of the switches and servers, multiple pods could be located on the same and/or different floors.

ACI requirements

One of the main requirements of ACI is that it requires a minimum of three APIC controllers; this allows a quorum to be reached between controllers, so two controllers must have a configuration change before it can be applied. In a large deployment, up to five controllers are supported.

Network design using ACI

From a hardware and cabling aspect, an ACI network will be the same as any leaf-spine network. The requirements are that all leaf switches are connected to all spine switches and no spine or leaf switches are connected together. Virtualized networks are created on top of the physical network to provide the necessary application policies. Refer to the following diagram:

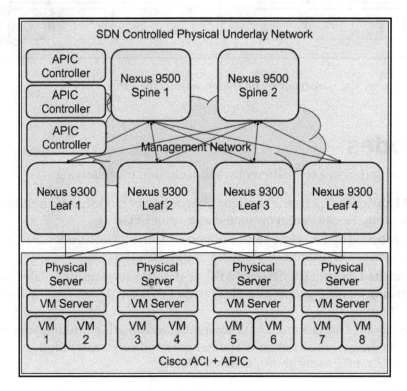

In this diagram, you can see that the network looks almost exactly like the one used for NSX, only the switches have been replaced by specific Nexus 9300 models and the virtualization is now generic. In this case, it does not matter what the virtualization system is. ACI is agnostic to the VM server but can interoperate with VMware and others.

Three controllers are necessary for production deployment, and by default two must agree with each other before a change is allowed. This is similar to how NSX works; it also requires three controllers.

As the ACI overlay is implemented, the virtual design will look similar to the NSX design. The main difference will be the concept of EPGs, which is similar to the way NSX handles VXLAN. EPGs are a set of devices that are treated similarly. By default, all EPGs are deny-all, so all traffic is dropped until rules are applied.

EPGs can be defined based on many criteria; a few of them are listed here:

- VLAN ID
- VXLAN ID
- System name
- Operating system

For example, you could create an EPG with the policy that any VM that starts with xyz or is running Windows Server is part of the EPG. You can also base the EPG on what the service type is, such as a database or web server. Refer to the following diagram:

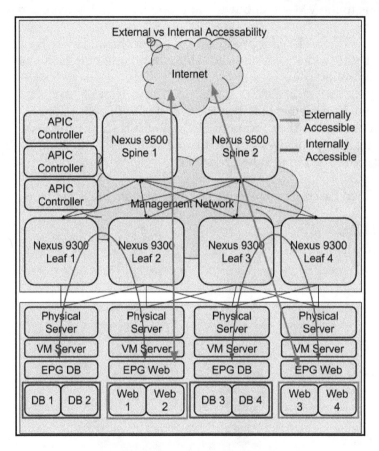

In this diagram, you can see that there are two types of VMs and Web. For this design, there are two EPGs: the **DB** and **Web**. **DB** is only accessible to **Web** (red link), but **Web** is accessible to the outside world (blue link). The simplicity of the design helps to keep the network and devices manageable.

In the preceding design, EPGs are based on the type of server **DB** or **Web** that is running on the system. While the design only includes two types of EPGs, up to 21,000 L2 or 15,000 L3 EPGs can be defined as of ACI v2.2.

Configuration via the GUI

The GUI for APIC is straightforward, with a menu and submenu tabs along with context-sensitive help. The **Quick Start** section is helpful when you are first setting up the system. Note that in this demonstration, we only have one controller instead of the three that are necessary for production deployment.

In the following diagram, you can see the main menu and the submenu. When we discuss buttons, we will refer to these this way:

If we run the **First setup for the ACI fabric** quick start, it walks us through the process of setting up the initial important data, such as the **Border Gateway Protocol Autonomous System Number (BGP ASN)**. For demo purposes, I am using my own ASN, 15096:

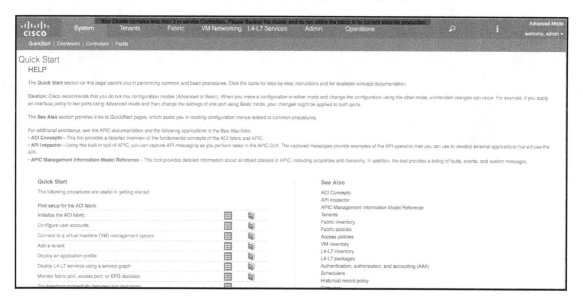

For configuring ACI, follow these steps:

1. In the event that you do not have an ASN, you can utilize the reserved ones from the block 64,512 - 65,534:

2. Here I have entered the ASN for the system but have not included any route reflector nodes. A route reflector is a router that reflects or mirrors the routes it receives to its neighbors:

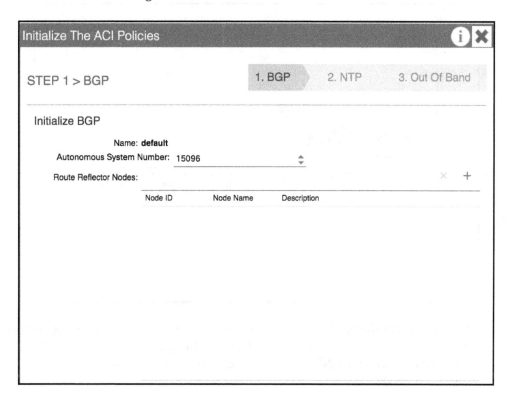

3. Next, set up **Network Time Protocol (NTP)**. I generally use the ntp.org pool for the area I am in; for example, us.pool.ntp.org is an alias for multiple NTP servers located near or in the US.

4. To add an NTP server, click on the + button in the following screenshot the **Management EPG** label on the right-hand side:

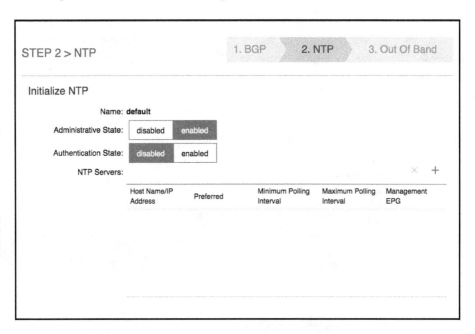

5. When you add the NTP server, you have a few options that can be set, including the polling interval (how often you check the time) and a management EPG that has connectivity to the NTP server. Here, you also choose whether it is a preferred server:

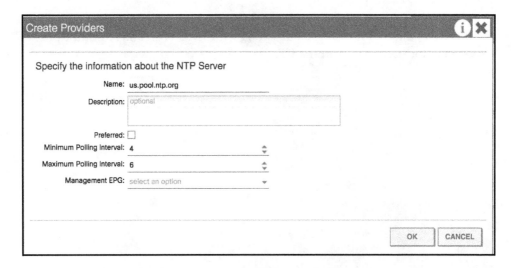

6. Once the NTP server is configured, you will see it on the page:

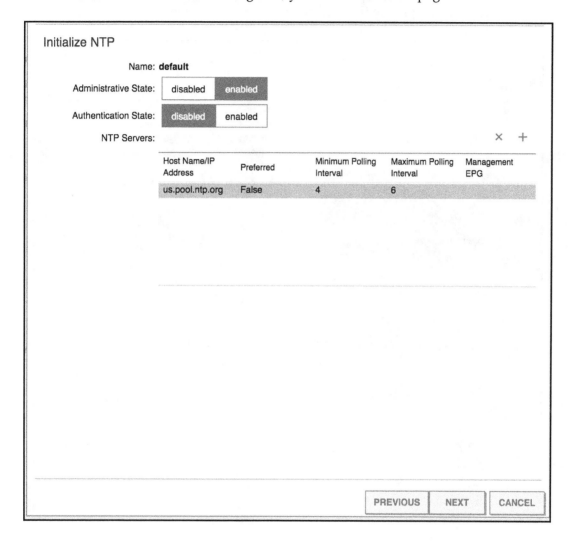

7. Next, you need to set up **Out of Band (OOB) EPGs**. In the following screenshot, they are all on private IP space in the `10.1.1.0/24` region:

8. Now we can add a user that can manage tenants. Go to the **Admin** menu and choose the **AAA Authentication** submenu. You should see something similar to the following:

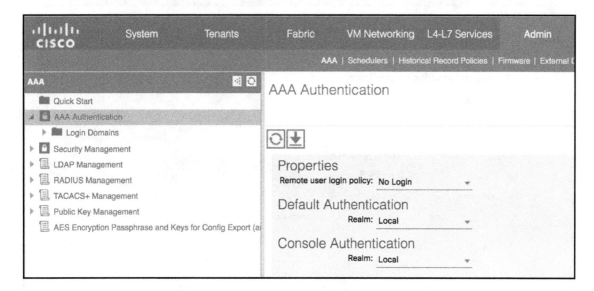

9. Now go to **Security Management** and choose **Local Users**. Under the **ACTIONS** tab on the right-hand side, choose **Create Local User**:

10. We start with security, adding the user to the correct security domain:

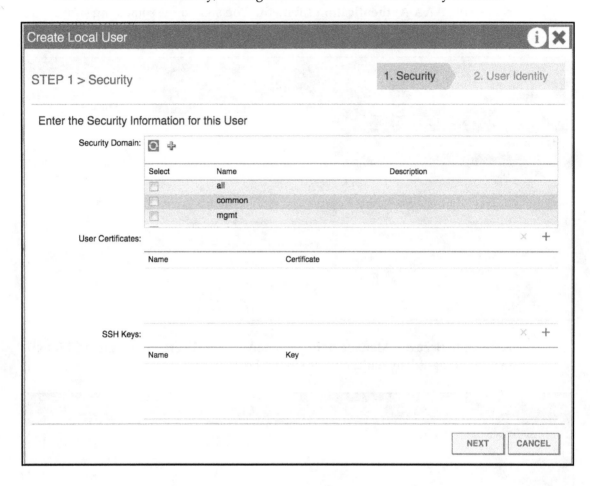

11. Set up the user to administrate tenants:

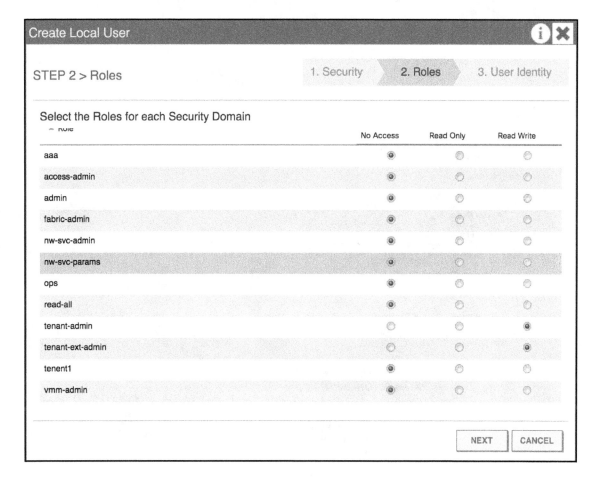

12. You can set an expiration for the user:

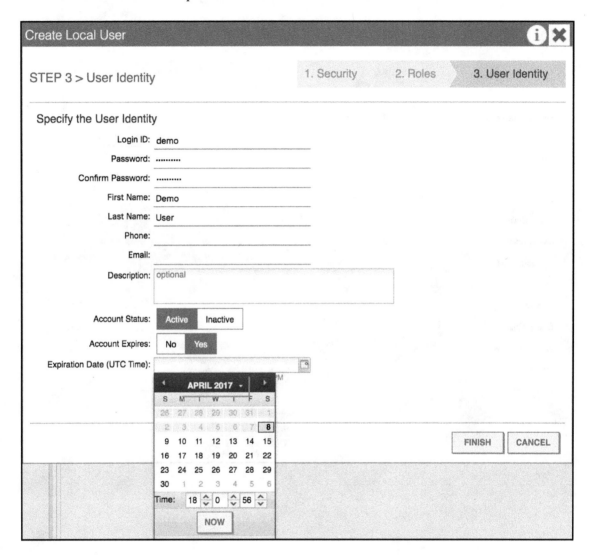

13. Now we look at the final user configuration. Determine whether it is correct and modify any data that is incorrect:

14. Hit **FINISH**. And we can now see the user:

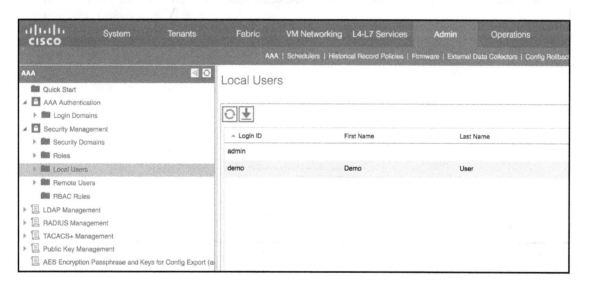

15. Now that we have set up the nodes, we can go ahead and browse fabric devices:

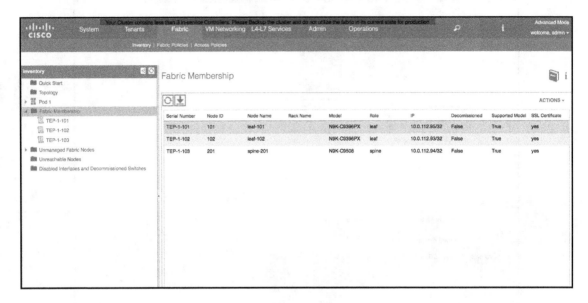

16. Here, we dig into the properties of a fabric system, in this case, **TEP-1-101**:

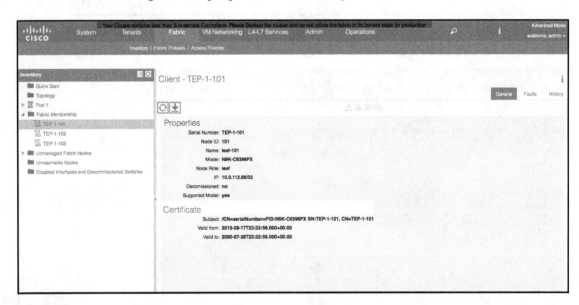

17. We can also view the health of the entire pod:

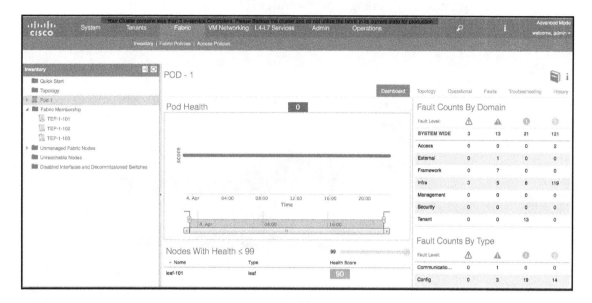

18. We can visualize the setup as well:

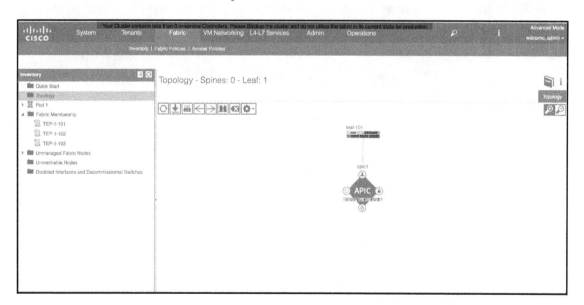

19. We can look at a picture of what the different boxes look like, with the ports showing configured (orange) or unconfigured (red):

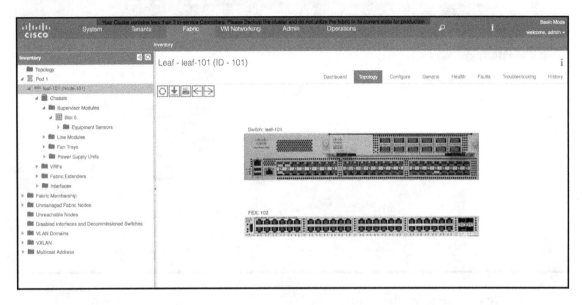

20. In the following screenshot, we can see the properties of the BGP configuration we set up initially:

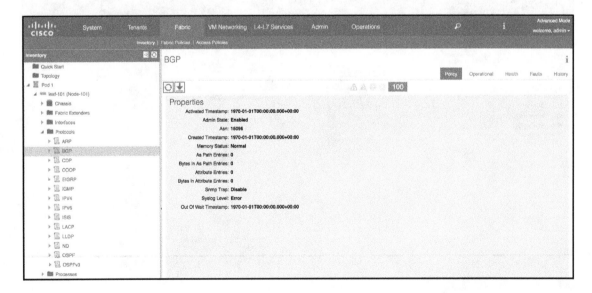

21. And finally in the following screenshot we can see the limitations of the system.

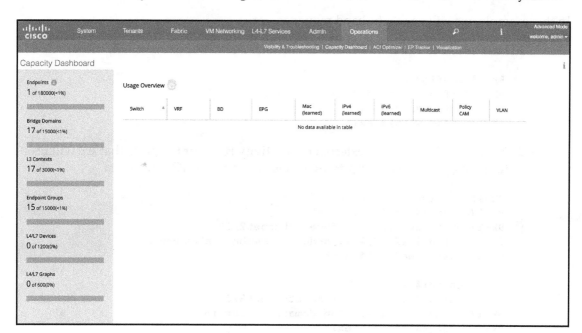

Configuration via the CLI

Configuring ACI via the CLI is similar to configuring NX-OS; in fact, you can configure ACI from the NX-OS CLI.

Example 1: **Adding a new user**

In the first example, we will add a new user to the APIC system:

```
9k-1# configure
9k-1(config)# username user1
9k-1(config-username)# password notagoodpassword
9k-1(config-username)# exit
```

Example 2 : Enabling in-band management

In this example, we will enable in-band management:

1. First, we need to assign a VLAN to the management ports; we will use VLAN 20:

```
9k-1# configure
9k-1(config)# vlan-domain inband-mgt
9k-1(config-vlan)# vlan 20
9k-1(config-vlan)# exit
```

2. Next, we will configure external connectivity rules for the ports that we will use for management. These ports are connected to the APIC controllers:

```
9k-1# configure
9k-1(config)# leaf 201
9k-1(config-leaf)# interface ethernet2/1
9k-1(config-leaf-if)# vlan-domain member inband-mgt
9k-1(config-leaf-if)# exit

9k-1(config)# leaf 202
9k-1(config-leaf)# interface ethernet2/2
9k-1(config-leaf-if)# vlan-domain member inband-mgt
9k-1(config-leaf-if)# exit
```

3. Lastly, we need to tell the system to use the inband management:

```
9k-1(config)# mgmt_connectivity pref inband
```

Example 3 - Create a new tenant and attach it to EPGs

For the next example, we will create a new tenant and attach it to the existing EPGs. Perform the following steps:

1. Enter the configuration mode and define the tenant and the VRF associated with it:

```
9k-1# configure
9k-1(config)# tenant demo
9k-1(config-tenant)# vrf context cli_demo
9k-1(config-tenant-vrf)# exit
```

2. Create a new bridge domain and attach the VRF to it:

```
9k-1(config-tenant)# bridge-domain cli_demo_bd
9k-1(config-tenant-bd)# vrf member cli_demo9k-1(config-tenant-bd)#
exit
```

3. Configure an IP address on `bridge-domain`:

```
9k-1(config-tenant)# interface bridge-domain cli_demo_bd
9k-1(config-tenant-interface)# ip address 192.168.10.1/24
9k-1(config-tenant-interface)# exit
```

4. Attach the tenant to the predefined EPGs, namely WEB and DB:

```
9k-1(config-tenant)# application 2-TIER
9k-1(config-tenant-app)# epg WEB
9k-1(config-tenant-app-epg)# bridge-domain cli_demo_bd
9k-1(config-tenant-app-peg)# exit
9k-1(config-tenant-app)# epg DB
9k-1(config-tenant-app-epg)# bridge-domain cli_demo_bd
9k-1(config-tenant-app-epg)# exit
9k-1(config-tenant-app)# exit
9k-1(config-tenant)# exit
```

Now that the tenant and services are attached to `bridge-domain`, the system is configured.

Configuration via wizards

Wizards allow system administrators to configure ACI easily by simply answering questions. One example is the tenant wizard:

```
admin@apic-demo:tenants> ./tenant.wiz
tenant
------
name : DemoCustomer
alias : DemoCustomer_tenant
description : This is DemoCustomer
monitoring-policy : default
private-network
---------------
name : DemoCustomer_net
description : DemoCustomer Network
bgp-timers : default
ospf-timers : default
monitoring-policy : default
bridge-domain
```

```
----------------
name : DemoCustomer_domain
description : DemoCustomer BD
network : ?
 default network
 inb network
 overlay-1 network
network : inb
Do you want to create another private-network (y/n): n
Do you want to view the corresponding commands? (y/n): y
---------------------------------------------------------------------
-----
mocreate DemoCustomer
cd DemoCustomer
moset alias DemoCustomer_tenant
moset description This is DemoCustomer
moset monitoring-policy default
cd /aci/tenants/DemoCustomer/networking
cd /aci/tenants/DemoCustomer/networking/private-networks
mocreate DemoCustomer_net
cd DemoCustomer_net
moset description DemoCustomer Network
moset bgp-timers default
moset ospf-timers default
moset monitoring-policy default
cd /aci/tenants/DemoCustomer/networking/bridge-domains
mocreate DemoCustomer_domain
cd DemoCustomer_domain
moset description DemoCustomer BD
moset network inb
cd /aci/tenants/DemoCustomer/networking/private-networks/DemoCustomer_net
cd /aci/tenants/DemoCustomer/networking
cd /aci/tenants/DemoCustomer
Do you want to commit changes? (y/n): y
Committing all the mos...
Committed mo tenants/DemoCustomer
Committed mo tenants/DemoCustomer/networking/private-
networks/DemoCustomer_net
Committed mo tenants/DemoCustomer/networking/bridge-
domains/DemoCustomer_domain
done
admin@apic-demo:tenants>
```

Configuration via REST

Cisco offers a RESTful interface to the APIC controller. In the previous chapters, we discussed how REST works and how tools such as Postman allow you to easily work with and test RESTful functions.

First, you need to build a login object:

1. Choose **POST** and enter
   `https://apic.host.address/api/mo/aaaLogin.xml`.
2. Choose **raw** for the body and put in `<aaaUser name='USERNAME' pwd='PASSWORD'/>` replacing it with your username and password:

3. Once you click on **Send**, you should be logged in to the APIC server. You can now continue and do other REST calls.

4. Here is an example of how to query APIC for a list of tenants. Choose **GET** from the Postman drop-down.
    Enter `https://apic.host.address/api/class/fvTenant.xml` in the request URL space:

Summary

In this chapter, you learned about Cisco ACI and how to navigate the CLI, GUI, and RESTful interfaces. We also discussed how to set up a new APIC-driven network; configure the management network, users, tenants, and interfaces; and add a BGP ASN to the configuration.

In the next chapter, we will put all of the data together to learn how to design a NGN.

9
Where to Start When Building a Next Generation Network

In the previous chapters, we discussed designs around hardware, designs around software, and generic concepts. Most of this work is simple when you already have a network that you are extending, but if you have a greenfield network, then there is more planning to do.

When you are done with this chapter, you should have the grasp of the following topics:

- A good understanding of network design fundamentals
- Ideas about what network hardware and software to use
- Knowledge of how to run a **Proof of Concept** (**PoC**) with a vendor
- An understanding of **Service Level Agreements** (**SLAs**) and what level of support is needed

Network design fundamentals

In the first eight chapters of this book, you learned about different technologies that are considered next-generation. No matter what hardware or software you decide to utilize, the physical design will be similar. The main differences will be whether you have physical firewalls, load balancers, or other network function devices in the path.

Going back to the concepts from our introductory chapter, we will review the most important ones.

A leaf-spine network uses the concepts of edge/leaf switches and core/spine switches. A network can be interconnected in a few different ways, including a full mesh, as in a Clos design, or partially meshed, as in a Benes design.

Multidimensional designs

The similarities between designs come from the fact that the physical act of networking has become simplified, with switches and routers able to handle all of the bandwidth requirements of the devices inside the rack. When designing, we focus on the concept of a **Point of Delivery** (**PoD**), which can be a partial rack, full rack, or multi-rack design that can be easily replicated to minimize troubleshooting effort and sparing.

PoD

A PoD is a construct that contains all the necessary parts to operate a service, such as compute, storage, and networking. As mentioned earlier, it can be almost any size, but is logically constrained to the smallest amount of equipment necessary—compute, storage, and network. These could all be contained in one-third of a rack up to a set of racks, normally no more than 16 due to switch port constraints.

Single-rack design

Designing the network in a single rack, where all the devices—such as servers, storage, and networking equipment—are in a single rack, is one of the building blocks of a PoD. In general, you will have two switches and/or routers in a rack to provide redundancy. Refer to the following diagram:

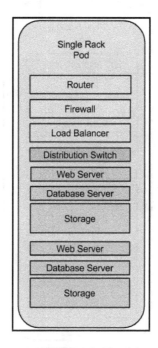

This is a simple rack design with a pair of **Web Server/Database Server/Storage**.

Multi-rack PoD design

Here is a multi-rack design where the center of the three racks is the main connection to the outside world:

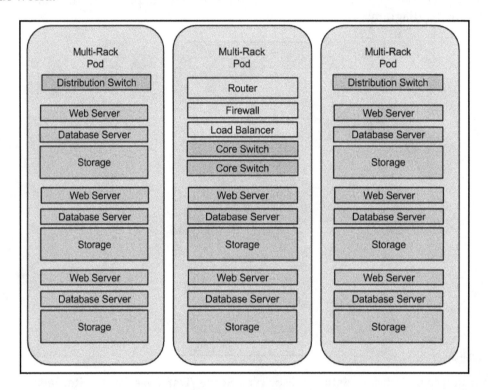

This design uses the middle rack as the main connection to the outside world.

The following is a simplified diagram of the physical design of a PoD:

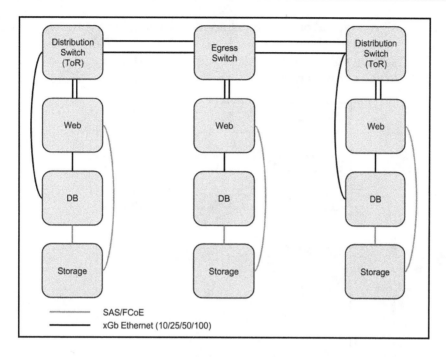

As shown in the preceding diagram, storage is connected to the database server and the web server via SAS/FCoE. Both the database server and web server are connected to the distribution switch / **Top of Rack** (**ToR**). If we collapse the design to show just the switches, routers, load balancers, and other network equipment, it will look exactly like any other design:

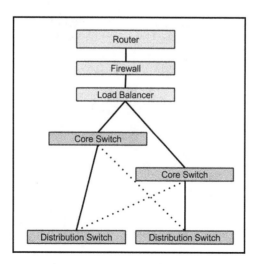

The preceding design is typical of a small data center where there are two core switches, otherwise known as **End of Rack (EoR)**, and two distribution or ToR switches. For a fully redundant design, you would need two routers, two load balancers, and so on with two separate uplinks to your provider(s):

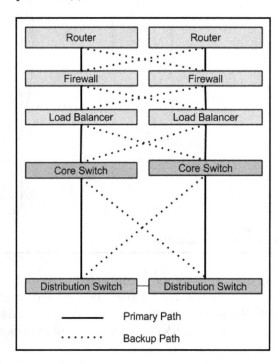

Here we see a fully redundant design. The links between the switches can be active-active (both paths are used and traffic is load-balanced), but the links between the core switches, load balancers, firewalls, and routers should be active-standby to avoid issues with traffic entering and exiting from different locations. When you use ACI or NSX, your firewalls and load balancers may be virtual, as seen in the following diagram where the routers and switches are physical, but the functions such as a load balancer and firewall are virtualized on the host server.

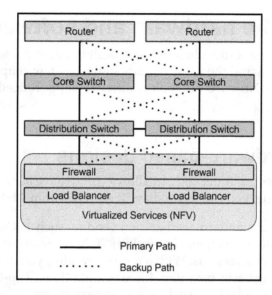

In a virtual design, even the uplinks are virtual; each server is connected to both the switches and then the firewall, load balancer, and other features are placed inside the server. If you expand the design to a multiple core switch design, you will see the Clos design implemented. Here's how it looks:

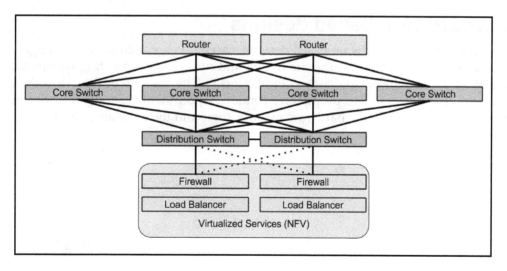

Deciding on the hardware and software

Open or closed, that is the question. In a network design, you can use both, but it's important that you understand the value of both. In the last few chapters, we've gone through both the options. Now we will look at different support needs and how they will affect our decision.

Proprietary hardware-based designs

Chasing a proprietary design limits you but allows you to have *one throat to choke* support, where if you have an issue, you can pay to have it solved within 4 hours.

In this space, you will find standard, well-known vendors such as Cisco, Juniper, and Dell. While Juniper and Dell do have **Open Networking** (**ON**) versions of hardware, they also sell proprietary, commercial versions. With a top-tier vendor, you have access to a bevy of support options, including basic, next-day, 4 hours, and others. Top-tier vendors also sell access to dedicated software and networking support engineers.

Cisco ACI and Juniper's Contrail are both SDN solutions. Contrail is offered as open source, but realistically you would want Juniper's support when deploying.

Open hardware-based designs

When it comes to open hardware-based designs, we could choose from Accton/Edgecore, Quanta, or Dell (ON series only) for our vendor and run an open operating system, such as Cumulus Linux, or a closed one, such as Pica8's PicOS. The cost will be much less than hardware plus software from a proprietary vendor. Support will generally be split across two organizations, namely the hardware manufacturer and the software manufacturer.

For example, if we take hardware from Edgecore, AS5712-54x being the most widely used (48x10 GB ports + 6x40 GB ports), and add software from Cumulus, we can assume that our costs will be *n+1* hardware (one spare for quick replacement) and the software license for Cumulus. If you utilize something like **Open Network Linux** (**ONL**) with **Open Route Cache** (**ORC**) and an open source routing solution, such as FRR (a fork of Quagga), there is only the hardware cost.

Support needs

First things first, we need to understand how much vendor support we are looking for, that is, do we want a 4 hour turnaround or can the networking team manage the network with 8/5-day support and keeping spare parts for their networking equipment in the event of hardware failure. Obviously, if the need is for a 4 hour turnaround, a vendor such as Cisco or Juniper needs to be involved as they are the only networking companies with the ability to support a customer with 24x7x365 plans. I remember back in Exodus, when we had the RP in a Cisco 7500 fail in a remote location, Cisco had a replacement RP on site within 4 hours and we were able to get the router back up. We paid a lot of money for the service, but it was worth it.

24x7x365 full support

If you need full support, including 24x7 phone and a 4 hour replacement guarantee, then you only have a few options: Cisco, Juniper, or Dell EMC. While Juniper does offer some ON switches, you will still end up working with their proprietary ones.

It is important to remember that, even with the best support level that Cisco, Juniper, or others provide, you will not get code fixes or modifications immediately. You may end up waiting for months for Cisco to provide you with a new version of the software for your switch unless there is a CERT issue (security issue) that needs to be fixed.

If we focus just on Cisco, we will look at the options provided with the Nexus 9000 and ACI. As a side note, ACI can integrate with VMware, so there are options where you can have both. The main issue with ACI tends to be the complexity of the design, so the addition of NSX to it will only complicate it further.

Business hours support

If you are able to handle most of the support and use resources sparingly, you can save a lot of money. If you use open source hardware and software and have a reasonably strong C programmer on your team, you can fix most issues and add features yourselves. Features will also be added by other members of the open source community. Issues with the base operating system will generally get patched quickly.

Sparing open networking equipment is simple as many switches can be used for multiple purposes.

Request for Information (RFI) and Request for Quotes (RFQ)

Both RFI and RFQ are part of the process of choosing a vendor. Normally, an RFQ will be filled with a lot of easy checkboxes for different protocols and features.

An RFI will contain different sections, such as physical and performance, and features such as MPLS and IPv6:

1. At the beginning of an RFI, you will have a cover sheet that will describe what you are looking for. In the following case, we are looking for two solutions:

    - **Core switching**: Core switching is simpler than SDDC as it only needs to handle transit packets. It is the spine of a leaf-spine design
    - **SDDC switching**: SDDC switching is more complex as it involves handling VXLAN traffic and performing **Virtualized Network Services (VNFs)**

Core & SDDC Services Switch

Engineering Request for Information
(RFI)

Customer is seeking responses for two classes of switching solutions:

1. **Core Services**

   A service-provider, carrier-grade platform supporting multiple
   interfaces and the ability to forward switched and routed packets
   at very high data rates. Addtionally, it must support various routing
   protocols and network service delivery mechanisms.
   Must include high availability and resiliency features and best-in-class
   manageability and health visability.

2. **SDDC Services**

   A service-provider, carrier-grade platform supporting multiple
   interfaces and the ability to forward, filter and modify switched and routed
   local and PoD specific packets and streams (IPv4 and IPv6)
   at very high data rates. It also includes but is not limited to, the termination
   of VLXAN based services, appliances, storage devices, etc.
   Must include high availability and resiliency features and best-in-class
   manageability and health visability.

2. After the cover sheet, it is good to have a simple description/objective list that covers what you are looking for and general legal disclosures:

Core & SDDC Services Switch - Engineering Request for Information (RFI)

I. Description / Objectives:

1. This request for information (RFI) is being issued by Customer's Engineering and Technology Team.
   Material contained within represents requirements from both Engineering and Customer's Network Management Department.
   Review and evaluation of submitted material will likewise be conducted by both the Engineering and Network Management teams.

2. It is understood that there may have been (or is currently underway), similar RFI/RFQ/RFP/etc. exercises originating from other departments within Customer. This particular request should be viewed (and completed) independently of said exercises.
   That said, information gleaned from the response to this request may be used in conjunction with prior/concurrently submitted material.

3. Customer is actively looking to quantify and qualify various capabilities of switches and switching solutions.

4. Customer is actively looking to understand the availability and timelines of switches and switching devices/solutions that meet specific criteria.

5. Customer is actively looking to understand the licensing and fee model(s) associated with switches and switching devices/solutions.

6. Customer is actively looking at various switch architectures and deployment models.

7. No assumption should be made with respect to differentiating various deployment models. That said, Customer is looking for two solutions. **One that is appropriate for servicing the "core" of a network and a second that is appropriate for SDDC services.**
   Respondents may submit different products/solutions to satiate the different requirements outlined immediately above.
   Respondents may also submit a single product/solution if they feel it well suited in either or both applications; please indicate as such.

   It is expected and required that respondents will submit a **SEPARATE and DISCRETE WORKSHEET** (Response Section "B")
   for each product / solution presented (e.g. one for a core switching solution and another for a SDDC switching solution).

8. The information contained within this RFI (plus all associated attachments, articles, appendicies, etc.) and the reponses thereto are to be considered <u>confidential</u> and under <u>non-disclosure</u>. This material is intended only for the person(s) or entity to which it is addressed and may contain proprietary information, which is privileged, confidential, or subject to copyright belonging to Customer. Any review, retransmission, dissemination or other use of, or taking of any action in reliance upon, this information by persons or entities other than the intended recipient is prohibited.

9. No contract will be awarded as a result of this RFI. This RFI does not in any way constitute a contractual obligation on the behalf of either party.

10. Customer shall not incur any obligation, liability, or cause of action whatsoever by reason of this RFI or any actions or inactions relative hereto. Respondents are solely responsible for all expenses associated with preparing and responding to this RFI. All RFI responses shall become the property of Customer and will not be returned to respondents.

11. Customer may, at its sole discretion, issue a follow-up Request for Proposal ("RFP") to some or all of the RFI respondents.
    Customer shall have no obligation to issue a follow-up RFP to any RFI respondent.

12. Customer is committed to a policy of nondiscrimination in its vendors, contractors and other suppliers. All qualified vendors, contractors and suppliers are reviewed without regard to race, color, religion, sex, national origin, ancestry, age, marital or veteran status, sexual orientation/ preferences or non-disqualifying physical or mental handicaps.

---

3. Here are a few simple instructions on how to fill out an RFI:

Core & SDDC Services Switch - Engineering Request for Information (RFI)

II. Instructions / Response Sections:

A. Respondent must include a one-page, executive-summary style descriptive outlining key differentiators of the submitted product/solution.

B. Respondent must complete the "Respondent Section" of the attached requirements worksheet in its entirety.
- A separate worksheet should be filled out for each viable product/solution submitted for consideration.
- No assumptions should be made regarding the network architecture in which the respondent's product/solution will be placed/integrated.
- The approximate retail "street" price must be included for each unit involved in the solution. No assumption of discounts should be made.

<u>**Capability field**</u> of the worksheet should be completed using the following values:
- "**5**" - Submitted product/solution **fully delivers** required functionality today.
- "**4**" - Submitted product/solution **can** fully deliver required functionality with only minor changes needed (< 1 month development time).
- "**3**" - Submitted product/solution **can** fully deliver required functionality with 1 - 3 months development time.
- "**2**" - Submitted product/solution **can** fully deliver required functionality with 4 - 8 months development time.
- "**1**" - Submitted product/solution **can not** deliver required functionality **but** there is a product roadmap to do so (future hardware platform, etc.).
- "**0**" - Submitted product/solution **can not** deliver required functionality nor is there a product roadmap to do so.
- "**NA**" - Required functionality is not applicable to the submitted product/solution
Notes: • *Please use the "Notes" field to provide relevant details pertaining to the product or solution's ability to deliver required functionality.*
      • *Please use the "Notes" field to describe capabilities that may exist above and beyond the required functionality.*
      • *If capability "1" is used, please use the "Notes" field to indicate the timeframe and details surrounding the product/solution roadmap.*
      • *If **any** amount of development time is needed to satiate the requirement, please use the "Notes" field to detail motivators:*
            • *NRE*
            • *Quantity commitments*
            • *Financial commitments*
            • *Etc.*

<u>**IPv4 and IPv6 fields**</u> should be completed as follows:
- "**Yes**" - Submitted product/solution **IS** fully "aware" and capable as it relates to the referenced protocol and to the stated line item.
- "**No**" - Submitted product/solution **IS NOT** fully "aware" and capable as it relates to the referenced protocol and to the stated line item.
- "**NA**" - The referenced protocol is not applicable or relevant to the stated line item.
- "**Notes**" - Submitted product/solution may be partially "aware" and capable as it relates to the referenced protocol and to the stated line item.
      Please use the "Notes" field to provide relevant details and/or time lines associated with full compatibility

<u>**B/L field**</u> of the worksheet should be completed as follows:
- "**B**" - Capability is included as a "base" feature; no additional licencing fees, procedural costs, labor fees or other financial dependancies are needed to enable or leverage the capability.
- "**L**" - Capability is available. However, additional licencing fees, procedural costs, labor fees or financial dependancies are needed to enable or leverage the capability.

C. Respondent must include and attach relevant product literature, specification sheets and diagrams with their submission(s).

D. Respondent must include a full list of protocols of which the solution is capable of routing and on which it can operate and report.

E. Respondent must include a description of both the process and fee structure associated with inserting a new feature request into the development queue.

F. A relevant, itemized example pricing worksheet for the suggested solution (with clearly noted assumptions), must be included.

4. In the next document, we describe some of the physical attributes we need to know about the switches, such as dimensions, weight, and the number of interfaces:

			RESPONDENT SECTION				
Corporate Engineering Team **Core & SDDC Services Switch - Engineering RFI** Response Section B			Response Target: ☑ Core Switch ☐ SDDC Switch	Vendor / Product Name: .... Model No.: .... Approx. Unit "Street" $:			
			please see instructions				

ITEM NO.	CATEGORY	DESCRIPTION	CAPABILITY (Value =5,4,3,2,1,0,NA)	IPv4	IPv6	B/L	NOTES
		FOUNDATIONS - PHYSICAL & PERFORMANCE					
1	Physical	Please detail physical dimensions and weight of all included components and indicate ability to rack-mount said equipment		NA	NA		
2	Physical	Please detail redundancy schemes available for the network and redundant components within the device		NA	NA		
3	Physical	N+1 and 1+1 redundancy capabilities (switch fabric, fan, power, etc)		NA	NA		
4	Physical	Please document what management and craft interface are available on the platform					
5	Physical	Please document solution's MTBF (mean time between failure) and MTTR (mean time to repair)					
6	Physical	Support for AC or -48 volt DC power. Please document start-up and operating amperages & how the number and type of cards influence the power requirements of the solution.		NA	NA		
7	Physical	Support for redundant power supplies (indicate how many)		NA	NA		
8	Physical	NEBS (network equipment-building system design guidelines) Level 3 certification		NA	NA		
9	Physical	Support for 10GigE interfaces (indicate port/card density and how many total supported in each box and across a pair/cluster). Please also indicate whether the ports are " blocking" or non-blocking"		NA	NA		
10	Physical	Support for GigE interfaces (indicate port/card density and how many total supported in each box and across a pair/cluster)		NA	NA		
11	Physical	Port support for: 1 Gbps (gigabit per second)		NA	NA		
12	Physical	Port support for: 10 Gbps		NA	NA		
13	Physical	Port support for: 40 Gbps (if not present today, please detail roadmap and time line. Also please describe what dependencies are required: e.g. upgrades to power supplies, augmentation or replacement of route processor modules, etc.)		NA	NA		
14	Physical	Port support for: 100 Gbps (if not present today, please detail roadmap and time line. Also please describe what dependencies are required: e.g. upgrades to power supplies, augmentation or replacement of route processor modules, etc.)		NA	NA		
15	Physical	Port support for: Logical (Null, Loopback, sub-interface, pseudo) (please detail)		NA	NA		
16	Physical	Please detail plans for terabit forwarding / switching capabilities					
17	Physical	Please document all available, supported physical interfaces and speeds		NA	NA		
18	Physical	Please detail the number of interface slots available and the available throughput per slot. Also please indicate if oversubscription is present and if so, please detail how this oversubscription is architected/handled.		NA	NA		
19	Physical	Please detail the maximum number of interfaces that can be operational in the switch		NA	NA		
20	Physical	Please detail any constraints on mixing different interface types in the switch		NA	NA		
21	Physical	Please detail any constraints on the number of operational interfaces due to addition of router resilience/redundancy features		NA	NA		
22	Physical	Please detail whether any type of interface restricts or limits the features supported by the router. Are particular features (QoS (quality of service), multicast, IPv6 Access Control Lists, GRE (generic routing encapsulation), etc.) restricted to, or limited by particular interfaces?		NA	NA		

5. In the next part, we talk about performance, MPLS, and general concepts such as L3VPN:

ITEM NO.	CATEGORY	DESCRIPTION	CAPABILITY (Value =5,4,3,2,1,0,NA)	IPv4	IPv6	B/L	NOTES
	CUSTOMER REQUIREMENTS		**please see instructions**				
48	Performance	Ability to scale beyond 10G of traffic throughput. Please document capabilities					
49	Performance	Ability to operate as either a complete Layer 3 router or purely Layer 2 switch					
50	Performance	Distributed processing of routing protocols					
51	Performance	Distributed processing of data forwarding plane					
52	Performance	Distributed processing of management plane					
53	Performance	Distributed processing of infrastructure services		NA	NA		
54	Performance	Please detail the number of hardware queues per port					
55	Performance	Nonstop forwarding (NSF)					
56	Performance	Ability to support software upgrades without impacting the deployed solution and with no subscriber traffic or state being lost (hit-less upgrades) (e.g. ISSU or In Service Software Upgrade)		NA	NA		
57	Performance	Ability to support hardware upgrades without impacting the deployed solution and with no subscriber traffic or state being lost		NA	NA		
58	Performance	Please detail which hardware components in the router may be hot swapped, which may not, and the impact on the router, and on packet forwarding of controlled and uncontrolled hot swapping.		NA	NA		
59	Performance	Please indicate and detail any other mechanisms, apart from redundancy, that enhance the overall reliability of the proposed router/solution					
60	Performance	"Feature Blades" - Please detail and describe available blades and their purpose/capabilities		NA	NA		
61	IPv6	IPv6 hardware compatibility		NA	Yes		
	SOFTWARE / ROUTING / POLICY DECISION & ENFORCEMENT / TRAFFIC MANAGEMENT						
62	General	Possess any embedded, included or underlying technologies and/or features that would permit derivative financial gain by the enablement thereof (please explain)					
63	IP Routing	IPv4 and IPv6 services and routing protocols (please detail supported service and protocols)					
64	Security	Modular operating system (please detail specific available modules if applicable)		NA	NA		
65	MPLS	MPLS (Multi-Protocol Label Switching) forwarding		NA	NA		
66	MPLS	MPLS L3 (layer 3) VPN					
67	MPLS	MPLS L2 (layer 2) VPN		NA	NA		
68	MPLS	MPLS TE (Multi-Protocol Label Switching Traffic Engineering)					
69	MPLS	MPLS-Label Distribution Protocol (MPLS-LDP)		NA	NA		
70	General	Ability to terminate MPLS Pseudo-wires into VPLS (virtual private LAN service) instances					
71	General	VPLS & LSP (label switch path) ping to isolate fault in the core					
72	General	L3VPN (please detail supported protocols)					
73	General	L2VPN (please detail supported protocols)					
74	General	L2 Circuits					
75	General	PPP encapsulation		NA	NA		
76	General	HDLC (High-Level Data Link Control) encapsulation		NA	NA		
77	General	Frame Relay encapsulation		NA	NA		

Proof of Concept (PoC)

Once a decision has been made about the equipment vendor(s), the next item of the business is to set up a PoC to determine that the equipment meets your needs. Companies such as Cisco and Juniper have PoC labs where they can assemble all of the networking equipment necessary to prove that the design works.

Once your RFI is done and all the general questions are answered, it's time to do a PoC. A PoC can be as big or small as the vendor can handle. Normally, you would have at least one instance of each device you expect to use and the expected workload information to test with. When I ran the customer simulation team at Procket Networks, we often hosted companies in our lab where we had two large routers, three small routers, some network testing equipment, and a few Cisco/Foundry/Juniper devices.

Before PoC, we would normally get a design from the customer and attempt to replicate it as best as possible. Often, we would not have all of the equipment necessary, but we could come up with a plan on how to demonstrate the ability of our systems.

Cisco and Juniper have much bigger PoC labs and more resources. If you are a reasonably sized customer, you can ask for a PoC and note the equipment that you would like to have. PoC is where you can test the equipment to make sure that the answers to the RFI are correct. Often, companies will report single dimensional numbers, such as the number of IPv4 routes they can handle, with no IPv6, ACL, or other items filling up TCAM memories.

When I worked for Cisco, I handled many PoCs on customer sites. One CRS PoC took three weeks and involved three different companies bidding for the business. As a highly qualified QA/tester, I arranged the test equipment from Spirent and handled the setup and testing of the different routers. One of the lessons I learned from this PoC was that some vendors claim numbers much higher than possible, based on well-designed tests that only looked at simple numbers.

Some of the tests we ran were highly unlikely to happen in real life, such as 40-byte packets at line rate across OC-192 (10G) links. These were things the customer asked for but understood were just checkboxes. This is because, realistically, no vendor can handle that type of traffic for any amount of time.

Designing a PoC

The most important thing in a PoC is to test the parts of your network design that differentiate you from the standard network design.

For example:

- The network may have the need for a high number of ACLs
- The network may have high latency or jitter-sensitive traffic, such as the needs of stock trading floors or video rendering/editing studios
- The network may need carrier grade NAT or 6rd (rapid IPv6 deployment over IPv4 network)
- These needs can be translated into tests, such as forwarding performance with 10,000 ACL rules installed on an interface

 This type of test needs to be done bidirectionally, with normal traffic crossing other ports on the same switch fabric to confirm the impact of the ACL rules.

For latency and jitter, you can run a test with important streams being heavily monitored, then send significant traffic to other ports to confirm that **Quality of Service (QoS)** is being handled correctly.

Running a PoC

In general, a PoC should take no more than a week, depending on the number of tests that need to be done. If advanced planning has been done, then the equipment should be set up, cabled, and configured with a base configuration that allows you to quickly add extra configuration items.

A PoC should have a tracking document similar to the RFI that would list the requirements and have places for checkboxes, numbers, and notes. For example, if you run a performance test with ACLs and during the test you are able to scale to 8,500 ACL rules without impacting traffic, you would note that in the PoC tracking document. If the test is done with only standard ACLs (source IP only) or extended ACLs (source IP, destination IP, protocol, and so on), that will also be recorded.

If a vendor has issues in completing any of the requirements, it is better to skip the test and let the vendor troubleshoot the issue than to immediately fail them.

Finishing up a PoC

Once the tests are complete, a final tally can be completed and vendors can be compared side by side. If there are problem areas with vendors where they are unable to show their equipment functioning as they stated, that should be taken into account.

Once you have all of the data, you can make a decision about what vendor you believe is the right choice and start negotiations about price and support.

Summary

In this chapter, we talked about choosing between open and proprietary hardware and software. We covered the support levels that can be expected and how your support needs may guide your decisions. We covered the RFI and PoC concepts and how to handle them.

In the next chapter, we'll have a detailed look at designing an altogether new next generation network, using all the concepts that we looked at in this chapter.

10
Designing a Next Generation Network

In the previous chapter, you learned about RFI, PoC testing, and the support differences between open and proprietary network devices.

By the end of this chapter you will able to do these:

- Determine the size and state of the installation (new or additional)
- Utilize the information from the RFI/PoC stage to determine the necessary equipment
- Assemble a final list of equipment that is necessary to build an NGN

Terminologies used in this chapter

We will use some new terms in this chapter; they are explained in the following sections.

Equipment racks – two post, four post, and enclosed

Essentially, there are a few different types of rack that are used in data centers. Most often, you will see an enclosed four post rack (I don't think I've seen an enclosed two post rack), which is essentially a cabinet with mounting brackets and the width of the equipment is 19 inches (or 21 inches for OCP) and 28 inches or more deeper. While you can have open four post racks, they are generally not used. Two post racks are racks where there is only one location to attach equipment and the equipment essentially floats outside the rack. In a two post rack, equipment can also be mounted in the center for more stability.

Two post and four post racks

Airflow

When looking at equipment, there are multiple ways the cooling fans can operate. In **Front to Back** (**F2B**), the fans take the air from the front and push it out through the back, like a standard computer. In **Back to Front** (**B2F**), the air is taken from the back and pushed out through the front. In side-to-side, the air comes in from one side and goes out the other.

In general, most equipment runs F2B; however, how you mount the equipment can change which airflow design you need. For example, a Cisco ISR router has all of the ports on the back, which means you should mount it backwards, with the Cisco bezel pointing inwards.

New versus old or greenfield versus brownfield

The concept of new versus old is very important to network design. You cannot properly design a network as an addition to an existing network without knowing all of the information about the old equipment including power use, heat, airflow, and weight.

Physical location

One of the most important parts of your design is based on whether the design is for a new location where the entire design is new or a current location where the design must fit together with other equipment. The deployment concept is called greenfield or brownfield, referring to a new site as green like new grass in a field and an old site as an old brown field.

When studying a new location, there are some pieces of information you will want to gather:

- What are the dimensions of the room/cage where the NGN will be deployed?
- What is the furthest distance from the core of the network to the edge or ToR switches?
- How is power distributed? Do you have access to 48V DC or just 120/240V AC? Are the power junction boxes coming from the ceiling or the floor?
- What floor is the deployment on? What is the amount of weight per square foot/**Kilo Pascals** (**kPa**)—the metric equivalent, supported?
- Do you have enough access to get the amount of fiber/copper into the room, accounting for physical firewalls in the ceiling?

Most, if not all, of this information should be known by the facilities manager. If there are questions about power, cooling, and so on, those may need to be referred to specialists. It is very important that all of the minimum specifications are met, otherwise when the equipment is installed there will be issues.

New location – greenfield

Since a greenfield network is much easier to deal with, we will start there. Once a site survey has been completed and the available power, cooling, space, and other important details are collected, the design can start.

Normally, the design will call out the specifications necessary for space and power and list the worst-case heat dissipation necessary. Some initial design concerns should be around airflow (F2B or B2F, never side-to-side), weight, and the type of rack (enclosed, four post, or two post).

Here, we utilize the RFI data about weight, size, and power usage to determine what the worst-case scenario would be. We also need to plan for upgrades and additions. The good thing is that over time the power per byte goes down, so a basic rule is to take double what you need to build the initial setup, and make sure that the minimum specifications meet those demands.

Old location – brownfield

In a brownfield network, the same rules as a greenfield network apply except that you will be restricted to the power, cooling, and space available. Your design will encompass the current network, the upgrade path, and plans. Most networks are replaced in situ, where parts are replaced one by one or in groups and then swapped over. At the end of the chapter, there is a small section on moving from the old network to the new one.

Care must be taken to confirm that new and separate power has been pulled into the location for the new devices to derisk the installation. Cooling and floor weight capacity must be verified and confirmed so it meets or exceeds the worst-case calculations for the new equipment.

In the event the equipment room was already designed to hold more equipment, you will want to verify that everything is correct and working. Often power will be reused by engineers to do what they need, without consideration for what the power is supposed to do.

If there is not enough power per rack for the design you are looking for, you may need to use more racks and limit the number of servers per rack, which will define how many ports you will use off the switches.

Using RFI/RFQ information to design the network

Now that we have the site survey information and the available power, cooling, and space, we can start designing and calculating what our needs are for the network. After the PoC, we will refer to the RFI, where we have physical specifications for each device. The data may also be available online, which is generally how we get data for open networking and white-box systems.

We will take the data from the PoC and RFI to determine the amount of equipment we will be using and the characteristics of the equipment. Remember, if you are using **Direct Attach Cables (DACs)** or fiber transceivers, we need to account for them.

Design the network for expansion; you may need to add more cards to certain devices later, but those devices should have available slots for expansion. For example, if your design is two racks in a pod with two router/switches, two aggregation (ToR) switches, and a significant amount of compute/storage hardware, you will want to design for the addition of two more racks, where the two main routers/switches will become the spine of the network.

In the following diagram, we have two rack pods where there is a router, firewall, load balancer, and two core switches in each:

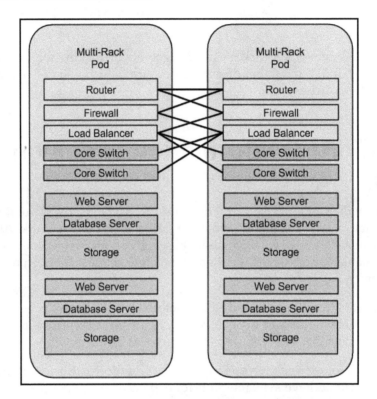

In this diagram, we have connected two more racks to the pod and are using the core switches as a spine:

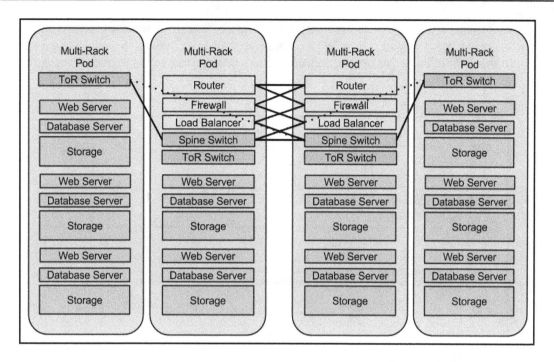

 Facebook created the CWDM4-OCP optic. These optics use less power than the standard CWDM4 and helped Facebook keep the design of their new 100G switch within the expected power and cooling range.

Designing using the Cisco ACI

Now we will do the calculations on a design using the Cisco Nexus 9000 series switches. From the RFI response, we know that the chassis alone weighs 84 lbs (38.2 kg), which is normal for equipment of this size. We should mount the switch lower in the rack if possible to avoid issues with the rack becoming unstable.

We can then use the Cisco power calculator, which allows us to input all of the specifications of the equipment and find out what the power needs are along with the amount of heat the equipment will generate.

For the power calculator, we will assume we are using two routers without redundant supervisor modules. We will put in 36 100G ports and 48 1/10G ports. We could use a single card, but it is best to have the uplink and downlinks on separate cards to avoid a complete outage.

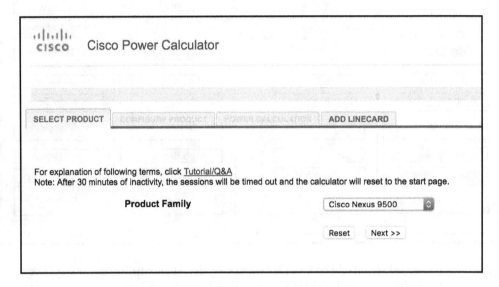

When you connect to the power calculator, you are asked what product family you will be working with. We are going to focus on the Cisco Nexus 9500:

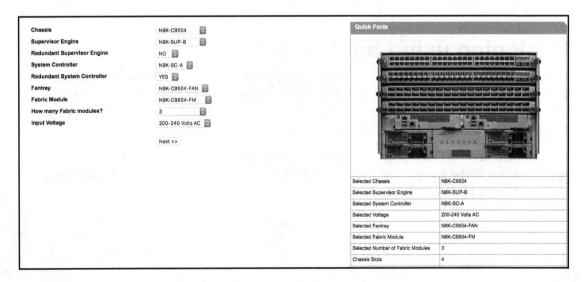

We will be designing a simple box with one supervisor revision, two system controllers, three fans, and three fabric modules. This is an *orderable* bundle called **N9K-C9504-B1** (Nexus 9504 Chassis Bundle with 1 Sup, 3 AC PS, 2 SC, 3 Fan Trays, and 3 Fabric Modules). We add in two line cards, one 36x40G, and one 64x10G.

When we run the power calculator with the two line cards we get an output:

Power Consumption/Heat Dissipation Summary			
Slot		Line Card	
1		N9K-X9636PQ	
2		N9K-X9564PX	
3		--EMPTY-SLOT--	
4		--EMPTY-SLOT--	
Minimum Power Supply		Percentage Of Power Used	
Single N9K-PAC-3000W-B in Combined mode		59.68 %	
First Alternative Power Supply		Percentage of Power used	
Dual N9K-PAC-3000W-B in Combined mode		29.85 %	
Total Output Current	**Total Output Power**	**Total Typical Output Power**	**Total Heat Dissipation**
8.14 Amps	2380.00 Watts	1723.00 Watts	7850.30 BTU/Hr

The power consumption of the system will be 8.14 Amps at 240V while generating 7850 BTU/hr of heat. A **British Thermal Unit (BTU)** is essentially the amount of heat necessary to raise one pound of water by one degree Fahrenheit. The chart also suggests other power units that can be used and the load that will be put on them. Using 60 percent of the available power is acceptable. You should never exceed 80 percent.

This data should be lower than the data in the RFI as the RFI should include worst-case numbers. If the RFI is lower, then it is important to confirm that the equipment is the same.

Some things that can throw off power calculations for chassis-based systems are as follows:

- The number of line cards inserted
- The type of line card used
- The number of supervisor/fabric cards
- The types of supervisor/fabric card used

With the Cisco 9500 series, you have multiple fabric cards that you can utilize. There is the standard card, the E Cloud Scale card supporting 100G and an S fabric that only supports one card, the 32 port 100G, (N9K-X9432C-S) line card, at this time.

If we redo the calculation with 100G-capable line cards and the FM-E fabric cards (four are required), we get a significantly higher number.

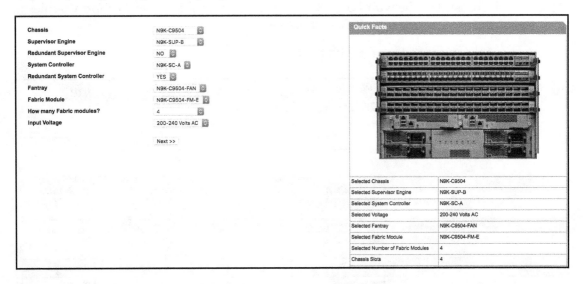

In all of the configurations, we are not using redundant supervisor engines.

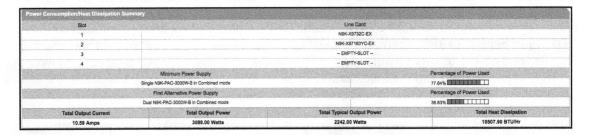

Here you can see that we are using 10.6 Amps at 240V and have 10508 BTU/hr. We have about the same number of ports available; it is just that now we have 100G instead of 40G. Note that we are very close to the 80 percent power usage, so it is advisable to use the next alternate power supply. It is possible to run the switch on two dedicated 15 Amp 240V circuits. The heat load being 10k BTU/hr will need to be confirmed with the facilities team.

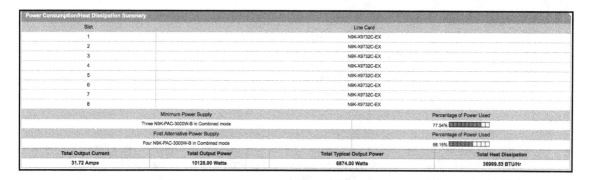

Power Consumption/Heat Dissipation Summary			
Slot		Line Card	
1		N9K-X9732C-EX	
2		N9K-X9732C-EX	
3		N9K-X9732C-EX	
4		N9K-X9732C-EX	
5		N9K-X9732C-EX	
6		N9K-X9732C-EX	
7		N9K-X9732C-EX	
8		N9K-X9732C-EX	
Minimum Power Supply		Percentage of Power Used	
Three N9K-PAC-3000W-B in Combined mode		77.54%	
First Alternative Power Supply		Percentage of Power Used	
Four N9K-PAC-3000W-B in Combined mode		58.15%	
Total Output Current	Total Output Power	Total Typical Output Power	Total Heat Dissipation
31.72 Amps	10128.00 Watts	6874.00 Watts	36999.53 BTU/Hr

If we upgrade to an eight-slot Nexus 9508 and fully populate it, to be comparable to open networking switches, you would need four 15 Amp 240V circuits as you will be drawing up to 10,128 Watts or 31.72 Amps.

By looking at the power calculations, we can see how important it is to understand what equipment you will be using and make sure that the proper power connections are installed.

For the 40G ToR, the Cisco 9372PX uses a maximum of 537W, which is about 4 Amps at 120V. With redundant switches, you need at least 8 Amps, so a standard 15 Amps circuit will be fine. The 100G ToR would be the 92160YC-X, which has 48 10/25G ports and six uplink ports of which four are 100G-capable.

The cabling necessary for the design includes cross connects between the ToR and EoR, ToR to ToR, and EoR to EoR. Assuming that the NGN is located in the same space as the existing (or is in greenfield) equipment, we will use DACs. For interconnects between the switches, we will use QSFP28+ cables (40/100G).

The equipment list will be straightforward, two 9504s and N ToR 9372PXs based on the number of pods we will have:

- **40G network**:
    - 2x N9K-C9504-B1
    - 2x N9K-X9536PQ 36x40G line cards
    - 2x N9K-X9564PX48 10G/1G and 4x 40G cards
    - 2/4x Nexus 9372PX switches

- **100G network**:
  - 2x N9K-C9504-B3-E
  - 2xN9K-X9732C-EX 32x100G line cards
  - 2x N9K-X97160YC-EX 48 10G/1G and 4x 40/100G cards
  - 2/4x Nexus 92160YC-X switches

Putting all this together allows you to get a quote and negotiate pricing. Smaller companies are normally required to buy from a reseller rather than Cisco directly. Cisco has a lot of tools available, mostly to compare with competitors. Here is what Cisco's tool shows for an ACI deployment costs versus NSX. The savings come from the switches versus the NSX overlay/underlay and in the cost of servers as NSX requires server hardware to provide NSX Edge services:

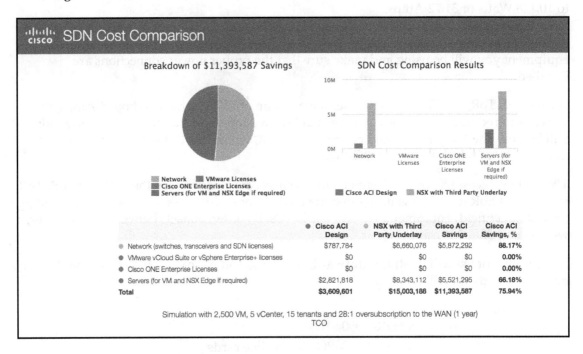

For simplicity, we will use a single Nexus 9500, firewall, and load balancer. Here the design is clear; the traffic, whether from the internet or intranet, enters the Cisco 9500 switch, and goes through a firewall and load balancer to the Nexus 9300 switches. The firewall / load balancer may be virtual representations made using ACI **Endpoint Groups** (**EPGs**).

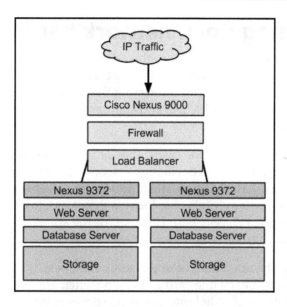

This design is simple to understand and expand; the actual ACI implementation is more complicated. The following is a representation of both the physical and virtual networks:

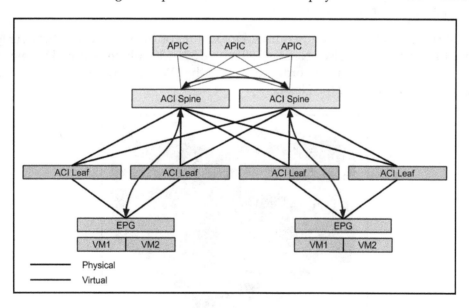

Here the black lines show the physical links including those to the three required APIC controllers. The blue lines show the virtual path between EPGs.

Designing using open network hardware

For the open networking design, we will use the Edgecore OMP-256X chassis switches for the spine and Edgecore AS5712 switches for the ToR. There is no power calculator, so the calculation has to be done by hand. One interesting thing about the OMP-256X is that it can be used in both OCP spec racks (21 inches) and standard racks (19 inches) by mounting the system so that the line cards are vertical.

The OMP-256X can support up to 8 line cards with 32 100G ports for a total of 256 100G ports when configured maximally. We will only use one 32x 100G card and one 48x 10G card as is used in the Cisco-based design. It would also be possible to build the design using 1U systems, where there are two levels of spines—a Benes or Clos design. However, to compare better, we will use a chassis-based system for the spine and a single **Rack Unit (RU)** switch for the ToR.

One thing to note about the open networking chassis switches, including the Facebook Backpack and 6-pack, is that each line card is its own switch and is configured in that way. You can see how the slots are divided into 16x 100G sections; this is because the front 16 ports use half of the connections on the Broadcom Tomahawk chipset and the other half of the connections go to the backplane, where they are used to connect to the other line cards. Essentially, it's a two-stage Clos in a box.

The OMP-256X when fully configured uses a maximum of 7000W, which is the average usage of a fully configured Cisco Nexus 9508 with 8 32x 100GbE line cards. This means that we can reasonably assume that, in order to expand the OMP-256, we will need four 15A 240V circuits, the same as for the Nexus:

The Edgecore OMP-256X

The division of the cards is even clearer when you look at the Facebook Backpack, which is four line cards supporting 32x 100GbE each. The design is essentially 8 Wedge 100 switches (16 ports front, 16 ports to the fabric) together in a single chassis:

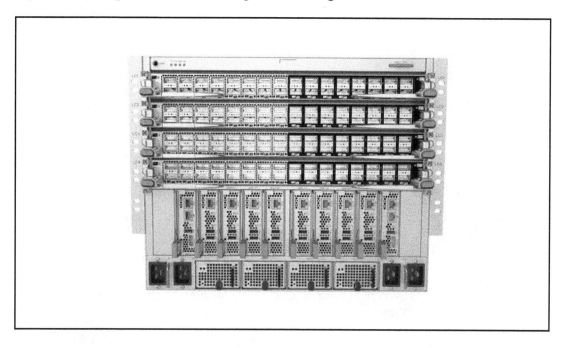

Here the slots on the left are color-coded silver, while the ones on the right are color-coded black. This is essentially 8 16x 100GbE switches in a single chassis. There are also another four fabric cards, which are essentially 32x 100GbE Wedge switches. Since they are using half of the connections from each line card, there are a total of 12 Wedge 100s in the chassis as each line card is equal to two Wedge 100.

An interesting note about the Backpack is that, when Facebook connects cables to the box, they put the longest ones in the middle as the middle has the shortest electrical trace from the port to the Tomahawk chipset and therefore the least interference.

For the ToR 40G switch, we will use the Edgecore AS5712-54x, which provides 48 10G and 6 40G ports. For a 100G solution, we would use the AS7312-54x, which provides 48 10/25G ports and 6 100G ports.

The preceding image shows the Edgecore AS5712-54X, one of the most deployed open networking switches in the World. The AS5712 is supported by software from multiple companies including Big Switch Networks (ONL, BMF, and BCF), Broadcom (ICOS), Cumulus Networks, and Pica8.

The AS5712 uses a maximum of 282 watts, which is about 2.5 Amps at 120V. Thus, you can have two switches on a normal 15 Amp 120V circuit.

The AS7312-54x uses a maximum of 350 watts, which is about 3 Amps at 120V. So you can operate two switches easily on a 15 Amp 120V circuit.

The 100GbE AS7712-32x, as shown, uses 310 watts without optics or a maximum of 550 watts with optics. The 40GbE AS6712-32x uses 227 watts under the following conditions as represented on the Edgecore website:

Energy Efficiency: 227 W typical power consumption under line rate traffic using 24 x passive QSFP DAC, 8 x 40GBASE-SR4.

The following is the equipment we will need to order to build the network:

- **40G network**:
    - 2x AS6712-32x
    - 2/4x AS5712-54x
- **100G network**:
    - 2x AS7712-32x
    - 2/4x AS7312-54x (or the AS7712-32x with breakout cables)

The design looks familiar if we use OpenFlow controllers to manage the switches:

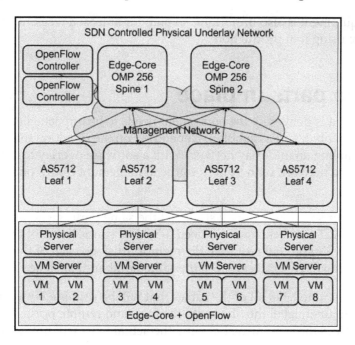

We can easily overlay the network with solutions from VMware such as NSX, or just use OpenFlow to manage all of the traffic by integrating with an OpenFlow controller such as ONOS or Floodlight.

Assembling the network

Let's see a few standard design points before we explore into the setup in depth.

Now that we know the power/cooling needs of the solution we have decided on, we can provide the data to the facilities manager and start assembling the necessary hardware, preparing the space, and ordering the accessories.

One thing that is important when planning the design is remote manageability. Some key pieces to have in the racks are remote management capabilities including power cyclers, console capabilities, and a secure management network.

For each rack, you will want at least two separate power circuits coming from separate panels, which will be used to feed any equipment with multiple power supplies. It is also key to log all of this data for future reference in the event that something happens.

Burning in the equipment is also important, so plan for at least a week of running the equipment before using it in production.

Putting the parts in place

When the equipment is delivered, the equipment needs to be unpacked and checked thoroughly, documented, and assembled. Depending on the direction the design has gone, you may be assembling an underlay network with a software overlay to manage the traffic like NSX, a standard network with built in traffic management (ACI), or an OpenFlow managed network.

No matter what your solution, you will still need the same parts, switches/routers, cables, and optics. For an ACI network, you will need 3-5 APIC controllers, for OpenFlow you will need two, and for NSX you will require CPU/memory/disk on each of the VMware NSX hosts. Each solution will generally contain the same number of switches and routers.

At this time, it is useful to label all of the cables that will be running between devices. If you are using SFPs with fiber, label the fiber with the local and remote ports. If you are using DACs, label the DACs the same way. Labeling the actual SFPs will not help when debugging.

If you plan to use any tools such as Puppet, Ansible, or Apstra, you will need the following information:

- Networking device MAC
- Serial number
- Type and use (ToR, spine)
- Which cables connect from the device to other devices and on which ports

If all of the devices are on an out-of-band network, you should be able to run most tools using this information.

Migrating to the new network

Migration from one location to another, or from an older pod design to a newer one, seems pretty simple—cut over the traffic and move on. In reality, it takes planning, extra configurations, and cooperation between all of the equipment owners/managers.

Stage one is to assemble the new network; whether in the same building or on the other side of the World, the new devices need to be accessible so that certain tasks can be completed.

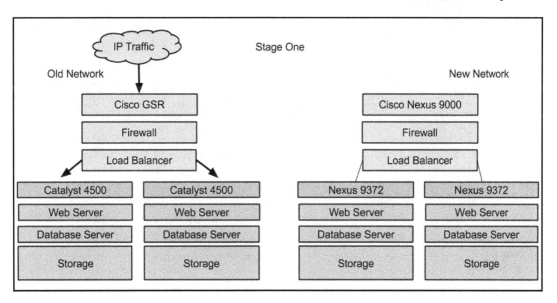

In the preceding design, we see that we have similar designs on both sides. On the left-hand side, you have these:

- A routing device, possibly a Cisco GSR 12810, CRS 4-slot chassis, or even Cisco Catalyst 4500
- A firewall, possibly also from Cisco, Palo Alto Networks, or any other firewall vendor
- A load balancer, necessary to balance the traffic between multiple servers and the server hardware itself

On the right-hand side, we have positioned the Nexus 9000 series switches in both the edge router space and as the ToR. The rest of the devices will be updated, but possibly from the same manufacturer. We can also see that all of the traffic is flowing to the network pod on the left, the legacy pod.

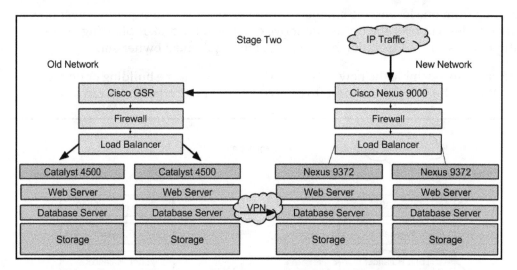

In the preceding diagram, we see a few things. Most importantly, there is a secure connection between the database servers, allowing data to be transferred between the two pods or sites. Second, the traffic is now flowing to the new pod/site, but is then redirected back to the old site. This allows for a slow migration from the old hardware to the new hardware.

While you are transferring data, you can start sending some traffic to the new pod to make sure that everything is working as expected. Important things to monitor are as follows:

- How evenly the traffic is split
- Whether the firewall is providing the expected protection and logging
- If the servers are handling the traffic correctly where the latency is the same as, or better than, the old pod/site

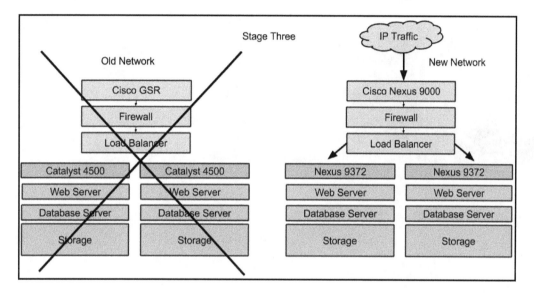

In this final diagram, we can see how all of the traffic has been migrated and the old pod/site has been shut down.

Summary

In this chapter, you determined the size and type of installation the equipment will be going in to. You also designed the network hardware layout based on the RFI/RFQ information and finally understood how to assemble a final list of equipment to construct the NGN.

In the next chapter, we will look at specific examples of different NGN designs including OpenFlow, SnapRoute, and ACI.

11
Example NGN Designs

In the previous chapter, we discussed how to design a network based on the information received from your RFI/RFQ and **Proof of Concept (PoC)**.

In this chapter, we will look at different NGN designs that are utilized by both service providers and enterprise networks. We will discuss large network designs along with smaller network designs for both enterprise and service providers.

At the end of this chapter, you should be able to understand different types of design, including the following:

- Open hardware with OpenFlow and OpenDaylight
- Open Hardware with SnapRoute managed via REST
- Cisco Nexus 9000 with ACI
- Open or proprietary hardware with VMware NSX

Designs used in this chapter

In this chapter, we will use two different designs. Most designs use either a Benes or Clos leaf-spine design. For comparison, we will use the core-aggregation design.

Leaf-spine design

As we discussed in earlier chapters, a leaf-spine design is the most common multi-rack PoD design. This design will be central to most of the different examples we will give.

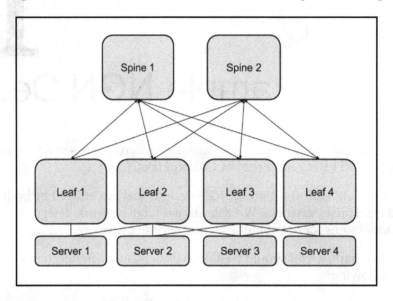

Core-aggregation design

In a core-aggregation design, multiple switches are connected to each other, necessitating using the spanning tree protocol or other methods to prevent network loops from forming. A network loop is where multiple switches send the same packets out of all their interfaces. Loops can cause broadcast storms, where devices send a massive amount of packets and receive multiple duplicate packets; this can take down the entire network.

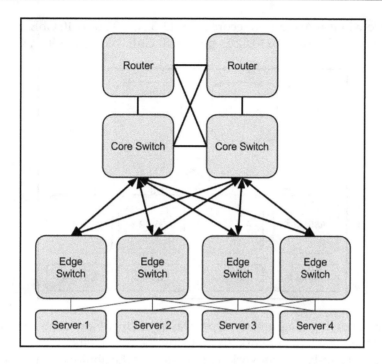

Using open hardware and software

In this section, we will talk about reference designs for a network using open hardware and software. We will cover both an active and controlled network, such as the one managed by OpenFlow, and a static one, such as the one that uses standard routing protocols with a software overlay.

OpenFlow designs

For the first OpenFlow design, we will use a standard leaf-spine with an OpenDaylight OpenFlow controller connected to it. The switches will be running Broadcom's OF-DPA with the Indigo OpenFlow agent.

For the spine, we will use Accton/Edgecore AS6812-32x, a 32 port 40 GbE switch. For the leaf, we will use AS5812-54x a 48x10 GbE, plus 6x40 GbE. We will build a 4-rack pod:

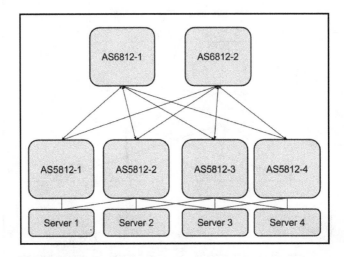

As shown in the following diagram, the OpenDaylight OpenFlow controller connects to the switches via the management network. By utilizing the management (out-of-band) network, changes in the public (in-band) network will not impact the ability of the controller to program the switches. This is the key to having a stable network.

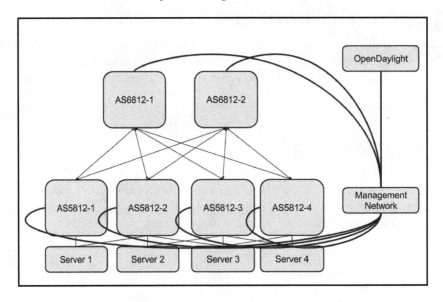

The out-of-band network is important for this setup as it provides a more secure channel to send commands to the switches. It also helps in setting up the switches as most switches do not have functional in-band ports on boot; they are available only after the configuration is set up or, in the case of open networking, once the SDK is initialized.

Once the initial build is done, all the switches are cabled, powered on, and have a **Network Operating System** (**NOS**) on them; OF-DPA plus Indigo should be installed. Refer to the following code:

```
root@switch:~# dpkg -i ofdpa_3.0.3.1+accton1.4-1-1_amd64.deb
(Reading database ... 15663 files and directories currently installed.)
Preparing to unpack ofdpa_3.0.3.1+accton1.4-1-1_amd64.deb ...
Unpacking ofdpa (3.0.3.1+accton1.4~1-1) ...
Setting up ofdpa (3.0.3.1+accton1.4~1-1) ...
```

This is a sample output from installing OF-DPA on Accton AS5712-54x; the version is specifically from Accton (the parent company of Edgecore) to run on their switches. Now refer to this code:

```
root@switch:~# /usr/sbin/brcm-indigo-ofdpa-ofagent --usage
05-29 20:59:49.856338 [ofagent] version 2.0.4.0 -- Built on Fri May 27 2016
at 09:10:39 UTC
Usage: brcm-indigo-ofdpa-ofagent [-?V] [-a AGENTDEBUGLVL] [-i DATAPATHID]
[-l IP:PORT] [-t IP:PORT] [--agentdebuglvl=AGENTDEBUGLVL]
[--dpid=DATAPATHID] [--listen=IP:PORT] [--controller=IP:PORT]
[--help] [--usage] [--version]
```

Here, we are running the Indigo agent with the `--usage` command, which gives us a short message about how to use it. The main information we need to know is how to connect the agent to the server. We will need to use the `--controller=IP:PORT` option to tell the agent the IP and port of the server. The port used before 2013 is 6633; the official port has been 6653 since 2013. Your application may use either.

Once installed, Indigo can be connected to OpenDaylight by putting in the IP address and port of the OpenDaylight controller.

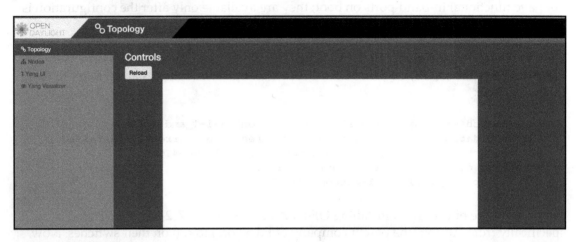

Initially, the OpenDaylight controller will show nothing in the topology. Once we connect the first switch, we will see it and a few hosts connected to the switch. Check out this example:

```
root@switch:~# /usr/sbin/brcm-indigo-ofdpa-ofagent --
controller=10.1.10.146:6653 -i 0x0000000000000273
06-02 18:53:40.938568 [ofagent] version 2.0.4.0 -- Built on Fri May 27 2016
at 09:10:39 UTC
OF Datapath ID: 0x0000000000000273
Initializing the system.
06-02 18:53:40.939101 [socketmanager] Initializing socket manager
06-02 18:53:40.940955 [ofagent] Adding controller 10.1.10.146:6653
06-02 18:53:40.941023 [ofconnectionmanager] Added remote connection:
10.1.10.146:6653
06-02 18:53:42.117282 [ofconnectionmanager] cxn 10.1.10.146:6653:
DISCONNECTED->CONNECTING
06-02 18:53:42.142504 [ofconnectionmanager] cxn 10.1.10.146:6653:
CONNECTING->HANDSHAKE_COMPLETE
06-02 18:53:42.240867 [ofconnectionmanager] Upgrading cxn 10.1.10.146:6653
to master
```

In the preceding exchange, the switch initially contacts the controller stating its data path ID of 273, then the controller connects to the switch and is promoted to the master. There are three hosts that are connected to the switch at connection time, as shown in the following GUI:

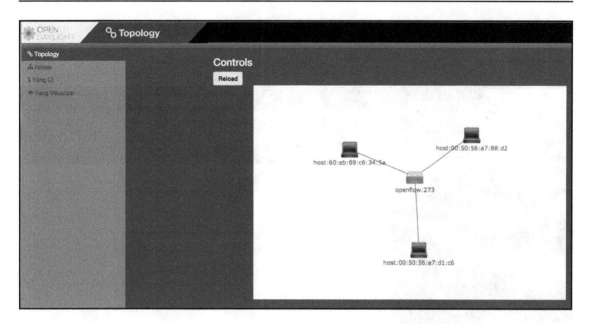

Our next goal will be to connect a fourth host to the OpenDaylight server. This allows us to confirm that the software is configured correctly and connectivity between the switches is functional.

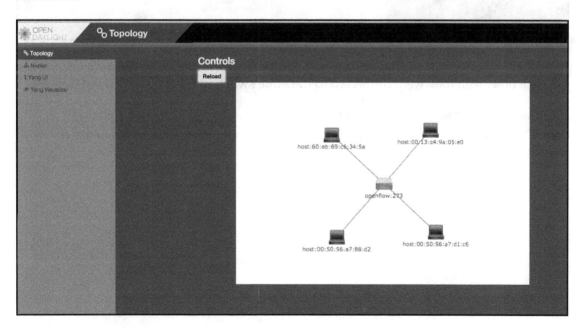

Now a second switch can be added with two hosts connected. The second switch is linked to the first switch to create a leaf/leaf ToR network. While we are only using two, larger configurations of hundreds of switches are supported by OpenDaylight.

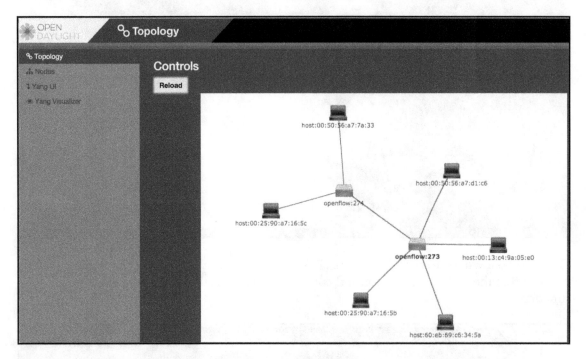

For forwarding, we will use the L2Switch application, which will allow different hosts to see each other as if they were connected to the same switch in the same broadcast domain.

An example would be where users of Internet2 (the educational only network) use OpenDaylight to configure connections between different universities that match their expected use.

Open hardware with SnapRoute

For the SnapRoute design, we will use two switches connected to each other running **Open Network Linux** (**ONL**) and SnapRoute's forwarding agent. The design will still be leaf-spine, but we will be running BGP between the switches:

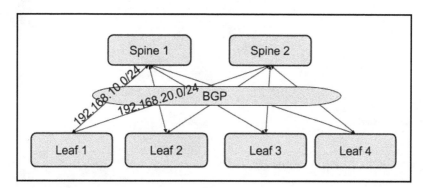

In the preceding diagram, links between **Leaf 1** and **Spine 1** and **Leaf 1** and **Spine 2** are given IP addresses corresponding to the configuration that will be applied.

Confirm that the FlexSwitch software is running using the system shell:

```
# service flexswitch status
[ ok ] FlexSwitch is running.
```

The next screenshot illustrates an example of using SnapRoute's RESTful API via Postman. We make a call to the API requesting the SystemStatus and receive data on how long the system has been running and what processes are running, such as ribd (**Routing Information Base** (**RIB**) daemon) and dhcprelayd (DHCP relay daemon).

As covered earlier in the book, RIB is a copy of all of the network information, whether it is used for forwarding, that is, put into **Forwarding Information Base** (**FIB**) or used for other functions such as to calculate the best paths to destinations.

```
GET  ∨     http://10.1.1.1:8080/public/v1/state/SystemStatus          Params    Send  ∨    Save  ∨

Body    Cookies    Headers (3)    Tests                      Status: 200 OK   Time: 62 ms   Size: 3 KB

Pretty   Raw    Preview    JSON ∨  ⇉                                      ⬒  Q   Save Response

 1 ▾ {
 2      "ObjectId": "",
 3 ▾    "Object": {
 4        "Name": "localhost",
 5        "Ready": true,
 6        "Reason": "None",
 7        "UpTime": "55h43m39.4793313s",
 8        "NumCreateCalls": "Total 8 Success 2",
 9        "NumDeleteCalls": "Total 0 Success 0",
10        "NumUpdateCalls": "Total 0 Success 0",
11        "NumGetCalls": "Total 18 Success 12",
12        "NumActionCalls": "Total 0 Success 0",
13 ▾      "FlexDaemons": [
14 ▾        {
15            "Name": "ribd",
16            "Enable": true,
17            "State": "up",
18            "Reason": "None",
19            "StartTime": "2001-07-02 19:51:07.59484187 +0000 UTC",
20            "KeepAlive": "Received 5 keepalives",
21            "RestartCount": 0,
22            "RestartTime": "",
23            "RestartReason": ""
24          },
25 ▾        {
26            "Name": "dhcprelayd",
27            "Enable": true,
28            "State": "up",
29            "Reason": "None",
30            "StartTime": "2001-07-02 19:50:48.148455384 +0000 UTC",
31            "KeepAlive": "Received 5 keepalives",
32            "RestartCount": 0,
```

In the following example, we will do the same query for system status using `curl` and the python `json.tool` to pretty up the output. In this example, we can see that the `vxland` or VXLAN daemon is running and has received 10 keepalive messages:

```
$ curl -X GET --header 'Content-Type: application/json' --header 'Accept:
application/json' http://10.1.1.1:8080/public/v1/state/SystemStatus |
python -m json.tool
  % Total % Received % Xferd Average Speed Time Time Time Current
  Dload Upload Total Spent Left Speed
100 3976 0 3976 0 0 260k 0 --:--:-- --:--:-- --:--:-- 277k
{
  "Object": {
```

```
"FlexDaemons": [
{
"Enable": true,
"KeepAlive": "Received 10 keepalives",
"Name": "vxland",
"Reason": "None",
"RestartCount": 0,
"RestartReason": "",
"RestartTime": "",
"StartTime": "2017-01-01 21:09:02.556083271 +0000 UTC",
"State": "up"
}
```

Configuring BGP

We will be configuring BGP between Leaf 1, Spine 1, and Spine 2. The management IP addresses of the switches are as follows:

- Leaf 1: `10.1.1.1`
- Spine 1: `10.1.1.2`
- Spine 2: `10.1.1.3`

To configure BGP, we need to first set the global settings; this will need to be done on all devices that run BGP. If you do not set the global settings, you will be unable to start BGP sessions as they will not have the necessary information, such as the local **Autonomous System Number (ASN)** or router ID.

```
curl -X PATCH --header 'Content-Type: application/json' --header 'Accept:
application/json' -d
'{"ASNum":"15096","RouterId":"192.168.1.1","IBGPMaxPaths":32}'
'http://10.1.1.1:8080/public/v1/config/BGPGlobal'
{"Access-Control-Allow-Origin":"*","Access-Control-Allow-Headers":"Origin,
X-Requested-With, Content-Type, Accept","Access-Control-Allow-
Methods":"POST, GET, OPTIONS, PATCH, DELETE","Access-Control-
Max_age":"86400","ObjectId":"f0c03caf-ec3b-4307-5f36-
e12b2a09b328","Result":"Success"}
```

As we do this command for each switch, the only change will be the router ID of the BGP configuration. For example, for Leaf 1, the router ID is `192.168.1.1`, while Spine 1 has a router ID of `192.168.1.2`.

When we query `BGPGlobal` on the REST interface, it will tell us the current global BGP configuration of the switch:

```
curl -X GET http://10.1.1.1:8080/public/v1/state/BGPGlobal | python -m
json.tool
 % Total % Received % Xferd Average Speed Time Time Time Current
 Dload Upload Total Spent Left Speed
100 238 100 238 0 0 145k 0 --:--:-- --:--:-- --:--:-- 232k
{
 "Object": {
 "AS": "15096",
 "Disabled": false,
 "EBGPAllowMultipleAS": false,
 "EBGPMaxPaths": 0,
 "IBGPMaxPaths": 32,
 "RouterId": "192.168.1.1",
 "TotalPaths": 0,
 "Totalv4Prefixes": 0,
 "Totalv6Prefixes": 0,
 "UseMultiplePaths": false,
 "Vrf": "default"
 },
 "ObjectId": ""
}
```

While there are many extra options for BGP, we have left most of them in the default state.

Building the network

There are a few necessary items you need to know to add a new BGP neighbor. You need to know the remote AS and the neighbors IP:

```
curl -X POST --header 'Content-Type: application/json' --header 'Accept:
application/json' -d '{"PeerAS":"15096","NeighborAddress":"192.168.10.2"}'
'http://10.1.1.2:8080/public/v1/config/bgpv4neighbor'
```

Here we are using a REST call to query the neighbors configured on the switch:

```
curl -X GET --header 'Content-Type: application/json' --header 'Accept:
application/json' 'http://10.1.1.2:8080/public/v1/state/bgpv4neighbors' |
python -m json.tool
 % Total % Received % Xferd Average Speed Time Time Time Current
 Dload Upload Total Spent Left Speed
100 887 100 887 0 0 348k 0 --:--:-- --:--:-- --:--:-- 433k
```

```
{
"CurrentMarker": 0,
"MoreExist": false,
"NextMarker": 0,
"ObjCount": 1,
"Objects": [
{
"Object": {
"AddPathsMaxTx": 0,
"AddPathsRx": false,
"AdjRIBInFilter": "",
"AdjRIBOutFilter": "",
"AuthPassword": "",
"BfdNeighborState": "",
"ConnectRetryTime": 120,
"Description": "",
"Disabled": false,
"HoldTime": 180,
"IntfRef": "",
"KeepaliveTime": 60,
"LocalAS": "15096",
"MaxPrefixes": 0,
"MaxPrefixesDisconnect": false,
"MaxPrefixesRestartTimer": 0,
"MaxPrefixesThresholdPct": 80,
"Messages": {
"Received": {
"Notification": 0,
"Update": 0
},
"Sent": {
"Notification": 0,
"Update": 0
}
},
"MultiHopEnable": false,
"MultiHopTTL": 0,
"NeighborAddress": "192.168.10.2",
"NextHopSelf": false,
"PeerAS": "15096",
"PeerGroup": "",
"PeerType": 1,
"Queues": {
"Input": 0,
"Output": 0
},
"RouteReflectorClient": false,
"RouteReflectorClusterId": 0,
```

```
  "SessionState": 3,
  "SessionStateDuration": "51.110675572s",
  "TotalPrefixes": 0,
  "UpdateSource": ""
  },
  "ObjectId": "b6920d65-385e-4819-7631-30b9fce97dd0"
  }
  ]
}
```

As you can see, there is a lot of information provided in the REST calls, including the number of peers, the number of prefixes, the time that the session has been up, and the maximum number of prefixes accepted from the session.

Moving forward, here is what the entire leaf configuration looks like when using `curl`:

```
curl -X PATCH -H "Content-Type: application/json" -d '{"IntfRef":
"fpPort1", "AdminState":"UP", "Speed":40000, "Autoneg":"OFF"}'
http://10.1.1.1:8080/public/v1/config/Port
curl -X PATCH -H "Content-Type: application/json" -d '{"IntfRef":
"fpPort2", "AdminState":"UP", "Speed":10000, "Autoneg":"OFF"}'
http://10.1.1.1:8080/public/v1/config/Port
curl -H "Content-Type: application/json" -d '{"IpAddr": "192.168.10.2/24",
"IntfRef":"fpPort1"}' http://10.1.1.1:8080/public/v1/config/IPv4Intf
curl -H "Content-Type: application/json" -d '{"IpAddr": "192.168.20.2/24",
"IntfRef":"fpPort2"}' http://10.1.1.1:8080/public/v1/config/IPv4Intf
curl -X PATCH --header 'Content-Type: application/json' --header 'Accept:
application/json' -d
'{"ASNum":"15096","RouterId":"192.168.1.1","IBGPMaxPaths":32}'
'http://10.1.1.1:8080/public/v1/config/BGPGlobal'
curl -H "Content-Type: application/json" -d '{"Name":"MatchConnected",
"ConditionType":"MatchProtocol", "Protocol":"CONNECTED"}'
http://10.1.1.1:8080/public/v1/config/PolicyCondition
curl -H "Content-Type: application/json" -d
'{"Name":"RedistributeConnectedBGP", "MatchConditions":"all",
"Conditions":["MatchConnected"], "Action":"permit"}'
http://10.1.1.1:8080/public/v1/config/PolicyStmt
curl -H "Content-Type: application/json" -d '{"Name":"ImportPolicy",
"Priority":1, "MatchType":"all",
"StatementList":[{"Priority":1,"Statement":"RedistributeConnectedBGP"}]}'
http://10.1.1.1:8080/public/v1/config/PolicyDefinition
curl -H "Content-Type: application/json" -d '{"ASNum":"15096",
"Redistribution":[{"Sources":"CONNECTED","Policy":"ImportPolicy"}]}' -X
PATCH http://10.1.1.1:8080/public/v1/config/bgpglobal
curl -H "Content-Type: application/json" -d
'{"NeighborAddress":"192.168.10.1", "IntfRef":"", "PeerAS":"15096",
"LocalAS":"15096", "ConnectRetryTime":30, "HoldTime":3, "KeepaliveTime":1}'
```

```
-X POST http://10.1.1.1:8080/public/v1/config/bgpv4neighbor
curl -H "Content-Type: application/json" -d
'{"NeighborAddress":"192.168.20.1", "IntfRef":"", "PeerAS":"15096",
"LocalAS":"15096", "ConnectRetryTime":30, "HoldTime":3, "KeepaliveTime":1}'
-X POST http://10.1.1.1:8080/public/v1/config/bgpv4neighbor
```

The configuration from Spine 1 is shown in the following code. It is similar to the leaf configuration other than having a different router ID. Spine 1 is connected to Leaf 1:

```
curl -X PATCH -H "Content-Type: application/json" -d '{"IntfRef":
"fpPort1", "AdminState":"UP", "Speed":40000, "Autoneg":"OFF"}'
http://10.1.1.2:8080/public/v1/config/Port
curl -H "Content-Type: application/json" -d '{"IpAddr": "192.168.10.1/24",
"IntfRef":"fpPort1"}' http://10.1.1.2:8080/public/v1/config/IPv4Intf
curl -X PATCH --header 'Content-Type: application/json' --header 'Accept:
application/json' -d
'{"ASNum":"15096","RouterId":"192.168.1.2","IBGPMaxPaths":32}'
'http://10.1.1.2:8080/public/v1/config/BGPGlobal'
curl -H "Content-Type: application/json" -d
'{"NeighborAddress":"192.168.10.2", "IntfRef":"", "PeerAS":"15096",
"LocalAS":"15096", "ConnectRetryTime":30, "HoldTime":3, "KeepaliveTime":1}'
-X POST http://10.1.1.2:8080/public/v1/config/bgpv4neighbor
```

The second spine, Spine 2, is configured in a similar way as the other switches, with one connection to Leaf 1:

```
curl -X PATCH -H "Content-Type: application/json" -d '{"IntfRef":
"fpPort1", "AdminState":"UP", "Speed":40000, "Autoneg":"OFF"}'
http://10.1.1.3:8080/public/v1/config/Port
curl -H "Content-Type: application/json" -d '{"IpAddr": "192.168.20.1/24",
"IntfRef":"fpPort1"}' http://10.1.1.3:8080/public/v1/config/IPv4Intf
curl -X PATCH --header 'Content-Type: application/json' --header 'Accept:
application/json' -d
'{"ASNum":"15096","RouterId":"192.168.1.3","IBGPMaxPaths":32}'
'http://10.1.1.3:8080/public/v1/config/BGPGlobal'
curl -H "Content-Type: application/json" -d
'{"NeighborAddress":"192.168.20.2", "IntfRef":"", "PeerAS":"15096",
"LocalAS":"15096", "ConnectRetryTime":30, "HoldTime":3, "KeepaliveTime":1}'
-X POST http://10.1.1.3:8080/public/v1/config/bgpv4neighbor
```

At this point, Leaf 1 is peered with both Spine 1 and Spine 2, and the forwarding information is being distributed.

Here is what the BGP sessions on Leaf 1 look like:

```
curl -X GET --header 'Content-Type: application/json' --header 'Accept:
application/json' http://10.1.1.1.1:8080/public/v1/state/bgpv4neighbors |
python -m json.tool
 % Total % Received % Xferd Average Speed Time Time Time Current
 Dload Upload Total Spent Left Speed
100 1707 100 1707 0 0 158k 0 --:--:-- --:--:-- --:--:-- 166k
{
 "CurrentMarker": 0,
 "MoreExist": false,
 "NextMarker": 0,
 "ObjCount": 2,
 "Objects": [
 {
 "Object": {
 ...
 "Disabled": false,
 "HoldTime": 3,
 "IntfRef": "",
 "KeepaliveTime": 1,
 "LocalAS": "15096",
 "MaxPrefixes": 0,
 "MaxPrefixesDisconnect": false,
 "MaxPrefixesRestartTimer": 0,
 "MaxPrefixesThresholdPct": 80,
 "Messages": {
 "Received": {
 "Notification": 0,
 "Update": 0
 },
 "Sent": {
 "Notification": 0,
 "Update": 0
 }
 },
 "MultiHopEnable": false,
 "MultiHopTTL": 0,
 "NeighborAddress": "192.168.10.2",
 "NextHopSelf": false,
 "PeerAS": "15096",
 "PeerGroup": "",
 "PeerType": 0,
 "Queues": {
 "Input": 0,
 "Output": 0
 },
 "RouteReflectorClient": false,
```

```
"RouteReflectorClusterId": 0,
"SessionState": 6,
"SessionStateDuration": "17h32m12.129971568s",
"TotalPrefixes": 0,
"UpdateSource": ""
},
"ObjectId": "1c4ab72c-6914-43b3-63c3-292b7401306c"
},
{
"Object": {
...
"LocalAS": "15096",
"MaxPrefixes": 0,
"MaxPrefixesDisconnect": false,
"MaxPrefixesRestartTimer": 0,
"MaxPrefixesThresholdPct": 80,
"Messages": {
"Received": {
"Notification": 11,
"Update": 0
},
"Sent": {
"Notification": 11,
"Update": 0
}
},
"MultiHopEnable": false,
"MultiHopTTL": 0,
"NeighborAddress": "192.168.20.2",
"NextHopSelf": false,
"PeerAS": "15096",
"PeerGroup": "",
"PeerType": 0,
"Queues": {
"Input": 0,
"Output": 0
},
"RouteReflectorClient": false,
"RouteReflectorClusterId": 0,
"SessionState": 3,
"SessionStateDuration": "22.845098904s",
"TotalPrefixes": 0,
"UpdateSource": ""
},
"ObjectId": "b5d9423e-151c-4f4a-63d2-ee6242cbfebc"
}
]
}
```

Here is the BGP routing state data pulled using Postman. The output shown in the screenshot is almost exactly the same as when we use `curl` and the Python `json.tool` to make it readable:

```
 1 ▾ {
 2       "MoreExist": false,
 3       "ObjCount": 2,
 4       "CurrentMarker": 0,
 5       "NextMarker": 0,
 6 ▾     "Objects": [
 7 ▾         {
 8               "ObjectId": "1c4ab72c-6914-43b3-63c3-292b7401306c",
 9 ▾             "Object": {
10                   "NeighborAddress": "192.168.10.2",
11                   "IntfRef": "",
12                   "Description": "",
13                   "Disabled": false,
14                   "PeerGroup": "",
15                   "PeerType": 0,
16                   "SessionState": 6,
17                   "PeerAS": "15096",
18                   "LocalAS": "15096",
```

The following code is a confirmation that an external BGP route is showing in the FlexSwitch routing table on the newly configured port (`fpPort3`), and it is shown as using EBGP due to having a different ASN:

```
{
"Object": {
"DestinationNw": "172.31.1.0/24",
"IsNetworkReachable": true,
"NextBestRoute": {
"NextHopList": null,
"Protocol": ""
},
"NextHopList": [
{
"NextHopIntRef": "fpPort3",
"NextHopIp": "192.168.30.2",
"Weight": 0
}
],
"PolicyList": [],
"Protocol": "EBGP",
"RouteCreatedTime": "2017-06-12 18:28:27.665878155 +0000 UTC",
"RouteUpdatedTime": ""
},
"ObjectId": ""
},
```

Cisco ACI

The Cisco ACI design will also be based on a leaf-spine design. One important thing to note is that APIC keeps a log of all changes to allow reversing if necessary.

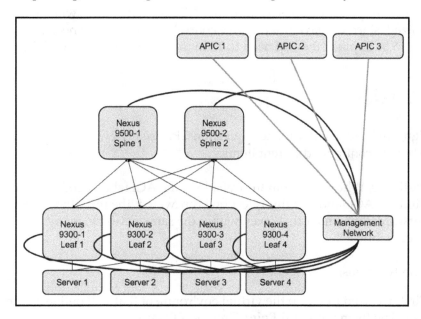

As discussed in chapter 8, *Cisco ACI*, a production ACI network requires three or five APIC servers, no matter how small the deployment is. In the examples from this chapter, we saw that the APIC controller will inform you that you do not have enough APICs to deploy to production. For this design, we use a similar design to the OpenDaylight one, but with three APIC servers.

For this design, we will put together a normal leaf-spine topology and wire the switches together and to the controller via the management network.

On first boot, we will run a fabric discovery to find all the switches. Once the switches have been located, we will configure the management network as shown in the preceding diagram. We then need to go into the APIC management tenant and configure static names for each of the devices.

The last and most important step is to configure NTP so that all the switches and controllers are synchronized, since we have three or five controllers, where you need a quorum for a configuration to be applied; they all need to be in the same time zone with the same time.

Design basics

For the design, we have to answer a few questions. Please review `Chapter 8`, *Cisco ACI*, for specifics on how to configure different items.

The first question is, Who/what from the outside of the ACI fabric needs to connect to devices behind the ACI fabric? If this question is answered, the rest of the configuration will be straightforward. Remember that, even within the same network, many users will be outside the ACI fabric.

We need to do two steps:

1. First, we need to set up the virtual environment that will define all the VMs and associate them with **End Point Groups** (**EPGs**).
2. Second, we need to add the EPGs to **Attachable Entry Points** (**AEPs**) on the physical side to group all the EPGs that need to communicate together.

Let's look into a sample customer:

You have an end user who needs access to a web-based billing application that resides behind the ACI fabric.

In order to provide connectivity, you will need to have an ANP for the billing application and an EPG for the web connectivity to the application. You will also need to create an EPG for the end users. The application EPG will be assigned to a provider contract that is created so that the billing application is reachable. The provider contract will allow the fabric to create the connection between the application and the end users. Refer to the following screenshot:

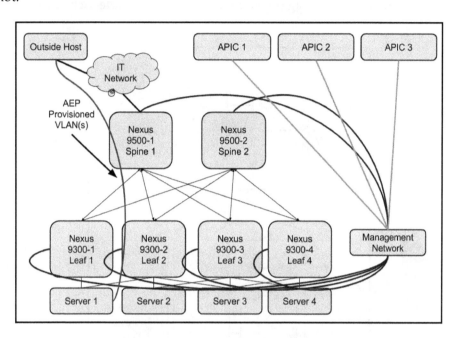

Here you can see the resulting VLAN created by the APIC when traffic needs to get to and from a server behind the ACI network. Refer to Chapter 8, *Cisco ACI*, where we talked about Cisco ACI to find information about the configuration.

Open or proprietary network with NSX

For the NSX design, we can use a combination of proprietary and open networking hardware or just one or the other.

For the design, we will use a core-aggregation design with compute racks and NSX Edge racks.

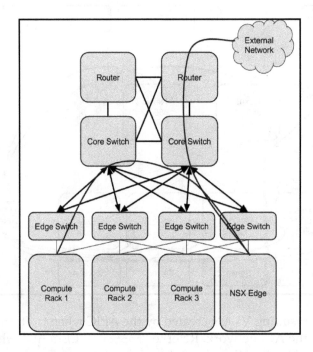

As we can see, traffic goes from **Compute Rack 1** to the NSX Edge and then out to the external network.

In Chapter 7, *VMware NSX*, you learned about configuring NSX. There was also a view of the network from the NSX overlay. Here is the same diagram for the preceding design:

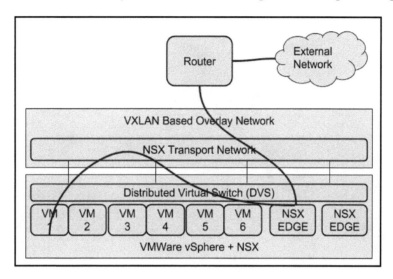

Notice that the **Distributed Virtual Switch (DvSwitch)** actually represents both the edge and core switches from the preceding design. The traffic flows from the VM through the DVS and is put into a VXLAN that is shipped to the NSX Edge and then out to the router and to the external network.

Summary

In this chapter, we talked about designs using OpenFlow, SnapRoute, Cisco ACI, and NSX to design and build networks. We referred back to earlier chapters, examining each one of them to see how to set up a deep configuration.

In the next chapter, we will talk about understanding and configuring **Quality of Service (QoS)**.

12
Understanding and Configuring Quality of Service

In the previous chapter, we looked at basic designs using OpenFlow, ACI, SnapRoute, and NSX. In this chapter, we will cover **Quality of Service** (**QoS**), which is an important part of any network. QoS is no longer an extra; it's a key part of networking, in both enterprise and service provider networks.

By the end of this chapter, you will:

- Understand what QoS is, both in layer 2 and layer 3 applications
- Understand how QoS is deployed and configured
- Know how to configure QoS using open source controllers
- Know how to configure QoS using NSX

QoS

QoS is the concept of providing different levels of service to selected traffic. With this, information is provided to devices to determine how to handle traffic crossing the devices when it is greater than the resources available. These resources can be bandwidth, access lists, processing, and other resources.

It's important to recognize that, while your traffic may not appear to exceed your link, micro-bursts of traffic can cause hard-to-trace issues. It is always advisable, even with QoS and other traffic management tools, to keep a link below 80 percent utilization.

QoS has two main ways in which it can manage traffic—either prioritizing specific flow(s) or limiting all other flows. On a standard device, QoS allows you to differentiate services based on any matchable packet header information, for example, source or destination address. Some devices that do deep packet inspection can match almost anything in the packet.

When applying QoS to a link, there are multiple ways to handle traffic that exceeds the limits set on the network, including tail drop, **Weighted Round Robin (WRR)**, **Random Early Detection (RED)**, and **Weighted Random Early Detection (WRED)**. All these queue management algorithms do the same thing—remove or reject packets from the queue. These are described next:

- **Tail drop**: This is the simplest way to manage traffic issues. With tail drop, when a queue or memory space is exhausted, the packets are dropped as they attempt to join the queue either on the input side or in the fabric.
- **WRR**: This algorithm was originally designed for ATM links where the packets are always the same size. When used with links that have random packet sizes, an average packet size must be calculated and then applied. WRR is not seen much in networks today and has been replaced by **Weighted Fair Queuing (WFQ)**.
- **RED**: Also known as **Random Early Discard/Drop**, this is a fairer queue management algorithm than tail drop. RED works by monitoring the output queue on the link and as the queue gets full, it starts to randomly drop packets attempting to join the queue; if the queue gets completely full, then all the packets are dropped. The main issue with basic RED is that it does not account for QoS priorities.
- **WRED**: This algorithm is a variation on RED. It allows queues to have multiple thresholds for packets based on the traffic class (ToS, CoS, or DSCP). As packets come in, if the average queue size is lower than the minimum threshold, packets are queued. As the queue gets full, lower-priority packets are dropped before higher-priority ones. Refer to the following diagram:

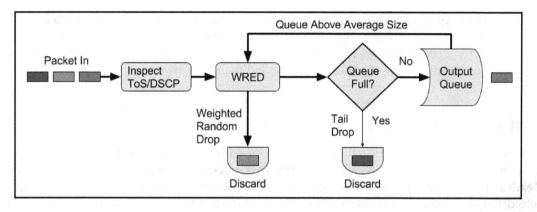

WRED example with three different types of packet

In this figure, you can see a few QoS technologies in use. First, there are three packets coming in—blue, green, and red. As the blue packet goes through, WRED is not applied, so the blue packet is passed on to the output queue; as the queue is not full, the packet is sent to the output queue.

When the green packet comes through, WRED is applied, but because the queue is higher than the average, the green packet is discarded.

When the red packet comes through, the queue is lower than the average, so the packet is sent to the queue; however, the queue is full, so the red packet is discarded.

If we add classification, that is, reading ToS/DSCP from the packets, we get something similar:

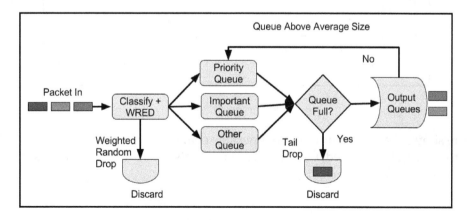

WRED with packet classification based on DSCP.

In the preceding diagram, three types of packet are coming in, each with a different DSCP value: blue being priority, green being important, and red falling in the general queue. The blue and green packets get through without any issue, but because **Other Queue** is full, the red packet is dropped.

Network behavior without QoS

Without QoS, traffic will normally be either dropped from the head or the tail of the queue while waiting to pass across a link. When traffic is stuck at the head of the queue, it is called **Head-of-Line Blocking (HoLB)**, which is one of the worst ways to manage traffic. Some networking equipment, such as the DEC FDDI GIGAswitch, had no way to prioritize traffic and therefore dropped traffic at the end of the queue when the queue was filled. Dropping traffic at the head of the queue is better in a HOLB type of a situation. Refer to the following diagram:

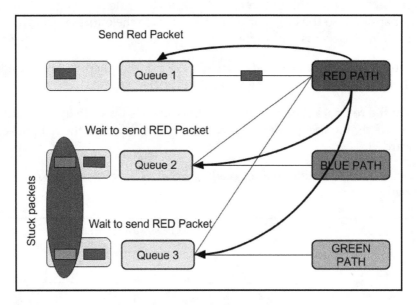

HoLB in a network with no QoS

This figure shows that, when multiple red packets come in, they stop the green and blue packets from being transmitted. Once all the red packets are sent, the other packets can be sent too. This is called HoLB.

HoLB and tail dropping, as we just discussed, are the two standard ways in which interfaces deal with congestion when no QoS policy is in place. In the preceding HoLB diagram, there is space for the blue and green packets on the line, but they cannot be sent as the red packets are being stopped.

Random drops are becoming more common-place. In some situations, such as bursting traffic or one-time events, this may not be an issue. Also, in other situations, such as when a site is under a denial of service attack, QoS may not help at all.

Generic traffic management

There are two different types of traffic management when using Ethernet, layer 2, and layer 3.

Layer 2 traffic management is designated as **Class of Service** (**CoS**) and used in 802.1Q, that is, VLANs and trunking. CoS does not guarantee latency or packet delivery. The CoS concept came out after 1995 along with VLANs.

Layer 3 traffic management was defined in RFC 791, the original **Internet Protocol** (**IP**) RFC as ToS using a three-bit precedence field in the packet. Over time, it has been refined to include differentiated services and **Explicit Congestion Notification** (**ECN**).

Layer 2 – focused QoS functionality

In layer 2 VLANs, there are eight values that can be attached to an Ethernet packet; they range from 0-7 and are defined by the **Institute of Electrical and Electronics Engineers** (**IEEE**) in the 802.1Q standard. The names of each priority will be stated based on both current naming conventions and their corresponding naming conventions from the RFC 791 (the original IP RFC) *Type of Service* section. Later, when we talk about DSCP, we will map those values to the CoS values to give a full picture. The following list describes the priorities:

- **CoS priority 0**: This is the default priority and delivers best results; in RFC 791, ToS priority 0 is stated Routine.
- **CoS priority 1**: This is background traffic; in RFC 791 ToS, priority 1 is stated Priority.
- **CoS priority 2**: This implies excellent effort; in RFC 791 ToS, it is stated Immediate. Priorities 0-2 are the lowest priority. All traffic in these first three CoS priorities is the first to be dropped when a link is congested.

- **CoS priority 3**: This is designated for critical applications and will be dropped after the first three. For RFC 791, this is named Flash.
- **CoS priority 4**: This is for video. RFC 791 states ToS priority 4 as Flash Override. Both CoS level 4 and 5 require low latency and jitter.
- **CoS priority 5**: This is for voice; in RFC 791, it is stated Critical.
- **CoS priority 6**: This is Internetwork Control for both IEEEs (telnet and other necessary communication tools).
- **CoS priority 7**: This is for Network Control (layer 2 control protocol traffic).

CoS is only available on trunk ports, not access ports. The following chart shows the CoS/ToS names:

CoS	CoS name	ToS name
0	Best Effort	Routine
1	Background	Immediate
2	Excellent Effort	Immediate
3	Critical Applications	Flash
4	Video	Flash Override
5	Voice	Critical
6	Internetwork Control	Internetwork Control
7	Network Control	Network Control

Layer 3 – focused QoS functionality

The first level of traffic management within the theme of QoS is the way TCP/IP handles congestion via exponential back off. TCP maintains a window (or the number of packets) that can be sent without an ACK (acknowledgment) from the other side. When a TCP flow does not get an ACK message from the receiving host, this means that a packet was not received by the other side or the ACK was lost on the way back. At this point, the sender will send the packet again. If this happens more than once, the sender will slowly back off and send data at a lower speed in order to try and stabilize the traffic.

Past having TCP/IP handle the congestion, the interface itself may handle the traffic in a reasonable way, such as randomly dropping packets rather than dropping the front or tail of the queue.

At one point in my networking life, I ran a large ATM-based nationwide network. While the ports were 45 Mbps, the allocated virtual channels (PVCs) were only 3-5 Mbps. When too much traffic was sent over the link, we would see normal congestion issues, such as higher latency and packet loss. At one point, Cisco updated the software on the line cards to drop packets instead of just queuing them. This caused a lot of issues as it was not immediately discovered. The solution to the issue was to upgrade the links as there was no specific traffic that we could prioritize.

QoS is implemented in different ways based on feature availability on the system that it is being applied to. Most systems support a minimum of ToS, which as explained earlier is an L2 packet attribute, and sets the priority in the packet header. ToS sets a field in the packet that defines the priority of the packet. As networking technology has evolved, ToS has been replaced by **Differentiated Services (DiffServ)**. This sets the **Differentiated Services Code Point (DSCP)** value, which provides a best-effort delivery of packets. DSCP can also be matched in the QoS configuration.

Outside the ToS/DSCP markings, QoS is normally handled by policy lists that define the traffic that is to be shaped. As mentioned earlier, these lists can define traffic using multiple different keys, including source/destination IP, source/destination port, and packet type. Normally, the first thing to do is limit ICMP packets if possible. This causes some confusion as `ping` will not work correctly to identify a problem. Incidentally, Juniper did this with their router interfaces to avoid having to process a lot of ICMP packets, which again caused people to assume that there was packet loss on the first hop.

The following chart shows DSCP/ToS and IP Precedence values. All values are represented in the decimal format rather than hex or binary:

DSCP (decimal)	ToS (decimal)	Precedence (decimal)
0	0	0
8	32	1
18	72	2
24	96	3
34	136	4
40	160	5
48	192	6
56	224	7

Utilizing QoS

Turning on QoS on traffic from a system is relatively painless. There will be an option in the operating system to enable either CoS or ToS.

Example of QoS in Linux

In Linux, you can see how traffic is being prioritized using the `ip link list` command, where it will show you what queuing discipline or `qdisc` you are using:

```
2: eth0: <BROADCAST,MULTICAST,UP,LOWER_UP> mtu 1500 qdisc pfifo_fast state
UP mode DEFAULT group default qlen 1000
 link/ether 74:d4:35:86:74:e6 brd ff:ff:ff:ff:ff:ff
```

Here we can see that `qdisc` is set to `pfifo_fast`; **First In, First Out** (**FIFO**). The `pfifo_fast` queuing discipline will honor some CoS/ToS tags, but this is not guaranteed. In order to utilize QoS, we will need to change the `qdisc` to something that can be configured, such as **Hierarchical Token Bucket** (**HTB**) disc.

HTB utilizes the token bucket algorithm, which does not need to know about outgoing interface characteristics, such as bandwidth. A fundamental part of HTB is borrowing tokens from parent interfaces if available. This means that, if the class has hit the minimum rate but not the ceiling or maximum rate, it will ask for more bandwidth.

1. To utilize the `qdisc`, attach them using the `tc` or traffic control command:

    ```
    tc qdisc add dev eth1 root handle 2: htb default 11
    ```

    The preceding command creates an HTB `qdisc` to `eth1` and assigns it the `handle 2`.

2. We can then create a class definition where there is a minimum and maximum guaranteed rate, such as the following where we set the minimum rate to `200kbps` and maximum rate to `500kbps`:

    ```
    tc class add dev eth1 parent 2: classid 2:1 htb rate \
    200kbps ceil 500kbps
    ```

    The preceding command defines QoS class `2:1`, attached to queuing discipline 2, and sets a minimum guaranteed bandwidth of `200kbps` and ceiling of `500kbps`.

3. Finally, a filter rule is created:

```
tc filter add dev eth1 parent 2: protocol ip match ip \
sport 22 0xfff classid 2:1
```

The filter applied is set up in such a way that traffic on source port (`sport`) 22 (SSH) belongs to the 2:1 class and is given a 200 Kbps guaranteed pipe, regardless of the traffic on the system.

Example of QoS in Windows

In Microsoft Windows, you can enable QoS by following these steps:

1. Choose **Start**, then **Control Panel**, and then double-click on **Network Connections**.
2. Right-click on the connection that you want to enable QoS on and then choose **Properties**.
3. In the box labeled **This connection uses the following items**, choose **QoS Packet Scheduler** and enable it.
4. You can now click on **OK**.

Hierarchical QoS

There are two main QoS designs—flat QoS, where one QoS policy applies to the entire physical interface, and **Hierarchical QoS** (**HQoS**), which allows you to provide multiple levels of service. For example, there may be no limits to traffic in general, but once there is congestion, voice and video traffic will be given precedence.

In the event that there is still congestion, voice traffic will be given precedence over video traffic. Refer to the following diagram:

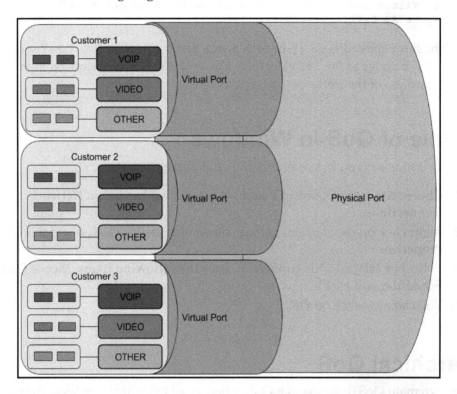

Here we have an HQoS design where three customers share the same physical port and there is traffic classification within the virtual ports assigned to each customer. HQoS is useful for multiservice providers, such as cable companies that provide voice, video, and the internet. With HQoS, they can carve out space for the video and voice and leave the rest for the Internet.

QoS in open source controllers

When looking to implement QoS in a network, it is important to understand the network design and layout. In an OpenFlow 1.3+ controlled network, QoS policies and queues can be built and connected to ports within the network. In general, we police outbound traffic, but you can police both outbound and inbound traffic if necessary.

For this configuration example, we will use **Open vSwitch (OVS)**:

1. The first thing that we will do is create a QoS policy on the switch and attach it to the port:

```
sudo ovs-vsctl set port et1 qos=@newqos -- --id=@newqos create qos
type=egress-policer other-config:max-rate=10000000 queues=1=@q1,2=@q2
-- --id=@q1 create queue other-config:min-rate=6000000
other-config:max-rate=6000000 -- --id=@q2 create queue
other-config:min-rate=4000000 other-config:max-rate=4000000
```

   This creates a pair of QoS queues—one set to 6 Mbps and the other to 4 Mbps; the max rate is set to 10 Mbps. The profile is connected to port et1 on the switch.

2. If we want to do something similar in OpenDaylight, we can do it via the Karaf interface. We need to install a few extra packages in the OpenDaylight Karaf interface:

```
karaf>feature:install odl-nic-core-mdsal odl-nic-console
odl-nic-listeners
```

3. Then, we need to create an intent. The syntax for this is as follows:

```
intent:qosConfig -p <qos_profile_name> -d <valid_dscp_value>
```

4. We will use DSCP_32 and the valid values are 0-63:

```
intent:qosConfig -p DSCP_32 -d 32
```

5. Then, we add the intent to the flow. The syntax for this is as follows:

```
intent:add -a ALLOW -t <DESTINATION_MAC> -f <SOURCE_MAC> -q
QOS -p <qos_profile_name>
```

6. Here we apply the intent to the flow between two boxes, tagging all traffic as DSCP_32:

```
karaf>intent:add -a ALLOW -t 10:00:00:00:00:01 -f 10:00:00:00:00:02
-q QOS -p DSCP_32
```

7. Here we use a command called `dpctl dump-flows` and confirm the flow is properly classified on the switch:

```
$ dpctl dump-flows

cookie=0x0, duration=11.873s, table=0, n_packets=3, n_bytes=294,
idle_age=11,
priority=9000,dl_src=10:00:00:00:00:01,dl_dst=10:00:00:00:00:02
actions=NORMAL,mod_nw_tos:128
```

In the preceding code, we see the flow is added to the switch with the ToS value attached (the ToS value is 4 x the DSCP value).

QoS in NSX

In VMware NSX, QoS is handled by setting the DSCP and CoS values for the virtual machine:

1. This is accomplished by opening the settings for **dvPortGroup** and choosing **Traffic filtering and marking**:

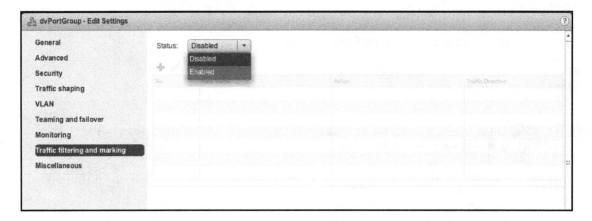

2. Once you have enabled traffic filtering and marking, you will need to create traffic rules. Next, we have a traffic rule named `Network Traffic Rule 1`, and we are setting it to tag traffic with either a CoS value, a DSCP value, or both:

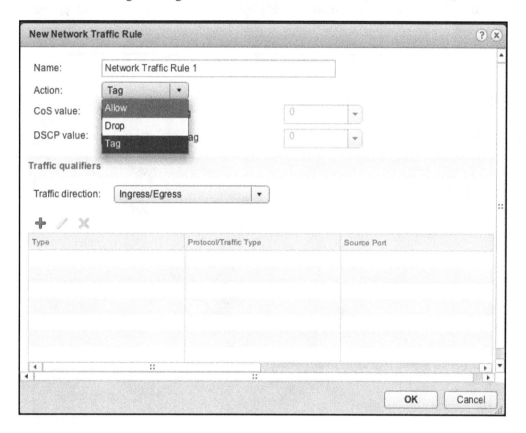

3. Now that we have chosen a tag, we can see a few more of the options, such as updating the CoS or DSCP tags. If CoS/DSCP is already set in the packet, we will remove it and replace it here to make sure that it follows the design. Also, the direction of the traffic we are modifying is chosen; it can be ingress, egress, or both:

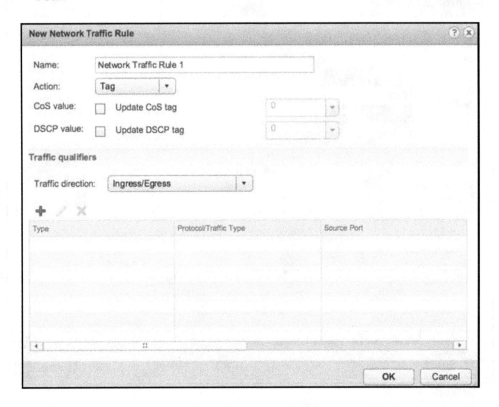

4. When we create a new traffic rule, we need to set up traffic for it to match to. For example, we can match by IP, MAC, or system traffic type:

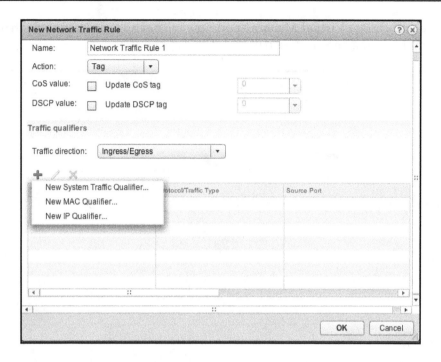

If we choose **System traffic type**, we get a selection box that holds predefined types of traffic, including **Management**, **Virtual Machine**, and **vMotion**. The qualifier box is set to **is**, and we can choose one of the predefined traffic types:

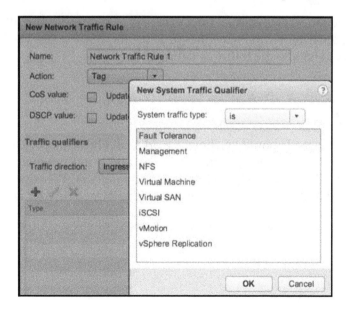

We will choose **Virtual Machine** and now we have a new traffic rule that updates any virtual machine traffic to use the DSCP code 63:

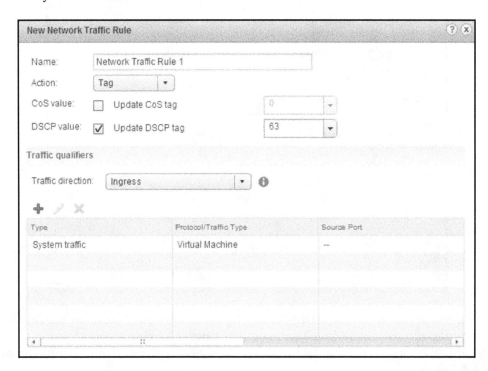

In the preceding sequence, you learned how to create a QoS profile and attach it to the system to mark traffic from virtual machines to a specific DSCP code. The DSCP setting allows the network to handle the traffic as defined.

Summary

In this chapter, you learned about QoS, how it works, and how to use it with NGN technologies. Examples of simple QoS on both Linux and Windows were shown along with the basic concepts of QoS in both OpenFlow and VMware NSX. We covered both flat and hierarchical QoS and their uses in both enterprise and service provider networks.

In the next chapter, you will learn how to secure a network using controllers, firewalls, and other security devices.

13
Securing the Network

In the previous chapter, we talked about how to utilize QoS in a NGN including flat and HQoS, layer 2 only CoS, and layer 3 ToS, along with DSCP and traffic shaping.

In this chapter, we will talk about securing a NGN using network controllers and other mechanisms, such as network taps and monitoring devices.

By the end of this chapter, you should be able to:

- Understand traffic steering
- Create a DMZ
- Send traffic through a firewall using open and proprietary network controllers
- Mirror traffic to a monitoring device

Terminology used in this chapter

In this chapter, we will be using a lot of specific terms from vendors that represent similar concepts. I will break down the terms into different areas based on their application. In order to compare and contrast the different solutions, there needs to be a way to evaluate them on a level field. We will learn the following types of terms:

- **Generic**: This refers to industry-standard terms that apply to all the different systems mentioned, including OpenFlow controllers, VMware NSX, and Cisco ACI
- **Cisco ACI-specific terms**: These are terms that are used specifically by Cisco to explain how to configure features and services
- **VMware NSX-specific terms**: These are terms used by NSX that correlate to other industry standard terms

Generic terms

Generic terms such as service chain are vendor-agnostic ways of naming features, functions, and hardware. As we move through the chapter, we will align vendor-specific terms with generic terms as needed. Here is a list of generic terms:

- **Service chain**: A service chain is a sequence of actions performed on the traffic to/from a device in the network. These actions can be performed by linking multiple virtual or physical services together, such as a firewall and load balancer.
- **Intrusion Detection System (IDS)**: An IDS is a service that monitors traffic and determines whether there is malicious traffic or behavior on the network.
- **Deep Packet Inspection (DPI)**: A deep packet inspector looks at not only the headers, but also the payload in IP packets and provides the information to the user and/or automated tools to handle.
- **Application Delivery Controller (ADC)**: An ADC offloads common tasks, such as SSL, from a host. ADCs can also provide compression, traffic shaping, and load balancing.
- **Tap**: This is a device that connects to a cable in the network and mirrors the traffic from the location to either a service or tap aggregator.
- **Tap aggregator**: It connects multiple taps together and allows traffic to be routed to different services, such as an IDS or DPI.

Cisco ACI-specific terms

Cisco ACI uses a few non-intuitive terms to describe generic functions. Here are their explanations:

- **Service graph**: Cisco's representation of a service chain
- **Function node**: A single service, such as a firewall or load balancer, connected to the service graph
- **Function node connectors**: The name for the connection used to link function nodes to the service graph
- **Service graph connector**: Used to connect multiple function nodes together
- **Terminal node**: Connects the service graph to the contract used by **End Point Groups (EPGs)**

VMware NSX-specific terms

VMware does a good job of using extended definitions of generic terms such as distributed firewall, which is a virtual firewall that is applied on a per-virtual-NIC basis. In the following list, we explain a few terms to clarify any questions:

- **Distributed Firewall** (**DFW**): A DFW is a firewall implemented in the VMware ESXi host, using hardware features in network cards when available
- **Rule table**: The rule table is a list of rules to apply to traffic crossing the DFW
- **Connection tracker table**: The connection tracker table is a cache of the current flow entries that use rules with a permit action
- **Service composer**: The service composer is a tool to create and apply network and security services to a virtual infrastructure

The evolution of security on the internet

The first rule of security is that you need to treat all devices on your network as if they are compromised and may be used against you. The second rule of security is to refer to the first rule. I say this not because security is impossible but more to point out that when securing a network, you need to separate or create segments/VLANs for the devices on the network to provide security against each other. This segmentation protects the network from an attacker connecting directly to an open port and having access to secure devices.

Right now, in mid-2017, the security issue all over the news is Ransomware, where computer files are encrypted or hidden from their owners displaying a screen on the computer stating this and that the user is to send money to the kidnapper. Before Ransomware, and continuing today, a big issue has been **Distributed Denial of Service** (**DDoS**) attacks, where thousands of compromised systems send traffic to a single destination to cause a service interruption or **Denial of Service** (**DoS**).

Before the current DDoS attacks, there were normal DoS attacks, including reflection and flood type attacks, where an attacker would send spoofed packets to have the target's IP address as the return-to locations that would return a lot of traffic. I remember clearly, back in 1997, one of my acquaintances determining that sending a packet to the broadcast address (x.x.x.255) of a network exchange point would return multiple packets. This behavior was disabled on most network devices soon after.

A broadcast address is an address that is flooded to all the devices on the same network block, so `192.168.1.255` would get responses from anything in the range of `192.168.1.1-192.168.1.254`.

In my career as a network engineer/architect, I have witnessed too many DoS attacks to count. Because I ran **Internet Relay Chat** (**IRC**) servers, the servers were a constant attack point for people looking to cause havoc or harass other users. One of the most memorable occasions was the high-profile attacks made by a person using the handle `Mafiaboy`, who managed to take down companies such as Yahoo!, Amazon, and others. The attacks were done during a meeting of the **North American Network Operators Group** (**NANOG**) that my employer at the time, Exodus Communications, was hosting. As the attendants were from multiple network service providers, we were able to create a **Network Operations Center** (**NOC**) where we worked together to try and solve the issues.

To state the obvious, the internet was not designed with security in mind; it was designed for connecting devices across the world to share information. Over time, security concepts have been developed to handle security on both the network devices and the end hosts. Initially, filters on the OS were used, then filters in the networking devices. Over time, concepts such as firewalls, virus scanners, and other security technologies were introduced.

One of the first clear signs that security was needed on globally networked computers was established by the Morris worm. In 1988, the Morris worm was a self-replicating computer program that infected many computers. It provided a clear picture of what issues can come out of having multiple computers networked. After the Morris worm, changes were made to systems to help secure them, though there was still a large number of *public* systems with anonymous access methods enabled.

Over time, it was recognized that while you could try to secure the computer, securing the network was just as important. Computers are constantly updated and new operating systems are released. Each time a system is updated, some issues are corrected, while more issues are created.

To this day, there are a lot of default services on newly installed computer systems that should not be enabled, such as mail servers. Most systems no longer need to run mail servers, yet by default they are enabled on most Linux distributions and must be shut off manually. Since a mail server has the ability to write to the file system, it provides a point of intrusion.

Though for a completely different reason, most home users are insulated from attacks to the mail system as most ISPs filter the mail port (25), both inbound and outbound, to limit spam. Also, most consumer and enterprise networks are behind **Network Address Translation** (**NAT**), where devices are not accessible from outside of the network directly, but only via rules that are created when the device connects to systems outside the network.

Traffic steering

Whether running a load balancer or a port redirector, traffic steering is an important part of security in networks. Traffic steering is the concept of redirecting traffic based on more than just the IP addresses. When traffic is only redirected based on the IP address, it is being routed. Traffic steering happens above layer 3, using TCP/UDP ports, session information, and applications to determine where to send traffic. In the Cisco ACI language, this is called a service graph.

The simplest version of traffic steering is load balancing, where all traffic goes to one or more load balancing network devices and is then redirected to the correct server. While load balancing is not security, it does use some similar concepts. Traffic comes into an IP address, which is connected to the load balancer, then the load balancer sends the traffic to one of the servers behind it based on how much traffic/load is on the servers.

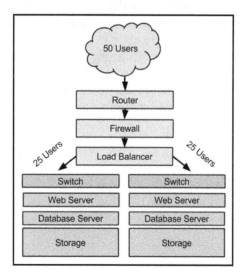

Simple load balancer design

Here we see 50 users visiting a website. The load balancer redirects 25 users to each backend server.

The added benefit of the load balancer is that, since it terminates all the connections and then creates a new session to the server, no incomplete or fake packets get through. Load balancers are not just for traffic sharing; they can also protect your servers from attacks such as a SYN flood.

 A SYN flood is where thousands to millions of SYN packets are sent to a device in order to block real traffic from getting through. When a SYN is sent and SYN-ACK is returned, the other side never acknowledges the packet and the connection eventually times out.

Traffic steering can be used to send users to a local cache of a site or content, such as movies. This saves bandwidth and money. It can also involve sending multiple copies of traffic or mirroring traffic, which we will discuss in the *Mirroring traffic to a monitoring device* section later.

Demilitarized/Demarcation Zone (DMZ)

A network DMZ is a location where network devices can be placed and accessed from the outside world directly. In most corporate networks, all of the internal systems are behind firewalls and filters. If there is a need to provide external access, a DMZ is created. The name DMZ comes from the concept of creating safe zones/areas where no military presence is allowed between countries or in contested areas. There is a demilitarized zone between North and South Vietnam, which also acts as the border. When we look at this from a networking perspective, DMZ is an area where there is less protection/monitoring, which is a similar idea.

DMZs are often used to host servers such as FTP, mail, and others that are likely to be compromised systems, such as DNS. A DMZ offers a secondary level of protection for your internal network by segregating dangerous traffic.

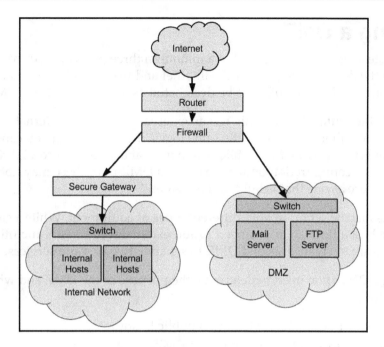

Design of a DMZ in concert with an internal network

Some companies, such as Cisco Systems, offer a DMZ where certain company-related, not managed, systems can be run. A famous one is `employees.org`, which sits behind the Cisco network on the DMZ. Other example systems that could be deployed would be devices with next generation services implementing new protocols, which may not be well supported by the current firewall/filtering technology, such as **Location/ID Separation Protocol (LISP)**. Publicly accessible systems, such as **Proof of Concept (PoC)** labs, will often be connected to the DMZ to allow controlled external access.

LISP is a way to disconnect the IP address of a system from a physical location, similar to how cellular phones have a number but not a fixed location.

DMZs are important for many reasons—the greatest being the ability to segment away devices that could be easily compromised. When designing a DMZ, pay close attention particularly to any connections, firewall rules, or other links that may allow devices from the DMZ easy access to your internal network; that is, any device on the DMZ should be accessed by the internal network the same way as any other device on the internet would.

Designing a DMZ

In order to create a DMZ, you will need at a minimum three ports on your router/firewall (depending on the design): one port for the internet and two ports for internal purposes, including the one that has the ability to be designated as or configured as a DMZ port.

If the router/firewall only has an external port and an internal switch (that is, all other ports are on the same logical network), then you cannot use it effectively as a DMZ. While you may be able to configure VLANs or use other configuration options to create a DMZ port, these may not be as secure as one that is built in the system.

Multiple DMZs may be set up to hold different types of equipment. While a single DMZ may be used to host a PoC lab, if you need to add external web servers and other services as well, you may want to create a second DMZ to separate two or more services.

When creating a DMZ, you need to determine the purpose of the DMZ and what features you will want to use:

- Do you want each device to have a public IP address?
- Which services will be hosted on the DMZ?
- Which filtering/firewall rules will you apply to the DMZ?
- Will you have more than one DMZ or DMZ port?

Once you have answered these questions, you'll be able to design the DMZ and the proper equipment ordered.

Implementing the DMZ

Now that the DMZ design is done and equipment ordered or already in place, we can set up a DMZ.

To set up a DMZ, we need to decide which ports will be used for what function. If we use a device with a DMZ port, things will be relatively simple as the DMZ port will have options for configuration and internal policies, which will avoid any issues with mixing networks.

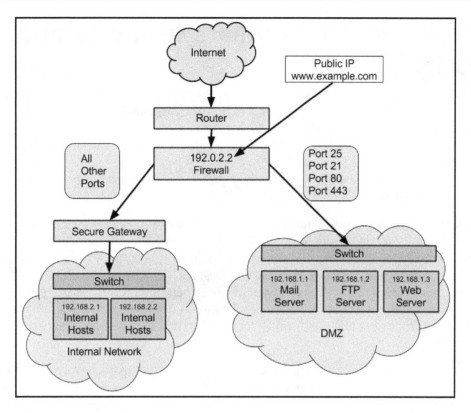

Here is an example where www.example.com points to a public IP that is assigned to the firewall

Here, we see an example where a single IP address, **192.0.2.2**, is used for both internal and DMZ traffic. The RFC 1918 block 192.168.1.0/24 is used for the DMZ network, and 192.168.2.0/24 is used for the internal network. When traffic comes into the web server, responses are sent through the firewall and NAT will return it back to the public IP of **192.0.2.2**.

The DMZ can also be set up with multiple IP addresses for each server: 1:1 NAT (where the public and internal address are the same but still filtered through the system) and other designs.

Using network controllers to implement security

Network controllers, whether OpenFlow, API, or the ones based on general automation, can reroute traffic through firewalls and other security devices, either virtual or physical. The concept is not new, but the implementations are. Projects such as OPNFV, an open source project under the Linux Foundation that brings together multiple components to create a single architecture, include a **Virtual Firewall** (**vFW**). OPNFV also provides OpenDaylight, ONOS, and much more, so we will utilize their projects as the basis for looking at open source controllers and VNFs.

The concept of inserting a virtual network function between devices is called **service chaining**. While it can also apply to physical devices, such as standalone firewalls, service chaining generally refers to virtualized services. Essentially, you insert a new service and put it in a chain and you can have multiple services, such as a firewall, DPI, and IDS. Different services can be brought in and out of use depending on the needs. Traffic can be routed in different ways through the devices. East-west (internal) traffic may be made to go through only a firewall, while north-south (external) traffic may be made to go through both a firewall and IDS.

As talked about previously, NFV allows features such as vFWs to be deployed in the network fabric or even at the edge of the network device. This functionality is required to easily route traffic through firewalls. While network steering could attempt to redirect traffic through a physical firewall, this firewall would need to be located within the same network area as the device being firewalled, which is expensive and not cost-effective.

Both Cisco ACI and VMware NSX provide the ability to configure vFWs and send traffic through them within the network on demand. VMware NSX has the concept of the DFW, which allows a virtual stateful firewall to be deployed within the fabric and enforced directly at the NIC on the VM server. Cisco ACI uses third-party solutions, such as the Palo Alto Networks VM series virtual vFW / physical firewall, which are directly integrated into the APIC using device packages; traffic is sent to them using the concept of service graphs.

Open source controllers and security

Using the OPNFV project as a basis for our designs allows the interchanging of controllers and virtualized services. The OPNFV project contains support for OpenDaylight, ONOS, and even Juniper's OpenContrail controller.

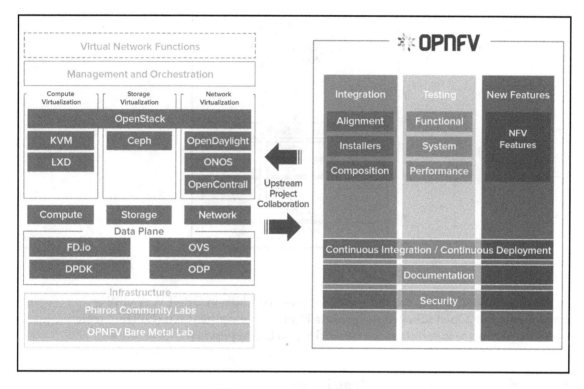

OPNFV Danube project diagram from wiki.opnfv.org

In the preceding diagram, you can see the layout of OPNFV and the different systems it supports, from data planes (DPDK and OVS) to **Virtualized Network Functions** (**VNFs**). Security is an important part of the OPNFV project and the VF and VNF are integral to security. The application of vFW to systems is very similar to how VMware NSX implements its firewall. Other virtual security appliances can be an IDS.

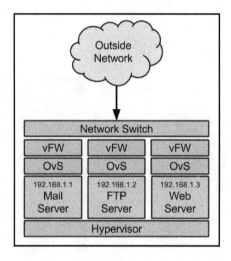

OPNFV vFW VNF architecture

In the preceding diagram, we can see the concept of VNFs in OPNFV. A vFW is implemented on Open vSwitch using **Data Plane Development Kit** (**DPDK**), which provides hardware integration for networking in the hypervisor.

Security using OpenDaylight

In OpenDaylight, there is the concept of a virtual tenant. The virtual tenant manager is a plugin that provisions VNFs such as a vFW. A vFW can be either commercial or open source. Palo Alto Networks provides a commercial vFW; pfSense and OPNSense both provide open source firewalls.

To get traffic to and from the firewall, flow filter rules will be created that send traffic that needs to be inspected through the firewall. Traffic can be north-south (to/from the public internet) or east-west (inside the network).

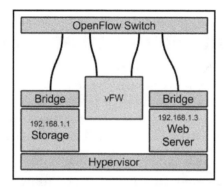

Routing server traffic through a vFW

Here, we have an OpenFlow switch routing traffic between hosts through a vFW, that is, service chaining. This is a common design for east-west traffic and provides protection for the data from the web server. If needed, a **virtual Intrusion Detection System (vIDS)** can be inserted in the chain for external traffic coming to the web server. A load balancer could also be added to the chain to allow more servers. Refer to the following diagram:

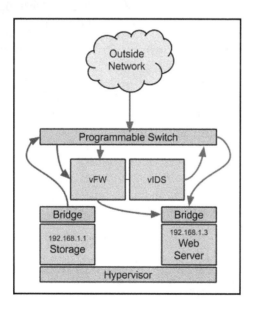

Service-chaining multiple VNFs

Here, we see a design where traffic between the storage and web server goes through a firewall, while traffic from the external network is sent through both a vFW and a vIDS. Internal traffic is shown in blue, and external traffic is shown in green.

Commercial controllers and security

Both Cisco ACI and VMware NSX use similar concepts to implement security. Each relies on information provided by the network manager to create the filters and firewalls necessary to control communication between devices. With Cisco ACI, an intent is created and ports can be assigned to the EPG connected to the intent. With VMware NSX, the devices are virtual, so templates could be created that automatically get different security implementations.

Since Cisco ACI is more hardware-focused, we will go through what the deployment of an application policy (intent) looks like and how it is applied to a hardware device. For VMware NSX, we will focus on how the system is secured using a virtual network.

Security using Cisco ACI

A quick overview of Cisco ACI shows what a firewall looks like once implemented through the ACI application policies. Here we are using a Palo Alto Networks V series vFW, which is supported in the APIC. Now refer to the following diagram:

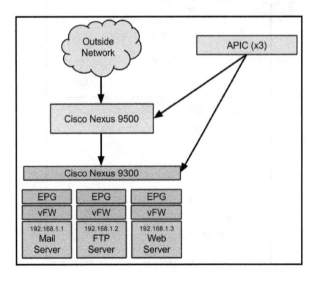

A simplified ACI virtualized firewall design

Here we can see a very simple picture of an ACI managing a vFW. The application policy applies the rules to different EPGs. In the next section, we will describe the way ACI functions.

When using Cisco's ACI, you first start with an EPG to which an **Application Policy Model (APM)** is attached. An APM consists of the following items:

- A set of EPGs, VMs, servers, and other devices with the same policy
- A set of rules defining communication between the EPGs
- A set of network services (VNFs) that are chained between the EPGs

In difference to other technologies, ACI believes in a zero-trust architecture. Any device attached to an ACI network is assumed to be untrustworthy until policies are assigned to the device or the device is attached to an existing EPG. This is a useful feature as it protects from unauthorized equipment being plugged into the network and getting access to important systems.

Because ACI was designed for multitenant solutions, **Microsegmentation (uSeg)** is a key part of ACI security. From the MAC layer up, ACI can provide separation, even with different systems on the same port or VLAN. Cisco calls their security concepts intra-endpoint group isolation, IP-based group isolation, and uSeg endpoint groups.

By default, any device in the same EPG can talk to any other device in the same EPG without requiring implicit permission. The idea with intra-endpoint group isolation is that you can block all the devices in the same EPG from being able to talk to each other, similar to the private VLAN concept. If you utilize intra-endpoint group isolation, you will need to create contracts for devices that need to connect to each other.

When using uSeg, the goal is to create security between specific devices on the same VLAN or interface rather than block all of the traffic between all the devices on the VLAN as with intra-endpoint group isolation. IP-based group isolation is generally used for physical interfaces but can be connected to different virtual solutions, such as those from VMware. All traffic management in layer 2 and 3 is handled according to the way the EPG is configured and what rules are applied.

ACI layer 4-7 service graph

This section will contain a lot of Cisco ACI-specific terms that we will explain in more general ways.

ACI utilizes as well as operates at layer 4-7 using the service graph. This graph represents the order in which the different networking devices (function nodes) will be applied. A function node is a single service function, such as a firewall or load balancer.

Function nodes are connected to the APIC via function node connectors and inserted into the path of two EPGs using a terminal node that attaches to the contract that specifies how the traffic will flow.

If this description is confusing, I have created a diagram to explain how the service graph works:

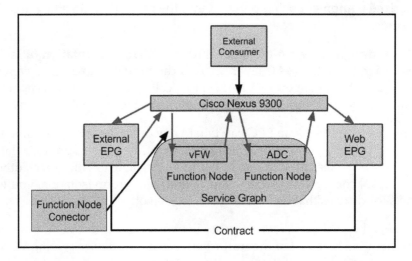

The Cisco ACI service graph

Here you can see a **Cisco Nexus 9300** running in ACI mode. I have left out the APIC as we have learned that at least three to five APICs are necessary for a production ACI design.

The blue lines represent traffic from the external consumer, which is being put into the external EPG, which then uses a contract to determine the service graph that will be followed. The service graph uses function nodes, such as the vFW and ADC, and connects to them using the function node connector. Once through the service graph, the traffic is delivered to the web server.

Security using VMware NSX

When using security within VMware NSX, the concept is very similar to Cisco ACI, and it involves using the Service Composer to create service chains. NSX contains a DFW, so no third party is necessary to get basic firewall rules. The rules are applied at the level of the **virtual Network Interface Card** (**vNIC**) using a kernel module that attaches to the physical network interface card. Because the work is done by the NIC, the performance is close to the line rate.

The DFW can run from layer 2 to layer 4 by default, with third-party add-ons going up to layer 7. As discussed earlier, layer 2 is the MAC layer, while layer 3 uses TCP/UDP source/destination information. At layer 4, the TCP/UDP ports are used as a filter. As explained by VMware, the DFW is done using two tables attached to the VM vNIC. The first table is the connection tracker, which caches the flow information for rules with permit actions. The second table is a rule table, which contains all the rules to be applied to the traffic.

As packets come in, they are run through the rule list starting from the top rule and progressing serially through the chain. The packets first go through the connection tracker table to check whether there is an entry for the flow; if not, the packet is sent through the rule table. Once the packet matches a rule, the action specified is done: forward/drop/modify/and so on. It is important to remember that because the rules are matched serially, you need to have more granular rules at the top and the default rule at the bottom.

VMware NSX uses what is called the Service Composer to configure service chains. The flow is similar to Cisco ACI:

1. The security groups and members are configured (EPGs in ACI).
2. The services that will be utilized are provisioned (service graph in ACI).
3. The services are applied to the groups (function nodes in ACI).
4. Last is the automation of application services by defining conditional rules.

Once the service is composed, it can be enabled to manage traffic as necessary. To add a new service to another tenant on the system, you simply add that tenant to the membership list.

Now we will build a firewall rule using the **Active Directory** (**AD**) service we configured in `Chapter 7`, *VMware NSX*:

1. First, we select a firewall and add a new section; we will call the section `Authenticated Users` and add it below the current first section:

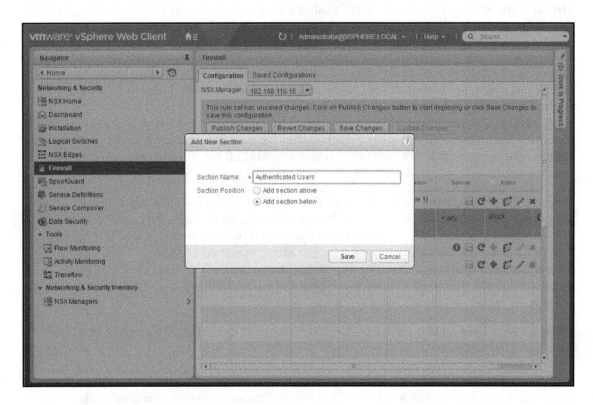

2. In the following screenshot, we see the **Define dynamic membership** tab where the criteria for being a part of the security group are configured. Here you can use the computer OS, VM name, IP address, and many other fields. We are using the **Entity** option and checking that it belongs to the **AppConfiguration** group.

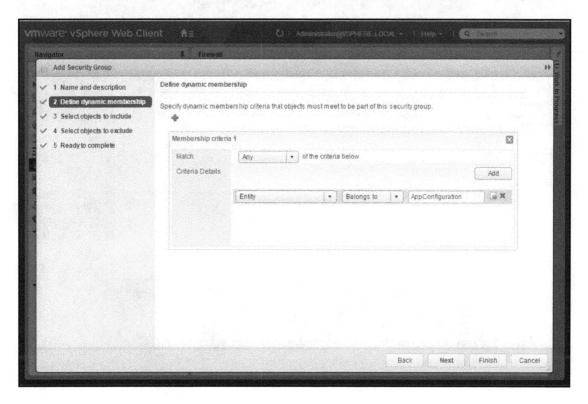

3. We will then add a source, which could be an IP, VM, or a myriad of other options. We will use **Security Group** and choose **Admins**.

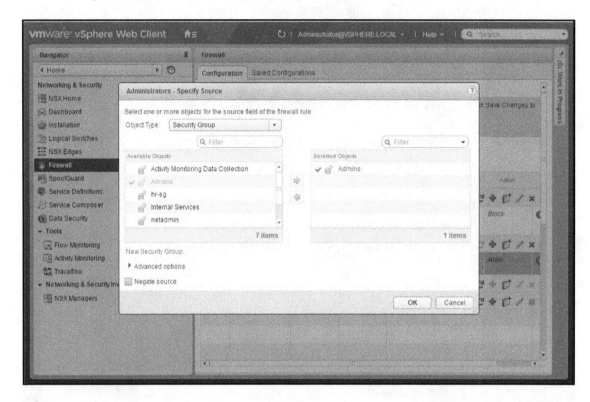

4. For the destination, we will use **Internal Services**, so people in the **Admin** group in the AD will be able to access internal services.

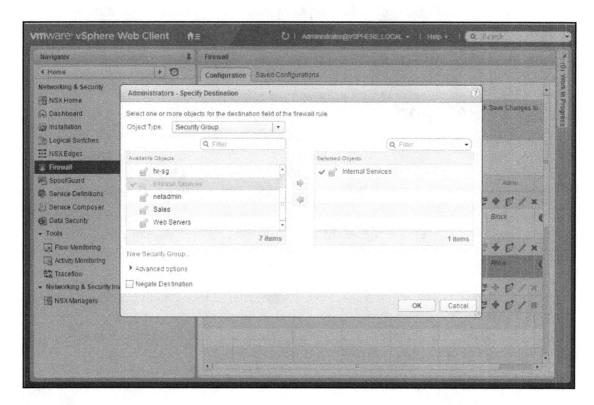

Mirroring traffic to a monitoring device

Mirroring traffic is a common way of monitoring the security of network devices. Mirroring can also be referred to as **Switch Port Analyzer** (**SPAN**). It can happen inline or out of band via network taps. While out of band is more common, inline tapping is being built over time. The value of inline tapping is that, when suspect traffic is noticed, it can be blocked/steered to an IDS or another inspection device.

In the beginning, we used physical taps, such as the vampire tap, which connects directly to the physical wiring and allows a copy of the traffic to be acquired. Earlier, networks used a coax cable that had a center wire and a metal shield around them. The tap would be physically pushed onto the wire, one part touching the center wire and the other the shield.

As networks progressed, physical inline taps were created. These taps allowed the traffic to flow normally, but they also sent a mirror of the traffic out to a special port on the tap. When tapping fiber optic networks, these types of tap are still common with different ratings, such as 10/90, where 10 percent of the light goes to the tap and 90 percent to the other side of the connection. The current technology in taps is that they not only mirror the traffic, but can also sample, slice, and otherwise modify the packets.

Using a SPAN port

A SPAN port is a physical port on a switch or router where traffic from other ports can be mirrored. When using a SPAN port, it is important to utilize one that is large enough to handle the traffic you send to it. For example, if you are mirroring multiple 1 Gb ports out of a single 1 Gb SPAN port, you may overload the port and lose traffic or worse.

SPAN ports can be created on OpenFlow switches relatively simply, as I wrote about in multiple posts on `sdntesting.com` back in 2014. The posts covered the same utilization of OpenFlow switches as taps.

In my testing, I have used Pica8 switches to replicate traffic, lots of traffic, using static OpenFlow commands. For example, here is a design where I take 10G of traffic and mirror it across five ports:

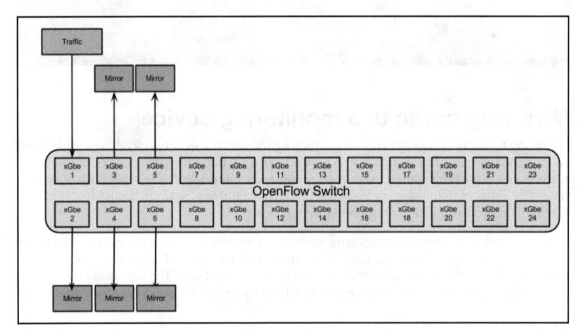

1. First, we need to set up a new bridge port and add interfaces to it:

```
# Add Bridge br0 - for PCAP Replication - 1st Port
##############################
# te-1/1/1 is input te-1/1/2, te-1/1/3, te-1/1/4, te-1/1/5, te-1/1/6
are output
#--------------------------------------------------------------
--------------------
$VSCTL add-br br0 -- set bridge br0 datapath_type=pica8
other-config=datapath-id=100
$VSCTL add-port br0 te-1/1/1 -- set interface te-1/1/1 type=pica8
$VSCTL add-port br0 te-1/1/2 -- set interface te-1/1/2 type=pica8
$VSCTL add-port br0 te-1/1/3 -- set interface te-1/1/3 type=pica8
$VSCTL add-port br0 te-1/1/4 -- set interface te-1/1/4 type=pica8
$VSCTL add-port br0 te-1/1/5 -- set interface te-1/1/5 type=pica8
$VSCTL add-port br0 te-1/1/6 -- set interface te-1/1/6 type=pica8
```

2. We then need to program the ports directly. This involves removing the default flow and inserting a new flow that mirrors traffic from port 1 to the other five ports:

```
# Remove Default Flow (not treating this as HUB!)
ovs-ofctl del-flows br0
# Add replication flow 1 -> 2,3,4,5,6
ovs-ofctl add-flow br0
in_port=1,dl_dst="*",dl_src="*",dl_type="*",dl_vlan_pcp="*",
dl_vlan="*",actions=output:2,3,4,5,6
```

3. As a final step, we need to ignore any traffic coming in the ports that we are using as SPAN/mirror ports:

```
# Drop ingress traffic from mirror ports
ovs-ofctl add-flow br0
in_port=2,dl_dst="*",dl_src="*",dl_type="*",dl_vlan_pcp="*",
dl_vlan="*",actions=drop
```

The preceding code is an extreme example of using a switch where the traffic that comes in port 1 is replicated out to five other ports, essentially creating ports where different packet inspection devices, such as DPI and IDS, can be located.

To expand on this idea, it is also easy to mirror multiple ports to multiple devices. In the following scenario, we will have four ports bridged so that they can talk to each other, with plus each port mirrored out to another port, as seen in the following diagram:

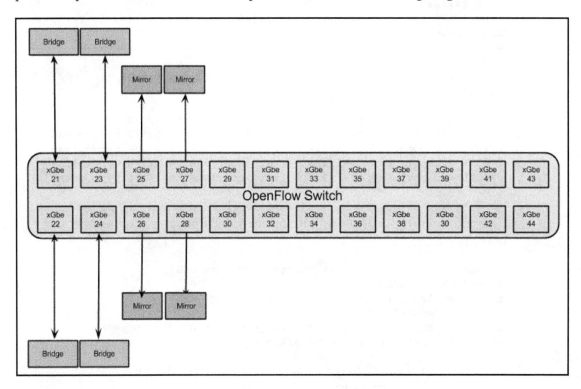

Here are the commands that are run to create the ports and the mirrors; the configuration is notated to explain the functions being done:

```
# Add Bridge br20 - for TAP Span - 1st Port
##############################################
# Bridged : te-1/1/21, te-1/1/22, te-1/1/23, te-1/1/24
# Output : te-1/1/25, te-1/1/26, te-1/1/27, te-1/1/28
#------------------------------------------------------
$VSCTL add-br br20 -- set bridge br20 datapath_type=pica8 other-
config=datapath-id=120
$VSCTL add-port br20 te-1/1/21 -- set interface te-1/1/21 type=pica8
$VSCTL add-port br20 te-1/1/22 -- set interface te-1/1/22 type=pica8
$VSCTL add-port br20 te-1/1/23 -- set interface te-1/1/23 type=pica8
$VSCTL add-port br20 te-1/1/24 -- set interface te-1/1/24 type=pica8
$VSCTL add-port br20 te-1/1/25 -- set interface te-1/1/25 type=pica8
$VSCTL add-port br20 te-1/1/26 -- set interface te-1/1/26 type=pica8
$VSCTL add-port br20 te-1/1/27 -- set interface te-1/1/27 type=pica8
```

```
$VSCTL add-port br20 te-1/1/28 -- set interface te-1/1/28 type=pica8
# Remove Default Flow (not treating this as HUB!)
ovs-ofctl del-flows br20
# Add replication flow from each bridged port to each of the other ports in
the group
ovs-ofctl add-flow br20
in_port=21,dl_dst="*",dl_src="*",dl_type="*",dl_vlan_pcp="*",dl_vlan="*",ac
tions=output:22,23,24,25,26,27,28
ovs-ofctl add-flow br20
in_port=22,dl_dst="*",dl_src="*",dl_type="*",dl_vlan_pcp="*",dl_vlan="*",ac
tions=output:21,23,24,25,26,27,28
ovs-ofctl add-flow br20
in_port=23,dl_dst="*",dl_src="*",dl_type="*",dl_vlan_pcp="*",dl_vlan="*",ac
tions=output:21,22,24,25,26,27,28
ovs-ofctl add-flow br20
in_port=24,dl_dst="*",dl_src="*",dl_type="*",dl_vlan_pcp="*",dl_vlan="*",ac
tions=output:21,22,23,25,26,27,28
# Drop ingress traffic from mirror ports
ovs-ofctl add-flow br20
in_port=25,dl_dst="*",dl_src="*",dl_type="*",dl_vlan_pcp="*",dl_vlan="*",ac
tions=drop
ovs-ofctl add-flow br20
in_port=26,dl_dst="*",dl_src="*",dl_type="*",dl_vlan_pcp="*",dl_vlan="*",ac
tions=drop
ovs-ofctl add-flow br20
in_port=27,dl_dst="*",dl_src="*",dl_type="*",dl_vlan_pcp="*",dl_vlan="*",ac
tions=drop
ovs-ofctl add-flow br20
in_port=28,dl_dst="*",dl_src="*",dl_type="*",dl_vlan_pcp="*",dl_vlan="*",ac
tions=drop
```

Now that we have looked at the open hardware, open source way to tap/mirror traffic, we can look at hardware and software that are commercially available.

Using an inline tap

The standard method of mirroring traffic is to put a purpose-built network tap between the switch and the host/network. This is not as flexible as using a built-in SPAN function of a network device, but it is believed to be more stable as the tap should go into bypass mode if anything happens, such as a power failure.

The inline tap will then generally be aggregated into a tap aggregator, which can then forward the traffic to the correct inspection device. The following diagram shows traffic being mirrored to the tap aggregator:

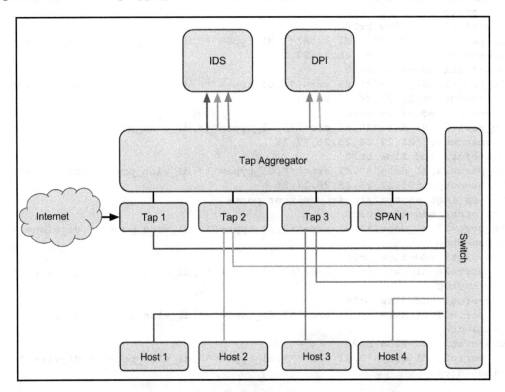

In the preceding diagram, we see different types of traffic being mirrored to the tap aggregator, including internal host traffic and internet traffic. Some of the traffic is routed to the IDS, and some to the DPI. Traffic can be dynamically routed to one or more inspection devices at any time.

GbE copper taps are inexpensive and very useful. Put together with an OpenFlow switch, as shown in the preceding diagram, a simple inexpensive tap aggregation network can be built. If you are attempting to tap higher speed links, such as 10 GbE, you will need to go for a more expensive solution.

While building the tap aggregation network, it is useful to determine whether you need smart taps. Smart taps offer packet slicing, packet filtering, and other features in hardware without loss.

Summary

In this chapter, you learned about general security concepts and how to apply them to different next generation systems. Using the OPNFV project, we looked at configuring switches using OpenFlow and vFWs. For Cisco ACI and VMware NSX, we used built-in tools, such as the NSX DFW, along with third-party software vendors, such as Palo Alto Networks, to create more secure environments.

Index